Mike McCarthy: Nobody's Underdog

Rob Reischel

Blue River Press
Indianapolis, IN

ISBN: 9781935628170
Library of Congress Control Number: 2012947159

Cover designed by Phil Velikan
Cover photo: Matthew Emmons, US PRESSWIRE
Editorial assistance provided by Dorothy Chambers
Packaged by Wish Publishing

Printed in the United States of America
10 9 8 7 6 5 4 3 2 1

Published by Blue River Press
Distributed by Cardinal Publishers Group
Tom Doherty Company, Inc.
www.cardinalpub.com

For Madison and Mia …

proof that angels do indeed walk the earth.

Love, Dad

Table of Contents

Sep 24, 2006; Detroit, MI: Green Bay Packers head coach Mike McCarthy talks to quarterback Brett Favre (4) during a timeout against the Detroit Lions at Ford Field. Mike registers his first victory as Packer's head coach with his team getting the 31-to-24 win in Detroit. (Tom Szczerbowski-US PRESSWIRE Copyright Tom Szczerbowski)

1

Nobody's Underdog

The Green Bay Packers' season — and Mike McCarthy's future as their head coach — were both on shaky ground. It was December 15, 2010, and the Packers were in crisis mode. Green Bay had just lost at Detroit, 7-3, in arguably its worst performance of McCarthy's five-year tenure. The loss left the Packers at 8-5, two games behind NFC North Division-leading Chicago and in a fight for their playoff lives.

Quarterback Aaron Rodgers, who left the Lions game with a concussion late in the second quarter, was listed as doubtful the following week. Deep down, though, McCarthy knew he wouldn't have Rodgers, a player who had quickly developed into one of football's elite signal callers.

To top it off, Green Bay was facing its toughest test of the year, a Sunday night road tilt at AFC power New England. The Patriots entered the contest having won 10 of 11 games, had the NFL's soon-to-be MVP in quarterback Tom Brady, and were averaging a league-high 31.9 points per game.

McCarthy was also facing growing dissatisfaction from the paying customers. In the nearly three seasons since Brett Favre had been traded, the Packers were 25-20 and hadn't won a single playoff game. In many places, that record would be just fine. But in the NFL's smallest city — one affectionately known as Titletown thanks to its 13 World Championships — McCarthy's future was extremely tenuous.

Now, all McCarthy had to do was go into New England without his best player and face football's finest team. To the oddsmakers, who installed the Patriots as 14-point favorites, the Packers were entering a gun fight with only a few pebbles.

Not to McCarthy. For five years, McCarthy had said little each time he met with the local media. McCarthy was always extremely "positive," using that word so often that many referred to him as Mike McPositive. McCarthy aimed to find the good in most situations, which meant he rarely made headlines with his words. His answers were generic. He was typically guarded, protective, cautious.

But on this Wednesday afternoon, four days before Green Bay met New England, McCarthy dramatically changed his approach. Instead of dishing out vanilla, McCarthy went for a scoop of Cherry Garcia. And everyone took notice.

"We're nobody's underdog," McCarthy bellowed when he was asked about facing the mighty New England Patriots. "We have all the confidence in our abilities. We've had challenges throughout the season. We've stepped up to those challenges, and we feel the same way going into this game."

Four nights later, the Packers met almost every challenge that came their way. Almost.

McCarthy, continuing his bold, new approach, opened the game with an onside kick. Backup quarterback Matt Flynn threw for three touchdowns and 251 yards. The Packers held the high-powered Patriots to 249 total yards and had nearly twice as many first downs as New England.

But a pair of critical Green Bay turnovers and some special teams breakdowns allowed New England to escape with a 31-27 win. Afterward, though, something had changed inside Green Bay's locker room.

There was a restored confidence. There was a belief and a certainty that had been missing for weeks now.

The Packers entered 2010 talking about a Super Bowl title but had disappointed many with a 3-3 start and an 8-5 record heading to New England. But McCarthy's "Nobody's Underdog" comment seemed to re-energize and rally his team, even though the mighty Patriots prevailed that night in Foxborough, Massachusetts.

"There's no doubt about it," Packers defensive tackle Ryan Pickett said. "New England wasn't just a good team, they were a great team. And when coach called us 'nobody's underdogs' it seemed to fire everybody up a little bit.

"If guys kind of needed a jolt, that was it. We knew we had a great team, but I know people were starting to doubt us, too. I guess it was time to show we weren't anybody's underdog, and that's what we went and did."

Packers right guard Josh Sitton agreed. "I think that New England game was definitely a turning point," Sitton said. "Obviously our goal is to go out and win every game, but we went and proved to them we can go frickin' play with anybody. I definitely think that was a turning point."

It sure was.

One week later, in a must-win game, Rodgers returned and threw four touchdowns in a 45-17 rout of the New York Giants. "We had our backs against the wall that night and came out and answered a lot of questions," former Packer center Scott Wells said. "We stepped up and peaked at the right time."

They sure did.

Green Bay's destruction of the Giants kicked off a six-game winning streak to close the 2010 season — a remarkable run that didn't end until the Packers defeated Pittsburgh in Super Bowl XLV and brought the Lombardi Trophy back to Green Bay.

There was a gutty 10-3 win over Chicago in the regular season finale, a game in which the Bears had little to play for but tried desperately to keep the dangerous Packers out of the postseason.

When the playoffs arrived, Green Bay was the hottest team in the tournament. The Packers won at Philadelphia, 21-16, in the wild-card round. Green Bay then annihilated top-seeded Atlanta, 48-21, in the NFC Divisional playoffs.

The Packers met Chicago, their most-bitter rival, for just the second time ever in the playoffs. Only this time, the NFC Championship was at stake. Thanks to a stellar defensive effort, Green Bay toppled the Bears for the second time in three weeks, 21-14. The Packers' first Super Bowl appearance in 13 years was next.

With a 31-25 win over the Pittsburgh Steelers in Super Bowl XLV, McCarthy and the Packers finally proved they certainly weren't anyone's underdog. Rodgers, the MVP, was brilliant and the Packers led wire to wire.

At the heart of it all was their 47-year-old coach, who took an extremely bold approach during the final two months of the season and saw it pay off in spades. "That took some guts," Packers nose tackle B.J. Raji said. "It's a league now where people don't say that much. Nobody's Underdog — that's only a couple of words, I guess. But they were big."

McCarthy's daring change in style wasn't limited to just the New England game, either. It was a two-month journey in which McCarthy suddenly changed from Bill Belichick to Rex Ryan.

Four days before the Packers met the Bears in the regular season finale, McCarthy said, "We'll play anybody, anywhere. ... we are fully ready for this contest on Sunday."

One week later, when McCarthy was discussing the 12 playoff teams, he said, "I don't want to say wide open, but we feel very confident with our chances."

Three days before heading to Atlanta for the divisional playoffs, McCarthy said, "Winning breeds confidence, no doubt about it. We are very confident in the way we are built as a football team, and really more importantly how we have been shaped throughout the season, especially the stretch run here, particularly the last three games. We are very excited about the opportunity to play in Atlanta. I am very confident in our abilities, and we are fully preparing and expect to win the football game."

And shortly before heading to Chicago for the NFC title game, McCarthy boldly stated, "We do a very good job in our preparation as far as the way we travel. We feel we're a very good road team. ... Playing on the road doesn't bother us at all."

Each and every time McCarthy spoke his mind, the Packers backed up his bravado.

Then, the night before Super Bowl XLV, McCarthy made the remarkably daring move of having his team fitted for Super Bowl rings. The game was nearly 24 hours away from being played, but McCarthy's celebratory plans were already in full swing.

"I felt the measurement of the rings — the timing of it — would be special," McCarthy said. "It would have a significant effect on our players, doing it the night before the game."

Bold, daring and almost arrogant. But also effective. This is how McCarthy operated down the stretch in one of the most exciting times this franchise has ever known.

"Some of it was probably psychological," Pickett said. "I'm sure a lot of it was because he believed it. It was all fine with me. It worked, didn't it?"

To the surprise of many, things have worked out for McCarthy since he was hired on January 12, 2006, as Green Bay's 14th head coach. McCarthy was a darkhorse candidate, at best, to replace Mike Sherman. But McCarthy emerged from a deep and talented field and was given his first head coaching job — anywhere — at the age of 42.

McCarthy inherited a 4-12 football team that was old, lacked playmakers, and was dysfunctional in Sherman's final season. But five minutes into his initial press conference, McCarthy made a proclamation packed with confidence.

"I'd like to acknowledge the fans of Green Bay and just to let you know that there will be an unconditional commitment ... to bring a world championship back to Green Bay," McCarthy said. "I think that's very important to state right up front."

It was one of the few things McCarthy said that ever made headlines. And at the time, many undoubtedly chuckled.

But five years after McCarthy's declaration, he had helped make it happen. It was far from easy, as the Packers began McCarthy's first season 1-4 and were later 4-8. But that team found itself and rolled off a four-game winning streak to finish the year.

One season later, McCarthy was instrumental in getting Favre to play some of the best football of his life. The Packers won 10 of their first 11 games in 2007 and eventually hosted the NFC Championship game. But Green Bay suffered a devastating 23-20 overtime loss to the New York Giants in what would be Brett Favre's final game as a Packer.

The ensuing offseason was the most tumultuous in team history. Favre, who was second in the MVP balloting in 2007, retired, then changed his mind and tried coming back to the team in late June.

Green Bay was ready to move on, though, and had turned the team over to Rodgers. Over the next month, nasty words were exchanged between Favre and the Packers, feelings were hurt, relationships were destroyed.

Finally, McCarthy and Favre met for six hours on the night of Monday, August 4 to see whether any type of amicable solution could be reached. It couldn't, and Favre — arguably the greatest Packer in team history — was traded to the New York Jets two days later.

"I was just looking for him to tell me that he was ready to play for the Green Bay Packers, and if we would have gotten to that point, then our conversation would have continued, OK," McCarthy said. "And it did not get to that point, and that's the facts. Because once again, it's about the football team.

"I clearly understand, appreciate what Brett has done for this franchise. He's a remarkable football player. I've enjoyed coaching him, he's fun to watch, and I'm sure I will watch him when he does play. But until we got past that spot, I was not going to expose the football team to that. I think that would have been very poor leadership and management on my part."

McCarthy and the Packers moved on with Rodgers, and the early returns weren't good. Green Bay went just 6-10 in 2008 after notching a 13-3 record the previous year. That seven-game slide was the largest in NFL history and put McCarthy back on the hot seat.

Green Bay rebounded with an 11-5 season in 2009, but lost at Arizona in the opening round of the playoffs. The Packers were scuffling in 2010, when McCarthy's brazen approach seemed to turn the season around.

Nobody's underdog? That's for sure.

Today, McCarthy is one of just four coaches in franchise history who has brought a world championship to the NFL's smallest city. And as the Packers readied for the 2012 season, McCarthy's 63-33 record gave him the fourth-best winning percentage (.656) in franchise history, behind Vince Lombardi (.754), Mike Holmgren (.670) and Earl "Curly" Lambeau (.668).

Green Bay has reached the postseason in four of McCarthy's six seasons and won two NFC North titles. Oh yeah, then there's that Super Bowl run, the one in which McCarthy left his comfort zone and his team stunned the football world and brought a world championship back to Green Bay.

"I think when Mike said that stuff about not being underdogs, everybody believed it," Packers wide receiver Donald Driver said. "That was a big moment in our season.

"We were down a little bit. We were struggling and fighting just to get into the playoffs. But I think that fired some guys up, and sure enough, we went on to win the Super Bowl."

McCarthy's hometown of Greenfield, PA. Upper left: Chaser's formerly owned by McCarthy's father. Upper right: McCarthy's photo decorates the wall in the bar. Lower left: the home of McCarthy's parents, Joe and Ellen. They've lived on the same street for 43 years. Middle right: St. Rosalia, the church McCarthy used to attend and still makes donations to. Bottom right: the little league diamond McCarthy played on as a child. He is also a sponsor of the league. (Photos by Rob Reischel)

2
Greenfield Macho

The day Ted Thompson hired Mike McCarthy to coach the Green Bay Packers, he referred to McCarthy's "Pittsburgh Macho" as a major factor in the decision. McCarthy never said so, but he probably wished Thompson had called it "Greenfield Macho."

Technically, Greenfield is a neighborhood in Pittsburgh, a member of the 15th ward with a population of roughly 8,000. But those who grow up in Greenfield aren't truly from Pittsburgh. They're from Greenfield — and that's where it all began for McCarthy.

"We don't say we're from Pittsburgh," said Bernie O'Connor, one of Mike McCarthy's 70-plus cousins. "We're from Greenfield."

A trip to Greenfield is like a step back in time. McCarthy grew up on — of course — Greenfield Avenue, a long, narrow and winding street where everyone knows everyone else. The houses are all made of brick and were built in the early to mid 1900s. Several homes have awnings, while the American flag flies from most. There are some homes, too, that still have antenna ears on the roof. The houses are so tight, neighbors can high-five from their upstairs windows. The yards are small and the driveways are tight.

Life isn't easy, but there's a terrific sense of community and neighborhood pride. "Greenfield is a place that knew me when I was developing," McCarthy said. "It is a place that made me who I am. Where I am today, I owe that to Greenfield."

He also owes plenty to his parents, Joe and Ellen. McCarthy was one of five children who grew up in an Irish-Catholic house, where the prevailing themes were hard work and discipline.

Joe McCarthy was a jack-of-all-trades, who worked as a fireman, a policeman and later renovated homes — including the one Mike was raised in. "My father's the hardest working person I've ever been around," Mike McCarthy said. "He doesn't waste time."

Of all Joe's occupations, though, he was best known for owning Joe McCarthy's Bar & Grill. Located at the end of a hill and no bigger than most homes in Greenfield, the bar became a hangout for a neighboring steel factory that's closed today.

"The bar was packed at eight in the morning, it was packed at 4 o'clock in the afternoon, it was packed at midnight," Mike McCarthy said. "That's just the way you grew up. It's a blue-collar environment. I just think people were brought up the right way."

Mike worked in the bar each Sunday immediately after church. Mike did a little bit of everything, just like his father. He stocked the place, waited tables, tended bar, and even cleaned the bathroom that was in the basement. "And Joe was harder on him than anybody else," O'Connor said. "Tough love."

Today the bar is called "Chaser's in the Run," and locals say it still looks exactly the same. There's a pool table that sits in the middle of the bar. There's a pull-lever cigarette machine. The beer is cold, the food is unhealthy, and the prices might be the lowest in America. There are a few subtle differences, though.

The bathroom has been moved upstairs now. And Mike's picture — taken on the day he was hired as Green Bay's head coach — hangs above a corner booth with McCarthy's signature. To many in and around Greenfield, McCarthy has become a hero and role model.

"I am very humbled to know that, yes, maybe there is a little kid who says, 'He grew up here and he is an NFL coach, maybe I can do it someday,' " McCarthy told the *Pittsburgh Post-Gazette* in 2008. "There is a responsibility, and to hear that

Pittsburgh people might look up to me is the ultimate compliment, as far as I am concerned, the ultimate compliment."

While Joe McCarthy did all he could to provide for his family, Ellen ran the house. She also worked as a secretary and part-time waitress to help keep the seven McCarthy's afloat. "I grew up the right way," Mike McCarthy said. Indeed he did. And in many ways, the "Nobody's Underdog" approach McCarthy took with his 2010 football team was a blueprint of his own life.

McCarthy was athletically gifted, but so are thousands of kids across the nation. What always set McCarthy apart was his drive and hunger to succeed. "He was always organizing something," O'Connor said of his cousin. "Basketball tournaments, stuff in the backyard, whiffle ball tournaments. He cared a lot and was really passionate. That's just how Mike was. He had a gift ... and he was like that right away."

Sports were always McCarthy's passion. And he was ahead of the curve from the start. McCarthy, a diehard Pittsburgh Steelers fan, was bigger than all his classmates. He attended St. Rosalia Academy, a Catholic school built in 1912 that also sits on Greenfield Avenue, a mile from where McCarthy grew up. McCarthy was a terrific basketball player at St. Rosalia, where he once helped the school go 39-1.

"Everything he picked up he seemed to excel at," said Marty Coyne, a youth baseball and basketball coach of McCarthy's.

Not far from St. Rosalia was Magee Park, a recreational facility that includes basketball courts, and a swimming pool and proclaims Greenfield to be "a fine residential community." It was there that McCarthy and his friends spent much of their summers.

McCarthy also competed in the Greenfield Baseball Association, where some of his best sporting moments took place. "He was the pitcher and I was the catcher," O'Connor said. "He was so much bigger than everyone else. There were times I thought he broke my hand."

McCarthy hasn't lived in Greenfield for nearly three decades now. But he still gives $100,000 a year back to his hometown — including $90,000 to St. Rosalia and $5,000 each to the Greenfield Baseball Association and the Greenfield Organization.

"The lessons I learned at Magee Field and at St. Rosalia are things that I think back on every day," McCarthy told the *Post-Gazette*. "When I think of Magee Field, I think of it as being our little inner-city country club.

"We had a pool, we had baseball fields, we had basketball courts ... there were always hundreds of people, and there was always something going on. And when I think of St. Rosalia, I think of discipline, academics, and I think of being taught how to live your life the right way. All of that, to this day, is very important to me, and it all started back in Greenfield."

St. Rosalia didn't offer football, though. So it wasn't until McCarthy arrived at Bishop Boyle High School in neighboring Homestead, Pennslyvania, that he started turning heads on the gridiron, too. Bishop Boyle has been closed since 1987. But some of McCarthy's achievements are still remembered fondly.

On the football field, McCarthy was a defensive end, a tight end, a kicker and a punter. Football was probably his third–best sport, though, and few would have predicted it would one day become his meal ticket.

But Baker University, an NAIA school in Baldwin City, Kansas, offered McCarthy a chance to play college football and continue chasing his dreams. It was there that McCarthy blossomed into a standout tight end, a captain and recently was recently inducted into that school's Hall of Fame.

"To have a Baker University athletic alumnus make it to the pinnacle of coaching as a head coach of an NFL team is just unimaginable," said Baker athletic director Dan Harris, who was an assistant football coach for the Wildcats in the mid-1980s, when McCarthy played at Baker. "Mike has created a new level of respectability for a traditional powerhouse NFL football program."

After graduating from Baker with a business administration degree, McCarthy landed a graduate assistant job at Fort Hayes State where he coached linebackers in 1987 and 1988. One of McCarthy's big coaching breaks, though, came in 1989 when University of Pittsburgh coach Paul Hackett hired him as a volunteer assistant.

McCarthy wasn't paid initially. But the staff he worked with included Marvin Lewis and Jon Gruden, who would both go on to become NFL head coaches. And McCarthy and Hackett forged a terrific bond.

"I think most of our staff at the University of Pittsburgh at that time has either coached in the NFL or still is coaching," McCarthy said. "I've been around a lot of very good football coaches, very good players that I was able to learn from."

It was during that time McCarthy moved back to Greenfield, and to make some money during the summer, he worked nights at the Allegheny Valley tollbooth on the Pennsylvania Turnpike.

"It was a summer job," McCarthy said. "It was something that I felt I needed to do between graduating from Fort Hays State University (in Kansas). You get your master's degree and you go and collect tolls. That doesn't quite add up, but that was my plan and path. Really, it was a good experience. It was something really just to make some money before the season started at the University of Pittsburgh, before we went to training camp.

"I know a lot has been made about it. I don't want to disrespect the Pennsylvania Turnpike. I did my job and I studied while I was there when there were no cars coming through the booth. It was a good experience. I always felt that was the normal way. You have summer jobs, you do those types of things, and I'm glad I took the path that I did, as far as a young man back then being exposed to those types of things."

Perhaps the most important thing McCarthy was exposed to at Pitt was the West Coast offense. Hackett had learned the offense from its master, former San Francisco 49ers coach Bill Walsh. And while McCarthy would later put his own stamp on it, the West Coast offense became his staple.

Hackett was fired after the 1992 season, but landed the offensive coordinator's job with the Kansas City Chiefs. Much to McCarthy's delight, Hackett — and Chiefs head coach Marty Schottenheimer — brought McCarthy along as an offensive assistant/quality control coach.

McCarthy was giddy. He was just 29 years old and had already achieved one dream of working in the NFL. McCarthy studied Schottenheimer's every move. And McCarthy has referred to him countless times since coming to Green Bay.

"I'm very grateful to Marty Schottenheimer," McCarthy said. "He gave me my first opportunity in the league. I have great respect for him on a personal and professional level."

McCarthy spent six years with the Chiefs, the last four as their quarterbacks coach. In that time, he worked with Hall of Famer Joe Montana, future MVP Rich Gannon, along with solid pros Elvis Grbac and Steve Bono.

It was also in Kansas City that McCarthy started believing he could become an NFL head coach one day. "Having the opportunity to be around Marty Schottenheimer and just the way he ran his program, his work ethic," McCarthy said. "I felt as an assistant coach that that's when it came to me that I felt that I'd be able to be a head coach in this league someday. I couldn't tell you an exact date, but it was at some point in my career in Kansas City."

Green Bay hired McCarthy as its quarterbacks coach in 1999, and he jumped at the opportunity to work with Brett Favre. But Packers head coach Ray Rhodes was fired after just one year, and McCarthy was on the move again.

The Rhodes debacle didn't hurt McCarthy's stock, as New Orleans hired him to be its offensive coordinator. But there was nothing easy about landing that job.

McCarthy laughs today about spending three days preparing his résumé at a Kinko's on Oneida Street in Green Bay. McCarthy then spent the better part of a week interviewing for the position with head coach Jim Haslett and assistant head coach Rick Venturi.

"We went to the office the first day and then every night about 10:00, 11:00, Jim Haslett and Rick Venturi, we would just start talking about football, different situations, different circumstances," McCarthy remembers. "And after about five days it was, I mean, it got to be monotonous. It was like, you asked me that question three times already.

"We were at dinner with (quarterback) Jeff Blake. We just signed Jeff Blake with a free-agent contract, and Jim said, 'You need to talk to him about what you're going to do on offense.' I said, 'Well, I don't even know where we are.' He goes, 'Oh, hell, you got the job. You knew that, didn't you?' That's how I found out I had it. Good experience."

So was McCarthy's time in New Orleans. Over the next five seasons, the Saints set 10 offensive team records, 25 individual marks, and they enjoyed the most explosive stretch in the franchise's 40-year history. McCarthy was named the NFL's Assistant Coach of the Year in 2000 and helped the Saints rank as the No. 1 scoring offense in 2002.

McCarthy became San Francisco's offensive coordinator in 2005, but the 49ers struggled immensely on offense and finished 32nd in the league. San Francisco was decimated by injuries that season, and 49ers rookie quarterback Alex Smith — the No. 1 pick in that April's draft — wasn't ready to play.

It all added up to a 4-12 season for the 49ers. Despite the disappointing year, McCarthy's stock remained high. "Mike is a very good football coach, very hard working and a great guy to work with," said Mike Nolan, who was the 49ers head coach in 2005. "He understands people and how important it is to have good people in the organization.

"Always wanted to know why we did what we did as a head coach, from my standpoint. I think Mike has paid a lot of close attention to the guys he's worked for. I know the circumstances, to some degree, the football team being 4-12 and not being very good statistically offensively. But Mike's an outstanding coach."

When the Green Bay Packers dumped Mike Sherman after the 2005 season, McCarthy applied. But most considered him a long shot — at best.

Packers general manager Ted Thompson would eventually interview seven candidates. Some were surprised McCarthy even made it that far.

"I've spoken with a number of people who have gone through this process, and they tell me over and over again that what you really think is going to happen turns out not to be the case," Thompson said after firing Sherman. "The person you think is going to be the right fit is not the right fit, and it turns out to be someone completely surprising to you.

"We're going to try to interview as many good candidates as possible and try not to have the answer before we go into the process. We'll let the process work itself out."

Thompson met with Dallas assistant head coach/passing game coordinator Sean Payton, Cleveland offensive coordinator Maurice Carthon, Chicago defensive coordinator Ron Rivera, San Diego defensive coordinator Wade Phillips, New York Giants defensive coordinator Tim Lewis and Packers defensive coordinator Jim Bates and Mike McCarthy.

Of those, Payton was the young, hot, assistant coach at the time, and many believed he was the favorite. But like Thompson had predicted, things rarely go the way you believe they will. The extremely cerebral and methodical Thompson took his time. He always does. And 11 days after Thompson fired Sherman, he made the surprising decision to hire McCarthy.

"I just can't tell you how excited and honored I am for this opportunity," McCarthy said.

There wasn't any one particular quality or a single mind-blowing answer that sold Thompson on McCarthy. Instead, it came down to a feeling that McCarthy was simply the best fit for the Packers in 2006 — and in the long term.

"I don't think there was any one," Thompson said of the factors that led him to McCarthy. "I think it was just the whole. I tried to obviously focus on the small things and the things I thought were really, really important.

"I had these long sheets of paper that I'd go through and I'd scribble, and at the end of it, I always had reminder things. And I talked to a lot of different people and I'd say, 'What makes a good head coach, what makes a good working relationship?' those kind of things."

Thompson fully believed that as soon as he finished interviewing the right man for the job, he'd know. But it wasn't quite that simple. And for a man as deliberate as Thompson, it made for some tense times.

"I had some marvelous conversations with seven different people, and after you get through with each guy you think, 'Boy, that was really good,'" Thompson said. "But I tried to concentrate and focus that I was going to go through the process. I was going to finish through the guys that I knew for sure I wanted to do interviews with.

"At the end of it, I felt that there were several candidates that would make excellent head coaches here. The difficult part for me was finally settling and saying, 'OK, this is the right thing.' There were a lot of things, a lot of different qualities, but a lot of these men had the same qualities, too, the same things you look for in a head coach. But at the end of the day I think Mike McCarthy is the right guy at the right time."

There was a long list of things Thompson liked about McCarthy. Among them was the fact McCarthy had worked with quarterbacks such as Favre in Green Bay, Brooks in New Orleans, and Montana, Gannon, Grbac and Bono in Kansas City. All of the signal callers excelled under McCarthy, giving him the reputation as a "quarterback guru."

Thompson liked what he referred to as "Pittsburgh macho stuff," a no-nonsense, tough-guy approach McCarthy developed in Greenfield — and continued throughout his coaching days.

Thompson liked McCarthy's familiarity with the Packers' organization. And he felt McCarthy's leadership abilities were just what a Green Bay team coming off a 4-12 season — its worst performance since 1991 — needed.

"What stood out to me in the interview process was Mike's leadership ability and the comfort level that he and I had on a personal level," Thompson said. "Mike is someone who is a tough, no-nonsense person. That appealed to me very much.

"And he is all about football. He has tremendous football knowledge, which was very clear throughout the interview process. Going into this, I wanted someone who would fit within this organization, with our players and in this community. I believe Mike has those qualities."

As important as all of that was, perhaps the most important characteristic Thompson went looking for was someone whom he could work well with. That certainly wasn't the case with Thompson and Sherman.

Thompson had replaced Sherman as Green Bay's general manager in January 2005, and Sherman never got over the demotion. While the two were professional, their relationship never grew into anything more.

McCarthy, meanwhile, was Green Bay's quarterbacks coach in 1999, a time when Thompson was the Packers' director of player personnel. The two developed a relationship then and Thompson believed they'd work well together again.

"I think it's important, especially in Green Bay with the way this organization is structured, for the head coach and the general manager to have a really good relationship, sort of a comfort level," Thompson said. "I don't know... maybe it'd be the same way any place. You need to be comfortable when you're sitting across the table and talking and being able to chew the fat and walk down the hall and say 'How you doing? How are the kids?'"

Thompson had his hand-picked head coach. And he fully believed McCarthy could lead Green Bay back to its accustomed place among the league's elite. "I studied his record. I talked to a lot of people. I talked to a ton of people, none of whom I could thank enough," Thompson said. "I talked to a lot of head coaches. I talked to a lot of general managers going through this process, and Mike's name was one that kept coming up.

"The fact that I knew him from before, I knew his work ethic. Everyone who ever worked with him spoke glowingly of him, I thought I'd bring him in. I didn't bring him in thinking, 'This is going to be the next head coach.' I tried to have no preconceived ideas. I'm very glad I did."

McCarthy was on cloud nine.

It wasn't that long ago he was working in his father's bar or in a toll booth. Now he was guiding an NFL team with more history and world championships (13) than any other.

"I think the opportunity of me sitting in this chair is a prime example that you can do anything in this world if you put your mind to it," McCarthy said. "That's something you sit there and try and tell your children.

"The bottom line, and I truly believe this, is that this is God's plan. I did not plan this. To sit here and say when I was 15 years old I planned on being the Green Bay Packers' head coach, that would not be true. But I had to do my part to make it happen. And this is not the accomplishment for me. The accomplishment is upholding the tradition. Trust me, I'm honored to be the head coach of the Green Bay Packers. But I'm not done yet."

Indeed he wasn't.

McCarthy eventually made good on his Super Bowl promise and turned "Nobody's Underdog" into a catch phrase. Just as important, he found peace and serenity in his personal life.

McCarthy married his high school sweetheart when he was young, and the two later had a daughter, Alexandra. When that marriage ended, though, Alex lived with her mother, and McCarthy was a bachelor for several years.

In Green Bay, though, McCarthy's professional and personal life both hit new heights. McCarthy married Jessica Kress in March 2008. It was the second marriage for both, and Kress had two sons, Jack and George, from her first marriage. As a couple, Mike and Jessica added two daughters to their family, Gabrielle and Isabella.

"It's been awesome," McCarthy said. "To me, (kids) are the reality check. This is a selfish profession. It's very demanding on your time and your energy, but more important, it's so demanding on your personal life. There's obviously benefits your family is able to experience ... but what they give up because of the time away from them is substantial.

"The opportunity to be with my family is of the utmost, highest priority. There's nothing like children. That's the greatest gift that I've ever been given.

"And right now, one of the greatest things is seeing my 20-year old (Alexandra) embrace her two stepbrothers and her two sisters. To have one in college and one in diapers is a pretty wide stretch, but it's been awesome. Very blessed."

Those who know McCarthy best, like former offensive coordinator Joe Philbin — who's now the head coach in Miami — have always been impressed with McCarthy's balance. And they believe it's a big reason for McCarthy's success.

"I think he's got great balance in a lot of areas," Philbin said of McCarthy. "His perspective is excellent. He's gotten very passionate about things that are important to him. I think that's clearly evident. And he's got balance, balance with the staff, balance with the players.

"He knows when to be tough, when to lighten up. He's got a good feel for those types of things, both with his coaching staff and his team. I think that's a real strength of his. And I think he's got a passion that the staff feels as well. The passion to achieve something special and honor the tradition and build on it and that's good. Those are two real good qualities that he has.

"He's very poised, and I think that's part of the balance he has in football and out of football. That's certainly different. We all hope you evolve and grow as a coach. Maybe he's a little bit more poised than he was earlier. I don't care how prepared you are, I'm guessing when you become a head coach there's pressures you weren't sure of, and probably until you sit in that chair you're not too certain about it. And so as he sat in that chair longer, I think he's gotten a good, wider perspective on things, and he's been able to deal with the ups and downs really well."

There would be plenty of ups and downs to come. But much of what McCarthy learned in Greenfield and along his journey to Green Bay were vital in handling them. "I think it's important to stay in the structure of my position and just be a consistent individual," McCarthy said. "I don't try to be liked. I don't try to be disliked, either. Because at the end of the day, being a head coach, it's lonely sometimes because you have to keep your eye on the target and be in tune with what's going on with the culture and structure. You don't have the time to maybe have that relationship that you did as an assistant coach or even a coordinator. And I miss all that.

"But to me, communication is the key to everything. I believe first and foremost communication is a two-way street. I've learned so much in life and coaching, not by talking but by listening. I think that's very important to practice what you preach.

"And I've talked about communication since the day I got into coaching. It's nothing that's new to any relationship that I've been a part of in the National Football League. Hopefully it's working."

The McCarthy Way would eventually work like a charm. But back in January 2006, McCarthy was just getting started. He had more work to do than anyone in football.

And not very many people were betting on him.

3

Getting to Know You

Tony Fisher didn't do himself any favors. The thing is, he wasn't alone. Fisher, Green Bay's veteran running back, was told his new head coach was named Mike McCarthy. Fisher admitted he never heard of McCarthy, then asked, "What's his name, Mike Mularkey?"

Mularkey was the head coach in Buffalo at the time. And while McCarthy didn't have great name recognition, it didn't take players long to understand what their new head coach was all about.

"I would say he's no-nonsense, but fair is even better," Packers fullback William Henderson said of McCarthy. "What he wanted was for you to come to work every day and give your best effort, whether it was practice or games. If that's no-nonsense, basically it's just asking you to be accountable."

Henderson was one of five players who finished the 2005 season on Green Bay's roster and who had also played for the Packers in 1999 when McCarthy was part of Ray Rhodes' staff. Nose tackle Grady Jackson was in New Orleans when McCarthy was the Saints' offensive coordinator.

Those most familiar with Green Bay's new head coach believed the Packers had themselves a keeper. "He impressed me and I think he'll be a great coach," Jackson said of McCarthy. "He's a good guy. I congratulate him."

At 42, McCarthy came to Green Bay as the third-youngest coach in the NFL. But he immediately laid out a vision for what he wanted, and he wasn't afraid to challenge those around him.

"Every team needs that," running back Ahman Green said of McCarthy's no-nonsense approach. "No-nonsense doesn't necessarily mean not a players' coach. No-nonsense means when he wants stuff done, he gets stuff done. He wants it done in a certain way, in a certain fashion.

"That's kind of how I played college football at Nebraska. Coach (Tom) Osborne was a no-nonsense guy, but he was a players' coach. And when he wanted things done, he wanted things done his way and almost to the point of perfection. And that's what I think Coach McCarthy is."

Henderson agreed. "I thought he did a phenomenal job working with Brett and some of the other quarterbacks that were here at the time," Henderson said of McCarthy's year in Green Bay. "And we had a successful year.

"Guys who didn't expect to have such successful years were able to have breakout years. We didn't do as well as a team. There were times we mishit on different cues, or whatever. But (McCarthy) was one of those guys who was consistent and had everybody's best interests at heart. And I thought (McCarthy) did a phenomenal job."

The problem was, McCarthy was inheriting a mess. Green Bay's new head coach would never come out and admit that publicly. But of the seven head coaching vacancies that existed after the 2005 season, the Packers' job was among the least attractive.

Mike Sherman's final team went 4-12, Green Bay's worst record in 14 seasons. Even more concerning, though, was that the Packers' best players were veterans largely past their prime.

Sherman had ruled the draft room for four seasons and flopped miserably in that role. So the Packers were now without talented youngsters who should have been in their prime. However, Green Bay's brass always put on a happy face when discussing the roster. The word "rebuilding" was never used.

McCarthy got the message pretty fast. "Well, I think in the National Football League, as I've had the opportunity to take different jobs, either you're purchasing the dream house or you're building the dream house," McCarthy said. "I think that my last two opportunities were building programs. New Orleans, we started from the ground up. And San Francisco, obviously this past year, it was the same type of scenario.

"I think the situation walking into here is clearly, I'm purchasing my dream house. Now, we may knock down a few walls and give all the rooms a fresh coat of paint. But, this definitely is not a rebuilding process. We're not building a dream house here.

"There's a great foundation. We have a tradition, resources that are second to none in the National Football League and I think that obviously gives us a springboard to get ready to compete for the upcoming season."

Few took McCarthy's "dream house" comment seriously, though. There were several reasons for that.

- When McCarthy took the job, he had no idea if quarterback Brett Favre would return. And even if he did, Favre was coming off the worst season of his career in 2005, when he led the NFL with 29 interceptions.
- Aaron Rodgers, Green Bay's No. 1 draft pick in 2005, was abysmal during his first training camp and exhibition season. If Favre chose retirement, McCarthy would be left with Rodgers or a veteran castoff to lead his first team.
- While Sherman's drafts were typically a mess, Thompson's first 12 months on the job weren't much better. Aside from safety Nick Collins, Thompson's first draft produced little immediate help. Thompson also allowed both of his starting guards, Mike Wahle and Marco Rivera, to depart in free agency. Thompson then tried to replace both players in free agency and struck out.

  Thompson gave Adrian Klemm an $800,000 signing bonus to play left guard, then watched Klemm struggle immensely and eventually get benched. Still, that was better than Thompson's plan of Matt O'Dwyer at right guard. The 33-year-old O'Dwyer was over the hill, showed nothing in training camp, and was released before camp ended.

- Although the defense ranked eighth overall in 2005, there were few precious playmakers. Green Bay forced just 21 turnovers, the third lowest mark in franchise history, and a total that ranked just 26th in football.
- Finally, the running game was in shambles because the interior of the line needed a total overhaul. In addition, running backs Green and Najeh Davenport were both unrestricted free agents coming off major injuries. And Samkon Gado had just eight games of NFL experience.

"I think the roster is OK," Thompson said. "I think we played with a lot of young guys (in 2005). We had to in some cases, but I think that experience should help us in the future. There are some question marks. We have to get some guys back who were injured and get them healthy and see how they're doing. But I feel pretty positive about our roster. We'll be OK."

McCarthy wanted to believe that. But as McCarthy readied for his first head coaching job, he was fully aware the odds weren't in his favor.

4

Summer of 2006

There's no doubt, McCarthy caught some breaks early in his Packers tenure. Without them, a tricky first season could have been disastrous.

First, quarterback Brett Favre decided to return for the 2006 campaign. It took Favre 113 days to make up his mind, but having him back in the fold was great news for McCarthy and his new staff. Sure, Favre was coming off a year in which he threw more interceptions (29) than touchdowns (20). His quarterback rating of 70.9 was his poorest since he became a starter in 1992 and ranked a miserable 31st in the NFL.

But Green Bay was playing from behind almost every week, causing Favre to play with a wild abandon he hadn't shown since his early years in Green Bay. The Packers' offense was also decimated by injury, and Green Bay was down to fifth-string running back Samkon Gado by the end of the season.

Many blamed Favre for Green Bay's woes. But McCarthy knew Favre's return was key for 2006. "To be honest with you, I don't think I played any differently in my approach last year than any other year," Favre said that offseason. "I know when we were winning games every week and being ahead all the time there's a different way of playing the game. And being 4-12 was obviously new to me.

"As the season progressed, we were playing from behind, and it was different. There was a different guy in the huddle all the time. Maybe I should have made some different decisions at times, but we had to try to win the ball game with whoever was in there.

"Sometimes you take chances and you know the odds are against you. But I'm not going to sit there and throw 3-yard checkdowns and let the clock run down. I'm going to take chances, and there are going to be people who agree with that and people who don't agree with that. And I really don't care."

McCarthy and offensive coordinator Jeff Jagodzinski needed only a few minutes with Favre to realize his golden arm was as powerful as ever. "I'll tell you this, his arm strength ain't no different," Jagodzinski said. "His decision making and seeing the whole field is as good as I remember."

But one of McCarthy's greatest challenges would be getting Favre to play with more discipline. During the 2005 season, Favre had virtually disregarded Mike Sherman's coaching and became arguably the greatest risk taker in football.

McCarthy believed he could corral Favre, though. The two had developed a solid working relationship in 1999 and picked up where they left off.

McCarthy also knew the gap between Favre and backup Aaron Rodgers was cavernous. So Green Bay's staff was thrilled when Favre decided to return in 2006 rather than call it a career. "It's important for him to play within the realm of the offense, which I think he always has," McCarthy said. "I've said it over and over again, when you call plays, the play caller and the quarterback have to be on the same page.

"You have to know when to push the envelope and pull back. If you push the envelope too much, a lot of times you may get away with it, but also you're in an area of turnovers and things like that that can happen to you. You've just got to be smart, got to be smart."

McCarthy's second big break that offseason came when general manager Ted Thompson signed cornerback Charles Woodson to a seven-year, $52 million free-agent contract.

Woodson, one of football's top corners for years, had no real interest or desire in coming to Green Bay. But when the NFL's other 31 teams showed no interest in Woodson, he had little choice but to accept the Packers' money.

"I wasn't happy that day," Woodson said of signing a free-agent contract with the Packers. "I wasn't happy whatsoever. I wasn't sold on coming here, but there were really no other options. It got to a point where I just had to accept what was going on. There just wasn't a lot of interest.

"I was talking to my agent every day and he was making phone calls to different teams, but nobody was interested. And every time I called him, he'd say, 'Well, Green Bay called.' And I'd say, 'Anybody else?' Man, I tried damn near every other team, but it wasn't happening."

Woodson's arrival and pairing with fellow standout cornerback Al Harris gave Green Bay's defense an enormous shot in the arm. The defense got another boost when Thompson signed free agent defensive tackle Ryan Pickett.

As McCarthy's first training camp neared, the rookie head coach was brimming with optimism. "What (would) I like to happen this season?" McCarthy asked. "Clearly, to win the Super Bowl. I mean, there's only one goal when you work in this business. That will always be our goal.

"I think parity in our business is very evident over the last 10 years in the league. I think you've seen turnarounds happen year to year, and I would not be comfortable ever standing in front of a group of men and telling them to go 8-8. That's not in my nature, and I don't think that's how you approach this business.

"I'm a big believer of playing the game a certain way. As long as you do that consistently, you're going to have an opportunity to win a lot of games. So we have a style of play and an approach of how we will play the game and we will adhere to that, and I feel we will be in a position to win a lot of football games."

McCarthy's first training camp was unlike any in the Green Bay Packers' 88-year history. On eight different occasions that summer, McCarthy conducted night practices on Clarke Hinkle Field. Under Curly Lambeau, Vince Lombardi, Mike Holmgren and every coach in between, the Packers practiced either in the morning or the afternoon heat. But McCarthy saw great benefits in shaking things up.

First, night practices allowed the players ample rest between practices and ensured they would spend less time in the mid-day sweltering heat. Second, after each practice there was plenty of time to review and make corrections before taking the field again.

McCarthy believed that schedule would keep his team fresher, while providing more time to make adjustments in the classroom. "The strength of practicing at night is really the way the schedule breaks down," McCarthy said. "You really operate on a one-a-day schedule and a two-a-day schedule. With this schedule, it gives you the ability to always meet and then practice and then go back to a meeting and correct and meet again before the next practice.

"So there's a lot of benefits to it, obviously, from the players' wear-and-tear standpoint, because they really only have the one, big, long 2 1/2-hour practice one-a-day. When you're on a two-a-day schedule, it's really not as long a practice.

"Today's game is different. It's different. You don't have as many people in camp, and the salary cap obviously is a focus. So that's definitely the benefit of it. Also, it's fan-friendly and it's coaching-friendly. There are just so many benefits of going to this schedule. I've done both and that's why we're doing this."

McCarthy picked up on the night practices while he was an assistant coach in New Orleans. The Saints practiced in Thibideaux, Louisiana, and McCarthy said working the night shift also helped take some of the monotony out of training camp.

"We'd have 8,000 to 10,000 people in the stands, and our players were sprinting through the walk-throughs," McCarthy said. "It was the whole level. Players liked it. When the lights come on and you put people in the stands, especially when you get into your second and third week of training camp, it's a great boost."

The Packers rented 30-foot rising lights from Magnum Products in Berlin, Wisconsin. Five sets of lights were lined on each side of the field, and another one was placed in the south end.

While the players enjoyed the night practices, the fans certainly benefited, too. Many times, the Packers faithful were forced to use vacation days to see training camp practices. Now, those in the surrounding Fox Valley area who worked during the day could still make it in time for a night practice.

"I've never practiced at night in training camp," Woodson said after the first practice. "And it was pretty cool. That was nice."

The quality of football, on the other hand, wasn't nearly as nice that summer. Green Bay lost three of its four preseason games and was a team that didn't appear to have many answers for its plethora of questions.

Rookie offensive linemen Daryn Colledge, Jason Spitz and Tony Moll were all green but would combine to be Green Bay's starting guards. The running game lacked pop, and the Packers were asking rookie Greg Jennings to become the No. 2 receiver.

Woodson struggled that summer and appeared disinterested at times. He and McCarthy had words after more than one practice.

The rest of the defense, which forced just 21 turnovers in 2005, remained a work in progress. Yet the word "rebuilding" never came from the lips of McCarthy or Thompson, despite the fact they'd have football's youngest team in 2006. "To me, rebuilding's more of a mindset from the chair I sit it. And if you want to justify your rebuilding, you usually can," McCarthy said. "Just look at the experience of our roster. I think rebuilding, I think youth, I think inexperience, I think injuries, I look at them all as excuses. I look at them as chinks in your armor that people are trying to either get at you with or justify.

"One thing I don't ever want to put in that locker room is self-justification on why something went wrong. It's all about what we need to do to make it right. I'm fully aware of how much experience we have and where guys are at in their development.

"But if you're on this football team, you have a responsibility to perform at a level that puts us in position to win football games. Period. That's the way I look at."

That was certainly a glass-half-full approach. McCarthy would soon discover that glass — at least at the start of the 2006 season — was closer to empty.

5

Off and Running

Mike McCarthy couldn't wait. It was only Wednesday, four days before the season opener against Chicago, the defending champs of the NFC North. And McCarthy seemed ready to go hit Bears quarterback Rex Grossman himself.

McCarthy had coached football for nearly 20 years in six different cities. But September 10, 2006, would be the first game McCarthy was a head coach.

"I'm obviously excited on a personal level," McCarthy said. "From a professional standpoint, it's obviously a job I've always dreamed of, and to have the opportunity to go out there and tee it up for the first time, I'm really looking forward to it."

McCarthy also couldn't wait to see his team perform. The NFL had become a league where the only certainty was its uncertainty. Teams came from nowhere each season to win divisions, playoff games and even conferences.

In 2005, for example, every division winner in the NFC was different from 2004. And of the six NFC teams that qualified for the playoffs in 2004, only one returned in 2005. Now, with his first game as a head coach looming, McCarthy believed the 2006 Packers could be one of those surprise teams.

"I think parity's very evident in the NFL," McCarthy said. "Usually one team jumps up every year. With that in mind, it's so important to play to who you are, offensive, defense and special teams. If you stay away from your weaknesses, play to your strengths, don't beat yourself, you'll be in every game, especially early in the season.

"Early in the season, more games are lost than won, and the probability of making the playoffs based on your first four games is a big indicator of how the team's going to do. Some people want to ask how many games we can win. Seriously, I'm trying to win them all. You tell me at the end of the year how many I won. Our intention is to win the division, get home-field advantage, and win the Super Bowl. That will always be the goal."

That goal looked a million miles away after the opener.

For much of Brett Favre's career, he had owned the Bears. Favre was 21-7 against Chicago during his first 14 seasons, and he had engineered a 10-game winning streak against the Bears between 1994-98.

In McCarthy's head coaching debut, though, Green Bay's offense was a wreck. The defense and special teams weren't any better, as the Packers suffered a 26-0 defeat before nearly 71,000 fans at Lambeau Field.

It was the first time in Favre's 15-year career with the Packers that he'd been shut out.

"I have to admit I was optimistic going into this game," Favre said. "I really was. Maybe I was the only one, but I felt like we could really surprise these guys and surprise a lot of people. That obviously is not the case. Maybe I was wrong, but I'm very confident in what I can do and my ability to lead the offense."

McCarthy, Favre and the Packers' offense were no match for the Bears on that day. Green Bay managed just 14 first downs and went 1-of-11 on third downs. Favre threw for just 164 yards, and the Packers lost the turnover battle, 3-1.

"Maybe we just ain't very good," Favre said. "I don't know."

McCarthy, who got the job in Green Bay thanks to his offensive background, wouldn't go that far. But he certainly didn't like what he saw in Week 1.

Grossman threw the ball at will against Green Bay, finishing with 262 passing yards, one touchdown and a 98.6 passer rating. And the Packers' pass defense, which ranked No. 1 in the NFL during the 2005 campaign, was completely out of sorts, as players such as safety Marquand Manuel, linebacker Brady Poppinga and cornerback Al Harris were torched all day.

"I know I let my guy catch too many," said Harris, who was largely responsible for Muhsin Muhammad's six-catch, 102-yard day. "I personally can't give up completions. That's how I look at it personally. No matter how long I have to cover, I can't give up completions."

Green Bay's special teams were equally miserable, as Noah Herron fumbled a kickoff, Nick Collins had a roughing-the-kicker penalty, and kicker Daye Rayner had a miserable field goal attempt from 53 yards.

To top it off, Bears ace return man Devin Hester returned a punt 84 yards for a touchdown early in the fourth quarter to complete the scoring. "We certainly had more negative things than positive things to show as results," Packers special teams coach Mike Stock said. "No question about it."

Without question, this was one of the roughest openers in team history. Green Bay, which began playing football in 1919, had 87 openers before McCarthy arrived. In just five of those had the Packers suffered a larger defeat.

"Any time you compete in the National Football League arena and you get shut out, that's not a good feeling," McCarthy said. "I'm not diving on no sword. We're 0-1 right now, we have some work to do as a football team, we will continue to work as a football team, and we've got a lot better days ahead of us."

Those days were clearly down the road, though.

Green Bay lost a second straight home game in Week 2, this time by a 34-27 count to New Orleans and its rookie head coach Sean Payton. Just one year earlier, the Saints were also 4-12, but Payton looked like he had his program ahead of McCarthy's.

Interestingly, Payton also interviewed for the Packers' head coaching job but lost out to McCarthy. Payton later got the Saints job, but he wrote in his book *Home Team: Coaching the Saints and New Orleans Back to Life* that the job he really wanted was in Green Bay.

"I'd flown up to Green Bay and had a terrific interview with the Packers," Payton wrote. "That's a great organization — a team I had followed since I was a kid. I felt optimistic about that possibility. ... I really thought there was a good chance I was getting the Packers' job. Without a doubt, Green Bay is where I wanted to go."

Payton was later in New Orleans, interviewing for the Saints' opening, when Packers' general manager Ted Thompson called.

"I had a message from Ted Thompson, the Packers GM," Payton wrote. "Ted got right to the point. 'Hey,' he said, 'the process has gone well. We've decided to go in a different direction, and I wanted to let you know as soon as possible. It hasn't come out yet. Please don't say anything until we announce it.' I wanted to cry. I appreciated the heads-up. But damn!"

On this forgettable Sunday, many Packers fans were probably wondering if Green Bay hired the wrong guy. Saints quarterback Drew Brees shredded the Packers, throwing for 353 yards, two touchdowns, and had six completions of at least 23 yards. Green Bay's offense showed signs of life, as Favre threw three touchdowns. But the Packers blew an early 13-0 lead, and afterward, questions immediately turned to team morale.

McCarthy knew he had to fix Green Bay's rotten pass defense, its shoddy running game and awful special teams. But two weeks into his first season, McCarthy had to ensure the Packers' self-esteem and confidence didn't go AWOL.

"It's hard, period, because human nature when you're down is just to give up," Packers defensive end Kabeer Gbaja-Biamila said. "You say, 'It's over, it's done.' I don't know why human nature is that way. It's a lot easier to quit. It's harder to just keep the faith.

"But the Bible says, 'A righteous man falls seven times, but he gets back up.' And what makes him righteous is not that he fell down, it's that he got back up. If I get back up, I can fight again. We have to keep fighting."

In Green Bay's last 19 games, it was just 4-15 (.267). In the 70 games prior to that, the Packers were 46-24 (.657). The losing was completely foreign to most of the veteran players. And McCarthy's challenge was making sure that defeat didn't become acceptable to anyone in the building.

"You worry about (the younger players) understanding enough of the fact that this isn't the way things are around here," Packers defensive end Aaron Kampman said. "Positive yes, that no one's going to go in the tank. Negative from the standpoint that they need to understand that this isn't the way things have been done around here. We don't start 0-2, and this has been two years now where we've been 0-for in the first couple games.

"All in all, bottom line is it's extremely frustrating being 0-2, especially starting our season at Lambeau. I hate saying this, I've said it for a while, but we're growing. We have to continue to keep swinging. It's a 15-round fight, and the decision for the bout isn't made in the third round. So we'll keep swinging."

After some early swings and misses, McCarthy and the Packers finally got it right in Week 3. Green Bay went to Detroit, where the Lions and rookie head coach Rod Marinelli were also off to an 0-2 start. Still, the oddsmakers installed Detroit as a 7-point favorite.

However, Favre was brilliant on this day, throwing for 340 yards, three touchdowns and no interceptions. Rookie wideout Greg Jennings had 101 receiving yards and a magnificent 75-yard TD in which he spun free of safety Jon McGraw and ran away from cornerback Dre' Bly. And the Packers made just enough plays during some tense final minutes to prevail, 31-24.

"That's the way you're supposed to spend Sunday afternoon," an excited McCarthy said afterward. "Excellent win for us. I'm just really happy the way they scrapped and fought for 60 minutes. I'm really pleased with the effort and the outcome.

"It's great to get the first one, and I'm looking forward to many more. But it's really a tribute to the players and coaches.

I thought they had an excellent week of preparation and then to go out there and cash in on their performance ... so I'm very happy for everybody involved."

The happy ending almost didn't happen. The Packers led, 31-24, and were running out the final seconds of the game when tailback Ahman Green fumbled at the Lions' 29-yard line with 54 seconds left in the game. McCarthy didn't blink, perhaps hoping to instill confidence in his beleaguered defense. Later, though, he admitted, "I think my heart rate went up a little bit, yes."

He wasn't alone.

For many Packers like Favre, who had seen the Green Bay find ways to lose games instead of win them over the past 12 months, Green's fumble had a "here we go again" feeling to it.

"You know, now I have to admit that right at the end of the game I'm thinking, 'We're going to lose this game,' " Favre admitted. "I don't want this to come across as being negative, but it's a hell of a lot easier to lose it in those situations than win it."

Detroit reached the Green Bay 45-yard line, and on the game's final play, quarterback Jon Kitna launched a Hail Mary pass. Packers safety Nick Collins knocked the ball down, and Detroit wideout Az-Zahir Hakim nearly made a sliding catch that could have forced overtime.

Instead, the pass fell to the ground and McCarthy could finally exhale. Moments later, his team gave him the game ball from his first-ever head coaching win.

Later, McCarthy was asked how he'd celebrate his milestone event. "Celebrate?" he wondered. "Just get a better night's sleep tonight than you usually do."

Nights of solid sleep were few and far between for McCarthy, though. The Packers followed up their first win with a 31-9 stinker in Philadelphia on "Monday Night Football." One day after the loss, Green Bay released former first-round draft pick Ahmad Carroll, who had been a disaster both on and off the field.

One week later, the Packers fell to 0-3 at Lambeau Field after a 23-20 loss to the St. Louis Rams. Trailing by a field goal, Favre drove the Packers to the Rams' 11-yard line with 44 seconds left. But St. Louis defensive end Leonard Little poked the ball away from Favre, and cornerback Jerametrius Butler recovered for the Rams.

Green Bay was now 1-4 and headed to a bye week with no momentum and what appeared to be little hope.

"There's a lot of work left to do," McCarthy said. "There's a lot of games to be played. I think it's evident the way our football team plays that that's not a concern of mine. We're not cashing in when it counts and that's really what it comes down to.

"If you want to get into statistical analysis and start talking about all different things, that's great. But when the offense isn't doing good, the defensive picks them up, and vice versa. Same thing with special teams. It's the three phases coming together, making plays and doing whatever you need to do to win. And we're not doing that right now."

Surprisingly, though, a little down time helped McCarthy's bunch win two games in a row for the first time since the end of 2004. First, Green Bay won at Miami, 34-24, when it intercepted Dolphins quarterback Joey Harrington three times. That was the Packers' first win in South Florida since the 1968 Super Bowl against Oakland, which coincidentally, was Vince Lombardi's final game as their head coach. Green Bay then downed visiting Arizona, 31-14, and improved to 3-4. All of a sudden, the Packers were in rhythm and having fun.

In Miami, Favre lifted wide receiver Donald Driver over his head after a replay reversal gave the Packers a 34-yard touchdown. Against the Cardinals, Favre had his first rushing touchdown in nearly five years, and the Packers didn't punt until the fourth quarter.

Perhaps McCarthy's first year wouldn't be a colossal disaster after all. "We've won three football games, and we're a team that's improving every week, we're a team that's getting better, we're a team that's starting to play with some momentum,"

McCarthy said. "And that's how you win in this league. We feel very good about the direction we're going in as a team."

The Packers still had plenty of momentum after splitting a pair of road games. Green Bay lost in Buffalo, 24-14, despite outgaining the Bills, 427-184. If ever there was a teachable moment, though, this was it.

McCarthy stressed turnover margin as much as any coach in the league. He always believed it was as important as any statistic in determining a game's outcome. And because the Packers lost that battle, 4-0, to Buffalo, they also lost the game.

Green Bay followed that up, though, with an impressive 23-17 win in Minnesota. Donald Driver had a remarkable day, with 191 receiving yards and a touchdown as the Packers won for the third time in four outings.

"You're looking at two guys that are on the same page," McCarthy said of Favre and Driver. "Brett has a very good feeling for Donald. They anticipate so well. That's really the strength of that group. They see it the same way. That's just the importance of doing the same passing concepts over and over and over again because of all the adjustments."

The Packers returned home feeling spunky, confident and optimistic. McCarthy told *Sports Illustrated* that week that he wanted the always-indecisive Favre back in 2007. Favre, while noncommittal, talked about how impressed he was with McCarthy's first year.

"I like Mike and his direction," Favre said. "I think he's already proven what he's capable of." But much of that cheery outlook was scrapped over the next three weeks.

First, Green Bay suffered an embarrassing 35-0 home loss to New England in a game Favre left with an injured nerve in his elbow. Backup quarterback Aaron Rodgers played the second half but suffered a fractured foot that caused him to miss the rest of the season.

"We can't jump on that roller coaster that exists," McCarthy said. "We took a step back today."

Favre returned the following week and made his 252nd consecutive start. But the Packers lost on a snowy Monday night in Seattle, 34-24.

Green Bay then fell to 1-5 at home when it was pummeled by the New York Jets, 38-10. With McCarthy's first season at the three-quarters pole, his team was a disappointing 4-8. The midseason momentum was gone. In fact, Green Bay seemed to be regressing.

Green Bay had been outscored, 107-34, during its three-game losing streak. The Packers had been shut out twice in front of the home fans, something that hadn't happened since 1934.

Suddenly, everyone around tiny Green Bay, Wisconsin, was wondering whether McCarthy was the right guy for this job. "I'm a big fan of Mike's," Green Bay long snapper Rob Davis said. "Mike came in here with a mission, and he's tried to stick to that plan, and the players have bought into it. I think he has a great relationship and rapport with the players.

"He has an open-door system, where if you have something you want to talk to him about, feel free to go talk to him about it. And that helps a lot of guys when they have a voice with the coach."

In fairness to McCarthy, not many first-year head coaches were experiencing much success through the first 12 games of the 2006 season. Of the 10 new coaches in the league that year, only New Orleans' Payton (8-4), Kansas City's Herman Edwards (7-5) and the New York Jets Eric Mangini had winning records. On a whole, the group was 49-71 (40.8%).

What was concerning to Packer Nation, though, was their team still lacked an identity. Green Bay expected its defense to be much improved, but it was dead last in points allowed (27.0). McCarthy also came in stressing a run-first philosophy, but his team was first in football in pass attempts.

Just who were the 2006 Green Bay Packers? No one could be quite sure. "We need to do a better job," McCarthy said. "It starts with me. And trust me, the coaches know exactly how I feel about their role in it and their responsibility to get this thing turned around, and the players will … know exactly about it. This is an emphasis business. When things don't go right, you emphasize it and get it turned around."

Get it turned around.

McCarthy had uttered these words hundreds of times in the 11 short months he'd been in Green Bay. By now, fans and media alike were beginning to wonder if that was possible.

Then, shockingly, the turnaround began to transpire before everyone's eyes. First, the Packers went to San Francisco, where McCarthy had coordinated the 49ers' 32nd-ranked offense in 2005. But on this day, McCarthy got the best of his former boss, Mike Nolan, and the Packers cruised to a 30-19 win.

"It was very gratifying," McCarthy said of defeating his former team. "I have a lot of respect for a lot of men in that locker room, players and coaches alike. Any time you have an opportunity to compete against your former family, it's special."

That performance was followed with a 17-9 win over visiting Detroit. It wasn't pretty as Favre was erratic and his receivers dropped five passes, but the Packers now had a two-game winning streak.

For the home fans who had been treated to just one win all year at Lambeau Field, it was a fun day. "All wins are good wins, but we have a number of things we have to clean up," McCarthy said. "I thought it was a very impressive performance by our defense. We need to get some things cleaned up on offense. But I'm very pleased with the victory. Our fans definitely deserve it. I thought they were outstanding, especially down the stretch in the fourth quarter."

The following week, Green Bay did little right on offense against Minnesota. Favre threw two interceptions, including one that Vikings cornerback Fred Smoot returned 47 yards for a touchdown. The Packers also managed just 46 rushing yards.

But Green Bay's defense continued to trend upward and limited Minnesota to 104 total yards and three first downs. And when Packers kicker Dave Rayner hit a 44-yard field goal with 1:34 left in the game, the Packers escaped with a 9-7 win.

"It's probably the most nervous I've been in my whole life," Rayner said afterward.

It's easy to see why.

Rayner had a rough night, falling on his backside and having a 38-yard field goal blocked in the first quarter. Then Rayner's 34-yard field goal attempt in the second quarter hit the left upright.

But when his late-game kick was true, the Packers had their first three-game winning streak since midway through the 2004 campaign. It also gave the Packers a season sweep over the Vikings and gave McCarthy a 2-0 record against Minnesota coach Brad Childress, who was also in the running for the Green Bay job the previous offseason.

"It's very satisfying," McCarthy said. "The rivalry speaks for itself. But it's a game our players and our fans really look forward to. I don't know how many times it's come down to a last field goal, so it's great to come out of there with a victory. And the adversity we had to overcome, particularly at the end, I'm very proud of our football team."

McCarthy's first season ended with a trip to Chicago, to face the 13-2 Bears. Less than four months earlier, Chicago had routed the Packers, 26-0, in the season opener. But on a New Year's Eve in Chicago, Green Bay returned the favor with a 26-7 beatdown of the Bears for its fourth straight win.

"I think it tells a lot about the character of the team, because we won some of these games in an ugly fashion," Favre said. "But a win is a win, and having a lot of experience, as I do, I think that works for you and I think that works against you. You kind of see things for what they are, and you kind of know what you're up against, whereas young guys, you're just kind of happy to be here.

"You don't realize at the time when you win the way we have won some of our games the last couple of weeks or you lose a couple, it builds character. It exposes it as much as anything, and the way this team has battled back and risen up to the challenge in certain situations, I think will do nothing but make this team better in the future. These four games, what better way to finish out the season?"

It was hard to quantify exactly how much improvement was made by simply judging the two Packers-Bears games. Chicago, which would reach the Super Bowl one month later, had already locked up the NFC's No. 1 seed and had little to play for.

But Chicago coach Lovie Smith made beating Green Bay his top priority after arriving three years earlier. And on this night, Smith played most of his starters for three quarters — a stretch in which the Packers dominated the football game.

"I've said this at the start of the season and maybe people are starting to see it a little bit more now: There are some talented guys on this team," Favre said. "Some talented young guys. How they handle success will be very critical in how far they go individually. Only time will tell that, but as far as what I've seen this year, there are some guys who can really be some stars in this league."

Green Bay's 8-8 record marked a four-game improvement from the previous season. The Packers also went an impressive 5-1 in the division, sweeping both Minnesota and Detroit.

As most of Green Bay's players now headed to Austin Straubel Airport to begin their offseasons, there was a definite optimism about McCarthy and his program.

"I think it's important, any time you establish a new program, a new structure and everything you're changing, you know you're going to have speed bumps along the way," McCarthy said. "And we definitely encountered those as we moved forward through the beginning of the season.

"We didn't win some of the tight games we had opportunities to win. We let some leads get away in the second half. But I'll clearly remember the stretch, because you saw a vision, you saw a plan, and you saw people stay to that plan and play very good football in the last four games. That's going to be my significant memory as we move forward."

With the offseason at hand, the Packers had several reasons to believe the future was bright. Over the final four weeks in

2006, Green Bay allowed an average of just 10.5 points and jumped to 12th in total defense, 13th against the pass and a tie for 25th in scoring defense.

"You could really say the last four to five weeks, we played as good a defense as anybody in the National Football League," McCarthy said.

Offensively, the greatest strides undoubtedly came up front. After the 2005 campaign, Green Bay had two glaring holes at guard and didn't know who its center would be. But rookies Daryn Colledge, Jason Spitz and Tony Moll all flashed in 2006, while first-year center Scott Wells played better than many expected.

"Fantastic," Favre said of his line. "They've got a ways to go, but I think they got better each and every week, I really do. They had their moments, but for the most part they got better, and I saw the confidence just rise with each game, and as the plays unfolded throughout the season, I could see that their confidence was building. At times maybe a little too high, but that's not a bad thing."

Despite the positive end to the season, Green Bay entered the offseason with a handful of issues. The tight end position was a mess, following the worst year of Bubba Franks' career. Green Bay needed a young running back, as the end was near for veteran Ahman Green. The Packers also needed more playmakers at wide receiver to take some of the burden off Donald Driver. Defensively, safety Marquand Manuel was overmatched. And cornerback Al Harris never seemed happy with his contract.

Of course, the 5,000-pound elephant in the room remained Favre, and whether he would return for a 16th season in Green Bay. But as McCarthy said goodbye to his team, he thought about how far they had come. He lamented the fact they missed out on a playoff berth.

But most importantly, he thought that this might just work. "I have mixed feelings," McCarthy admitted. "I'm proud of a number of things we accomplished. I'm proud of the smaller successes that we have accomplished since we all came together here in February, and I'm proud we have those in place and are able to build off them. But I'm disappointed we didn't get in the playoffs.

"I'm disappointed that I couldn't lead this team in the playoffs and see what happens. Because I think right now we're extremely healthy, we're playing our best football of the year, and that's what you want. So I'm disappointed in that, and I'll never be completely satisfied until we reach the top. I'm proud of a number of things we accomplished, but we still have a lot of work to do."

6
Turning Things Around

By early February 2007, McCarthy got a late Christmas gift: Favre was coming back. Favre, the master of indecision and waffling, had dragged his retirement saga on for several months in past offseasons. But this time, his decision came four weeks after the regular season ended.

"I am so excited about coming back," Favre told the *Biloxi Sun-Herald*, his hometown paper. "We have a good nucleus of young players. We were 8-8 last year and that's encouraging. My offensive line looks good, the defense played good down the stretch. I'm excited about playing for a talented, young football team."

Still, the Packers lost running back Ahman Green and tight end David Martin in free agency. Fullback William Henderson was released. And the only free agent general manager Ted Thompson signed was cornerback Frank Walker.

There was a good deal of young talent on the roster. But as training camp neared, McCarthy's team had plenty of questions, including:

- Could running backs Vernand Morency and rookie Brandon Jackson fill the large cleats vacated by Green?
- Would Green Bay's offense, which ranked 31st in the red zone in 2006, find a few more playmakers?
- Who would get the leg up in the kicking competition between Dave Rayner and rookie Mason Crosby?
- Could the Packers get anything out of rookie defensive tackle Justin Harrell, who had a history of injury problems at every level?

- And would Green Bay's tight ends, a nonfactor in 2006, rebound?

Despite the uncertainty, Packers general manager Ted Thompson made his feelings about the roster clear in late July. "For me personally, I'm ready to win," said Thompson, who was just 12-20 during two years as Green Bay's G.M. "I think it's time for this team to win and I think we're ready to do that."

During his first official press conference of the 2007 season, McCarthy didn't run from that. In fact, he again talked about winning a Super Bowl, a consistent message since the day he arrived.

"We're trying to win every football game," McCarthy said. "We're going to win the world championship here in Green Bay again. That's the view, that's the vision. We've made progress toward that goal, and we need to continue to have those small successes as we build toward that goal, and that's the way I view it."

McCarthy refused to address specific goals when it came to wins and losses for the 2007 Packers. But he clearly believed his team was ready to improve on last year's .500 season and second-place finish in the NFC North.

Few others believed that. *Pro Football Weekly*, the bible of football publications, picked Green Bay to go 7-9 and miss the playoffs. *PFW*'s list of the top 50 players in the NFL also didn't have a single Packer on it.

"We want to get better. We want to get better every day," McCarthy said. "To make progress, you want to win more games than you did last year. I think all those things are obvious. We're moving forward. We're working to move forward and very pleased with what we accomplished here in the past few months, and looking forward to taking the field (for training camp) as a football team."

While Green Bay's defense struggled for most of 2006, it closed the year strong and seemed in better shape than the offense.

The Packers ranked just 22nd in points scored in 2006 with 301, an average of just 18.8 per game. That was the Packers' third fewest points since Brett Favre began quarterbacking the team in 1992.

Favre played with greater control in 2006 than he did in '05, when he threw a career-high 29 interceptions. Still, his quarterback rating of 72.7 was the third-lowest of his career.

The Packers didn't have a proven wide receiver other than standout Donald Driver, who was sidelined during the start of camp with a nagging shoulder injury. The tight end group was a mess. And the red zone was more like the dead zone for Green Bay's offense.

Somehow, someway, though, McCarthy believed his team would be better offensively — even if he was in the minority with that opinion.

"The improvement, number one, has to come as a whole," McCarthy said. "You can go through every position. Our offensive line group will be a better group this year, just based on experience. The tight end group, we need to get more production out of that group, and they probably had the most learning for the perimeter group on offense as far as doing things they hadn't been asked to do before, so I look for that group just to improve based on their experience.

"And we've added some guys to the wide receiver group, and the wide receiver group needs to get healthy, frankly. So I just think we will improve from within. That's what I'm selling, doesn't sound like you're buying, so we'll have to wait and see."

Another challenge McCarthy faced was reversing Green Bay's recent trend of slow starts. In both 2004 and 2006, Green Bay opened 1-4. In 2005, the Packers began 0-4. That was a combined record of 2-12 over the past three seasons.

McCarthy's solution came by tinkering with the training camp schedule. McCarthy excused his team on three different Wednesdays during camp in hopes of keeping them as fresh as possible for the start of the season.

Green Bay needed to be sharp, too, as four of its first five opponents were playoff teams a year ago. "It's important to start fast," McCarthy said. "I think every year you say that in the National Football League. You look at the statistics, how important fast starts are, the percentage that applies to your football team making the playoffs and so forth. So I don't think there's a football team in the league that doesn't come in worried about the fast start. Maybe a more veteran football team.

"I don't think it's critical and things like that because you have to play it one game at a time. But to answer your question, we have stressed the fast start. The way we structured our scheduling gives us, I think, the best opportunity to start fast, because we're getting our work done and we should be fresh coming out of camp and so forth. ... We need to start fast. It's important."

McCarthy also knew how critical his second season was to his long-term future in Green Bay. McCarthy signed a three-year contract when he was hired in January 2006, making this a huge year for him. With a big season, McCarthy could warrant an extension before the 2008 campaign. If the Packers went backward, McCarthy could be jettisoned or enter 2008 as a lame-duck coach.

"Ted and I talked about my situation after the season for about five minutes, which was probably about two minutes longer than we needed too," McCarthy said of his contract. "But I'm comfortable. You're given options to sign a first contract, and I took the one I did for a reason.

"This business has really gotten to be a one-year deal anyway, so I really don't think about it. I'm not sweating it. I think you really have to keep your eyes on the short term. I'm more focused on the day-to-day things. That's what I think about, because if you take care of things in the short term, the bigger things will happen. So I really don't sweat the contract.

With that backdrop, the 2007 season was here. Optimism is great for 32 teams each September, but McCarthy seemed to truly believe this wasn't false hope. "I clearly believe that every football team has a path to reach and to win the Super Bowl," he said. "And I feel that every team I've been a part of, there's so many things that need to go the right way and so many obstacles you encounter during the course of a year that there's never just one way to win a world championship. So I think it's real important to be in tune with who you really are, set the course that's going to get you to a world championship, and I think that's why everybody has so much confidence in their program right now. Clearly, we do, too.

"We feel that we have an opportunity, long term, to play for a world championship. Also, we know we need to take it one week at a time and there's things we have to stay and adhere to and not get too far away from. And we know there's definitely going to be some challenges we have to overcome."

The first challenge was a Philadelphia Eagles team that won the NFC East in 2006 and was picked by many to reach the Super Bowl in '07. The Eagles, led by quarterback Donovan McNabb and running back Brian Westbrook, came to Lambeau Field as three-point favorites in their Week 1 matchup. Three hours later, though, Packers rookie kicker Mason Crosby drilled a 42-yard field goal with just two seconds remaining that propelled Green Bay to a surprising 16-13 win.

"I kind of got thrown into the fire in the first test," Crosby said afterward. "But that's kind of how I like it. It's exciting."

That kick capped a whirlwind summer for Crosby, who, drafted in the sixth round, faced the daunting challenge of unseating incumbent Dave Rayner. Granted, Rayner wasn't exactly knocking on the door of the Pro Bowl in 2006, when he made 74.3% of his kicks and ranked 26th in the NFL. But Rayner had a powerful leg, was well liked in the locker room, and seemed to have far more confidence than a year ago.

None of that ever phased Crosby, though, who was almost robotic in his approach. By the end of training camp, Crosby had connected on 101 of 118 kicks in games and practices (85.6%), while Rayner was 95 of 117 (81.2%).

"I just kept doing what I could do and control that and then just hope for the best," Crosby said. "I didn't know if I had an advantage either way. I felt that I was kicking well, and I'm just happy to be part of it now."

The Packers needed Crosby after a day when the offense was pedestrian. Green Bay managed just 215 total yards, and the rookie backfield of Brandon Jackson and Korey Hall were part of a running game that produced just 46 rushing yards.

But the Packers got a special teams touchdown when Tracy White recovered a fumble in the end zone. They held McNabb to a 60.6 passer rating. And Crosby played hero with his third field goal of the day.

"The bottom line is to win games," McCarthy said. "But I'll just tell you this, I'm not OK with the way we played on offense. It may sting more than normal. As a head coach, you have to be conscientious of that when you're in front of the football team. I don't want to ever tarnish a victory because the offense didn't play well. We're going to win them any way we can, and if it's with a great defense, which I think we have, that's OK. But we're also working to have a great offense, too."

The oddsmakers weren't impressed with Green Bay's opening week win. In Week 2, the Packers traveled to the New York Giants — who had been routed by Dallas in their opener — and again were a 3-point underdog.

But something magical happened that day in East Rutherford, New Jersey. Green Bay, which had talked openly about becoming one of the NFL's elite, took a major step toward doing exactly that.

The Packers led 14-13 heading to the fourth quarter. Green Bay then ripped off 21 unanswered points in the final period and cruised to a 35-13 win. Favre threw three touchdowns and became the NFL's all-time winningest quarterback, with 149 victories. Rookie running back DeShawn Wynn gave life to Green Bay's moribund running game with two touchdowns, including the game clincher from 38 yards with just four minutes left. And for the first time since 2001, Green Bay began a season 2-0.

"We have a lot of energy around here," McCarthy said. "I think it was evident and really started coming off of last season. The offseason program, through training camp, and really now with the two wins, I just see the confidence building.

"I think it's real confidence. It's not manufactured, and I think that's important. Our guys believe. They know they can improve. They believe in the work week and what it takes to get ready for a football game. It's growing, a lo1t of energy in the building."

The energy went to new heights the following week, when the San Diego Chargers came to town. San Diego featured the best running back in the NFL and arguably the league's best player in LaDainian Tomlinson. Quarterback Philip Rivers was a star in the making. And the defense, led by linebacker Shawne Merriman, featured one of the league's top pass rushers.

Las Vegas still wasn't buying Green Bay and installed the Chargers as 5 ½-point favorites. But the Packers' passing game, which had been mediocre at best since McCarthy's arrival, had its best day of the McCarthy era.

Favre looked like he was 27, not 37, throwing for 369 yards and three touchdowns. The top three wide receivers — Greg Jennings, Donald Driver and James Jones — showed that the Packers' passing game was in better hands than anyone imagined a few months back. And Green Bay's aerial circus sparked the Packers to a stunning 31-24 win.

"We got something to prove," Jennings said afterward. "Our wide receivers corps is young, with the exception of Donald, but he gives us great leadership. We're just coming out here trying to get better week in and week out, day in and day out. We're trying to do that from right now on to the Super Bowl."

Jennings, who missed the first two games of the year after pulling a hamstring, was outstanding in his return. Jennings caught four passes for 82 yards, including a 57-yard game-winning TD with just more than two minutes left. That score also vaulted Favre into a tie with Dan Marino for the most TD passes in NFL history, with 420.

Driver was absolutely leveled by San Diego safety Marlon McCree midway through the first quarter, a play in which he lost his helmet. But the fearless Driver got up and went on to have a brilliant day, with six catches for 126 yards and one TD.

Finally there was Jones, who resembled a 10-year veteran more than a rookie. Jones continued his blistering start with six catches for 79 yards. And through three games, Jones led all NFL rookies in receptions (14) and yards (183).

"I thought we did some really good things in the passing game," Packers offensive coordinator Joe Philbin said. "We were pretty crisp." That's putting it mildly.

Green Bay abandoned the run early against San Diego's terrific front, which was led by Pro Bowl nose tackle Jamal Williams. Instead, McCarthy's team threw the ball on a remarkable 77.6% of their 58 plays.

Green Bay operated largely out of an empty backfield formation and made the Chargers play with mostly their dime defense. And when the offensive line held up its end of the bargain, the Packers' wideouts made San Diego pay.

The biggest play of the game belonged to Jennings, who beat cornerback Antonio Cromartie on an inside slant nine yards downfield late in the game. Cromartie whiffed on the tackle, safety Clinton Hart took a bad angle and blew the tackle, and Jennings was off for a 57-yard TD that gave the Packers a 24-21 lead with 2:03 remaining.

It was a huge moment for Jennings, whose last touchdown had come on October 8, 2006. In the time since, Jennings battled injuries while questions about his toughness were starting to pop up.

"It was just one of those plays where the corner was kind of pressed, kind of headed out to the outside," Jennings said. "I knew he was coming to me, so I had to give him a little time, work the corner, and everything else kind of played out."

All of a sudden, the 2007 season was playing out better than McCarthy could have ever dreamed. Green Bay was an underdog in each of its first three games yet was now one of just two unbeaten teams in the NFC.

McCarthy's passing game was light-years ahead of where it was the previous season. His young offensive line was growing up before his very eyes. And Green Bay's defense was beginning to look like one of football's top units.

"We're 3-0. We're a team that's improving," McCarthy said after the San Diego win. "We beat a very good football team today. That's an excellent win. I thought the environment was incredible. I thought the fans were outstanding. They were with us every step of the way.

"It's a very big team win for us. I think it's one you can point to as far as building your program. I'm happy with the energy that we're playing with. I thought they played physical. The urgency coming out of the gate, we knew they were going to try to run the football on us and be physical with us. I thought it was an excellent team win."

Green Bay followed that with a 23-16 win at Minnesota, improving to 4-0 in the process. This was Favre's day, as his 16-yard first-quarter TD pass to Greg Jennings allowed him to set the NFL record with 421 career touchdown passes.

"I'm so glad we won the game. There was so much emphasis on this record and not the game itself," Favre said. "Everyone's like, 'What are you going to do? Are you going to have a big celebration?' Put yourself in my shoes. I want to help this team win. I do not want us to get blindsided by this record and what we're actually here for."

After a 27-20 home loss to the archrival Chicago Bears, Green Bay rolled off six straight wins and improved to a remarkable 10-1. There was a hard fought, 17-14, win over defensive-minded Washington. That was followed by a 19-13 overtime win on a Monday night in Denver in which Favre and Jennings hooked up for an 82-yard TD on the first play of overtime.

"I feel like I've been on some better teams, but it's hard to doubt this team," Favre said. "That was fun. I can't wait to watch the tape."

Green Bay went to Kansas City as a 2 ½-point underdog, scored the final 17 points of the game, and rallied for a 33-22 win. Jennings continued his breakout season with two touchdown catches, and cornerback Charles Woodson returned an interception 46 yards for a TD.

There was a 34-0 rout of visiting Minnesota and convincing wins over Carolina and Detroit. In the final four games of Green Bay's winning streak, it averaged 33.8 points per contest. At the heart of the offensive eruption was Favre.

Favre was in the middle of a five-game streak in which his passer rating was at least 100.0 — the first time in his career that happened. In that time, Favre completed 131 of 178 passes (73.6%) for 1,641 yards, threw 13 touchdowns, allowed just two interceptions, and had a passer rating of 121.5. Clearly McCarthy's magic in working with quarterbacks — young or old — was doing wonders for Favre.

"I don't recall coaching a quarterback that's had a run like Brett's had in all my years," McCarthy said. "He's really in tune with the offense as far as getting in and out of the different personnel groups and formations, and he has been very consistent taking what the defense gives you. His decision-making has been outstanding. His ball accuracy has always been a strength of his. But this is as good a run of a quarterback that I've been a part of."

McCarthy was in the midst of an awfully good run of his own. His play calling had been aggressive and imaginative. He had opposing defensive coordinators on their heels. And Green Bay's offense was humming.

"I feel good about it," McCarthy said of his play calling. "The biggest thing with play calling is being on the same page as the quarterback and the rest of the offense. We're hitting our stride, our rhythm, for a large part of the games. I think we're doing OK there."

The Packers were 10-1 for the first time since 1962. They were headed to Dallas to face a Cowboys team that was 10-1 for the first time in the franchise's 48-year history. And for just the eighth time in NFL history, two teams with records of 10-1 or better were set to square off.

"They're a great football team, and the reality of it is, we're a good football team and so are they," said Cowboys

Nov. 29, 2007, Irving, TX. Green Bay Packers head coach Mike McCarthy with quarterback Brett Favre against the Dallas Cowboys at Cowboys Stadium. (Photo by Mark J. Rebilas-US PRESSWIRE)

quarterback Tony Romo, who grew up in Burlington, Wisconsin. "Whoever wins this game is obviously going to have a little bit of a lead to gain that advantage going into the playoffs, but I said it before, too. This game right here is not going to decide the season.

"It's an important step for both teams to put themselves in position for the playoffs, but it won't decide how it's going to finish at the end. But you want to go out here and you want to improve and you want to become a better football team and continue to improve."

In this showdown that many believed was a preview of the NFC Championship game, the Cowboys certainly improved. The Packers, on the other hand, went backward.

Favre had never fared well in Dallas and carried an 0-8 career record at Cowboys Stadium into the game. For many other Packers, this was undoubtedly the biggest game they'd ever played in.

And when the bright lights went on, Favre, McCarthy and the Packers simply weren't ready. Favre struggled miserably, threw two early interceptions, then exited with an elbow injury with the Packers in a 27-10 hole. Backup quarterback Aaron Rodgers played well in relief, but the early deficit was too much and Green Bay suffered a 37-27 loss.

"I look at it as an opportunity that we didn't take advantage of," McCarthy said. "We're 10-2. That tells you exactly where we are. They're a good football team. This game may affect the playoff seed. That's fine, but we still have a lot of football left. I think you need to keep it in perspective there, and we have as a football team.

"We're disappointed because this is an environment that we have not played in as a young football team. I thought it was very important for us to come in and win this football game because we will be playing in a lot of championship atmospheres as we move forward. This is an opportunity that we need to learn from, because we did not play our best football tonight."

If there was one highlight, it was Rodgers' performance. Stuck on the bench for nearly three seasons, no one had a clue what the Packers had in Rodgers. Sure, Rodgers had performed well the past two summers, but that was against backups and many players now out of the league. On this night, though, Rodgers went 18 of 26 for 201 yards, threw his first NFL touchdown, and posted an impressive quarterback rating of 104.8.

Rodgers entered the game with nine minutes, 53 seconds left in the second quarter and the Packers trailing by 17 points. On the Packers' second possession with Rodgers in charge, he engineered an eight-play, 74-yard touchdown drive that pulled Green Bay within 27-17 at halftime. On Green Bay's first drive of the second half, Rodgers was back at it again. This time, he led a 12-play, 69-yard march that pulled the Packers within 27-24.

"To me, Aaron Rodgers played way better than Brett Favre," Cowboys linebacker Bradie James said afterward. "Brett Favre was just throwing the ball up. I don't know if we'd rather have him in there or Rodgers."

Green Bay never could get over the hump, but Rodgers won over a lot of people with his performance that night. And it was clear that Rodgers had also benefitted greatly working with McCarthy the past two years.

"I just can't say enough about his preparation, because I didn't even blink," Packers coach Mike McCarthy said of Rodgers. "I didn't throw anything out.

"I've been in that position before when you have to go to your backup or go to your third guy or even your fourth guy. I went through it in San Francisco, and you just start crossing plays off the chart, and that wasn't the case. I thought Aaron did an excellent job."

Even Favre — who was far from the ideal mentor — sang Rodgers' praises afterward. "I thought he played great," Favre said of Rodgers. "Gave us a chance to win. I thought he was ready to play. I was hoping it would be in different circumstances ... but I thought he did a fine job."

Rodgers' play helped ease the Packers' mind four months later when Favre announced his retirement. But that saga was for another day. As for the here and now, McCarthy and the Packers had several issues to address.

Tony Romo and the Cowboys had just shredded Green Bay's defense. Favre had to shake off his poorest game in several years. And the following week in practice, Rodgers suffered a hamstring injury and was inactive the final four weeks of the regular season.

Running back Ryan Grant helped Green Bay forget those issues, though, during the Packers' 38-7 rout of visiting Oakland the following week. Grant, celebrating his 25th birthday, ran for a career-high 156 yards, averaged 5.4 yards per carry, and scored for the third consecutive week.

When the season began, the Packers had virtually no ground game with the hodgepodge mix of Brandon Jackson, DeShawn Wynn and Vernand Morency. Now, Grant had balanced Green Bay's offense and given them their best back since Ahman Green was in his prime four years earlier.

"Ryan is really evolving into an outstanding back," said Packers center Scott Wells. "He seems to have good field knowledge and field vision, he makes his cuts at the right places, and he runs with his pads down.

"And the most important thing is he takes care of the football. He's really come a long way since Week 1, and he's taking advantage of the opportunity they've given him."

Back in September, Grant was buried behind Brandon Jacobs, Reuben Droughns and Derrick Ward on the New York Giants depth chart. And even though New York planned to keep Grant, he was the fourth-string running back.

The Packers had watched Grant closely throughout the preseason and felt he'd be a natural in their zone scheme. Grant was big (6-1, 224), powerful, fast and had tremendous vision.

Knowing the Giants had more backs than they needed, Thompson offered a sixth-round draft choice and the Giants accepted. Now, New York probably wished it would have sent a different back to Green Bay.

"Surprised, just a little shocked," Grant said of the trade. "I didn't really think that I would be traded. It was something that I looked at the positive in it. It was an opportunity to play for this team that wanted me. They traded for me at that point in the season. For anybody to trade for you is a good thing. That's how I took it."

The following week in St. Louis, Favre broke Dan Marino's record for career passing yards (61,361). Favre jumped to No. 1 with a simple seven-yard slant pattern to Donald Driver, and when the day ended, Favre held the new mark at 61,405.

Green Bay also routed the Rams, 33-14, and clinched a first round bye in the playoffs. Now 12-2, these Packers were once again tied with Dallas for the best record in the NFC, and they still had a chance to become the first group in franchise history to win 14 games in the regular season.

"It's something I haven't thought about," McCarthy said of winning 14 games. "Any time you say the first time in Packers history, that means a lot. I think those are the types of things, when the season is completed, that you look back on and appreciate. That would be an excellent accomplishment.

"We came out of training camp relatively healthy and started fast. That's always important. We just stayed focused on winning games and improving.

"I thought we won some games early that you probably didn't look the way you wanted it to look. But as we won games our confidence grew. We really developed into a very good football team. We need to continue to stay the course."

They didn't.

One week later, the Packers went to Chicago's Soldier Field and saw all hopes for the No. 1 seed in the playoffs disappear. On a bone-chilling day where winds gusted up to 40 miles per hour, Favre was abysmal. Green Bay's special teams were just as bad and the defense was nonexistent. It all added up to a frustrating 35-7 loss that left some fans doubting just how good this team was.

"I've been playing 17 years, and that was the worst conditions I've ever played in," Favre said. "Excuse? No excuse. It was, but they handled it better than we did. We have historically handled it well. It's kind of our ace in the hole, but today, obviously, it wasn't."

Favre threw two interceptions, one that was returned 85 yards for a touchdown by Chicago linebacker Brian Urlacher. Favre had just nine passing yards in the first half, and the Packers' offense never could get untracked.

Green Bay's special teams were equally ineffecctive. Punter Jon Ryan had two punts blocked, dropped a snap, and had one punt that traveled just nine yards.

"They coped, we didn't," Packers special teams coach Mike Stock said. "I think they found a way and we didn't. That's the bottom line. We knew we had to contend with the problems ... and they did a better job than we did."

Green Bay's backups drubbed Detroit, 34-13, the following week. But few were impressed. The Lions were again one of the league's doormats and dropped their 17th straight game on

Wisconsin soil. What everyone wondered was whether these 13-3 Packers were ready for the postseason.

"We're playoff ready," McCarthy insisted. "We'll be playoff ready in two weeks. We're not going to change our approach. We're going to continue working on improving and getting ready to win football games."

The regular season was a smashing success. Few ever thought this team — one that was 4-8 late in the 2006 campaign — would win the NFC North and earn the conference's No. 2 seed. Dallas, which also finished 13-3, earned the No. 1 seed thanks to its head-to-head win over the Packers in November.

Favre had a magical year, throwing for 4,155 yards — the third most in his career — and 28 TDs. Favre also posted a 95.7 passer rating — the third best of his career — and finished second in the NFL's Most Valuable Player voting.

The Packers finished the regular season second in total offense and passing offense and climbed to 11th in total defense. But could Green Bay beat the NFC's heavyweights and reach the Super Bowl for the first time in a decade?

The Packers had been shredded in Dallas just over a month before. The Bears had exposed Green Bay's special teams and showed that Favre's days as a cold-weather stud might be history.

"It was only a few days ago where we were a little bit concerned, and that concern hasn't changed," Favre said after the Lions game. "I'm always concerned.

"I'm pleased with the way we played (against Detroit) ... but there's a lot of areas we can improve. Once again, if you go back to (Chicago) — and I know the conditions were tough — we have to play our best football in order to go where we want to go in the playoffs."

7

Slaying the Seahawks

There are ghosts around every corner in tiny Green Bay. That's what happens with a franchise steeped in tradition and packed with championships. Curly Lambeau won six NFL Championships. Vince Lombardi won five.

And on January 12, 2008, Mike McCarthy was set to coach his first-ever playoff game. And when he looked to the opposite sideline, McCarthy saw Seattle head coach Mike Holmgren, a man who brought the 12th world championship to Green Bay in 1996.

"Unusual?" McCarthy asked in the days leading up to his biggest game yet. "I think it's probably the most unique situation in pro football. I don't know if anybody else has had to do that."

On top of that, there were plenty of ghosts from playoff pasts for McCarthy. From 1993-98, McCarthy was an offensive assistant and later the quarterbacks coach under Marty Schottenheimer in Kansas City. Those Chiefs teams were typically outstanding during the regular season, winning three AFC West titles and reaching the playoffs four times. But the postseasons were a nightmare.

During McCarthy's first year with the Chiefs, Kansas City reached the AFC title game. But the Chiefs lost there, dropped the next three postseason games McCarthy was part of, and were mired in a six-game postseason losing streak.

In 1995 and 1997, Kansas City's playoff losses were extremely painful. In both years, the Chiefs went 13-3 during the regular season and earned the conference's No. 1 seed in the postseason. Both times, Kansas City proceeded to lose its first playoff game — on its home field, no less.

McCarthy also went 1-1 in the playoffs during his five years as an assistant coach in New Orleans. But it was those playoff failures in Kansas City that stuck with McCarthy—and everyone who was part of the Chiefs' organization during that time.

Now McCarthy got his first chance as a head coach to erase past playoff failures. But he had to do it against the last man to bring a title to Green Bay, a man whose popularity still dwarfed McCarthy's.

"I look at it more as our football team versus his football team," McCarthy said. "Mike Holmgren calls the plays for their offense, and I call the plays for our offense. So as far as going up chess match-wise, that's really, there's not as much of that actually in the game.

"But as far as the week, preparation, getting your team ready to play, that's all part of it. I think any time you have an opportunity to compete in the playoffs against a coach of his stature, it's something you really look forward to."

There were several other story lines that added to the intrigue of Green Bay's first playoff game under McCarthy. Packers general manager Ted Thompson spent five seasons as Seattle's vice president of football operations and had a hand in bringing several current Seahawks to town. Seahawks quarterback Matt Hasselbeck was a former Packers backup who had developed into one of football's elite signal callers.

And when these teams last met in the playoffs in 2003, Packers cornerback Al Harris intercepted Hasselbeck in overtime and went 52 yards for the game-winning touchdown in Green Bay's 33-27 overtime win.

Many of the players from that game still remained. But all eyes were on the coaches. "I'm just tickled pink that they haven't taken my street signs down," said Holmgren, who has a street, Holmgren Way, named after him. "My time there was special, it was good."

McCarthy was hoping for something special to happen now. "I'm excited. This is what you work for," McCarthy said. "I think coaches, as a whole, you get caught up in the process. You get caught up in the journey.

"Just walking in here today I've never given any thought to this being my first (playoff) game. I've moved past that. I may feel different when I walk out on the field Saturday. I'm excited for this opportunity."

Less than four minutes into this contest, though, McCarthy's mood had changed from excitement to irritation. In the game's first 69 seconds, Packers running back Ryan Grant had lost two fumbles. That's right, two. And that quickly, Seattle capitalized and grabbed a stunning 14-0 lead.

"It's unfortunate what happened," Grant said of the two early fumbles. "But everybody … backed me the whole time. From the training staff to the coaches to the players, everybody just said, 'Stay with it. You know what you've got to do. Let it go.' "

Grant did just that. And by the end of the day, the largest crowd in Lambeau Field history (72,168) had watched Grant pull off one of the most stunning turnarounds in NFL playoff history.

After his atrocious start, Grant reversed field and went from goat to hero. Grant ran for 201 yards and three touchdowns and led the Packers back to a stirring 42-20 win.

Grant's rushing total set a new franchise postseason record. His rushing mark was also the seventh-highest in NFL postseason history. Not bad for a guy who was going to have to wear fake glasses and a wig around town throughout the offseason if his day didn't improve.

"Ryan's a talented young man," McCarthy said. "Ryan's very consistent. That's what I like about Ryan. You have the same player every day. He works extremely hard. There isn't a whole lot of variance in his performance. That's very useful for a coach, particularly in the game plan.

"I think his consistency is the thing I like best. He plays with a lot of confidence. He's very confident. I never questioned him and we did not blink. (Running backs coach) Edgar Bennett handled it very well. It did not surprise me that he ran the way he did today."

What may have been most surprising was Grant's early woes. During 218 touches during the regular season, Grant had just one fumble. On the first play of the game, though, Grant caught a swing pass in the right flat, fell and tried getting up. When he did, Leroy Hill forced a fumble, Lofa Tatupu recovered and returned it to the Packers 1-yard line to set up a TD.

On Green Bay's next possession, Grant ran for eight yards off left tackle on first down. But on his next carry, Grant again fumbled, and Seattle cornerback Jordan Babineaux recovered. That set up a second Seahawks touchdown, put the Packers in a 14-0 hole, and had the Green Bay faithful in an early panic.

"The good thing about spotting them 14 was that we did it so quick, we still had plenty of time left, and I knew Ryan could have a big game," Packers quarterback Brett Favre said. "Any time he touches the ball he can have a big game.

"And I came over, he was on the bench and I said, 'Hey, you know what, believe me if there's one person that knows what it feels like to be in his shoes, it's me.' I said, 'Forget about it. You're going to have plenty of opportunities.' He gave me the old, generic answer, 'Yeah, I know.' Same thing I would have said. But I said, 'Go down swinging, man. Don't worry about it.'"

Grant certainly didn't seem to. Two series later, Grant ripped off a 26-yard run that seemed to fully restore his confidence. Grant finished that drive with a one-yard TD run, then had a three-yard touchdown shortly before halftime that gave the Packers a 28-17 lead.

Then in the second half, Grant ran wild. Grant busted a 24-yard run that set up Green Bay's first TD of the second half and gave the Packers a 35-17 lead. Then Grant ripped off a 43-yard run late in the third quarter that set up his third TD, one that put Green Bay ahead, 42-20.

"We feel confident with this team and we know when we don't turn the ball over and we don't make mistakes on our end, we're pretty dangerous as an offense," said Grant, who was traded to Green Bay eight days before the 2007 season opener. "I've been playing football for a long time, and I understand there are ups and downs and I've got to keep fighting no matter what."

Grant did just that. And by the time the day was over, his list of accomplishments also included:

- most rushing TD's in franchise history
- second-most points in a playoff game (18) in team history

"What a day," said Packers director of pro personnel Reggie McKenzie, the man largely responsible for finding Grant the previous summer. "He's fun to watch. He's fun to watch. He runs hard, he runs tough and he's fast. He's fast. We just saw something in preseason and he made us say, 'We need to add this guy to our stable.' And he's been outstanding. We put his foot in the door and the rest was up to him. And he showed himself and proved himself."

So did Brett Favre. The 37-year-old quarterback was considered washed up by many prior to the 2007 campaign. But after a memorable regular season, Favre had one of his best playoff games ever. Favre completed 18 of 23 passes (78.3%), threw three touchdown passes, and posted a 137.6 passer rating — his best in 21 playoff games.

"He's a special player," McCarthy said of Favre. "He's clearly one of the all-time greats or the best that's ever played the game."

While the performances of Grant and Favre were certainly memorable, the game also became notable for the bizarre weather it was played in. All week, local meteorologists had called for light flurries ending by kickoff. But that forecast was entirely off base.

The snow was falling lightly when the game began at 3:33 p.m. CST. By the middle of the first quarter, however, things had intensified and the snow was beginning to stick on the field. Light flurries continued throughout the first half, then things got crazy.

Around the 10-minute mark of the third quarter, the snow dramatically picked up. The flakes were enormous. Snow piled up on the field, and workers with brooms, shovels and plows emerged to keep the yardage markers visible. Even the cheese wedges that sat on the heads of fans had an inch, or more, of snow accumulating on them.

"It was unbelievable, man," defensive tackle Ryan Pickett said. "I've never been a part of anything like that. It was unbelievable with the snow and the weather. I've never played in a game like that anywhere. You come to Green Bay, you expect games like that, though. And it was a lot of fun. We had a ball."

The players themselves felt like they were in a snow globe. A couple inches of snow quickly piled up on the field. And both vision and footing became major issues.

Green Bay was leading, 35-17, when the snow became the heaviest. Passing the ball became extremely difficult, but the Packers certainly weren't complaining.

"Third quarter, it started coming down a little harder," wideout Greg Jennings said. "Fortunately we were in the position where we could just run the football. It definitely was getting a little thick out there and was hard to see. We were able to execute, move the chains and keep getting first downs."

Tight end Bubba Franks, who played his college football at Miami and returned there every offseason, was one of many Packers who had a blast in the blustery conditions. "It was good. It was fun out there," Franks said. "Once it started coming down hard, it kind of looked like a snowy Christmas day.

"We were able to put some points on the board before it got too ugly, and once it got ugly, this is what we live in. So you're playing our football."

The game was somewhat reminiscent of Green Bay's loss in Seattle in 2006. That night, snow fell hard early in the contest, and the weather improved as the game went along. On this night in Green Bay, though, the weather got progressively worse. And the team with the lead—in this case Green Bay—held a huge advantage.

"It was tough to see people," Hasselbeck said. "That was crazy weather out there, but they were playing in the same conditions and they handled it pretty well."

After Green Bay took a 42-20 lead early in the fourth quarter, quarterback Brett Favre made a snowball and drilled wideout Donald Driver in the back. Driver later retaliated with a snowball to Favre's head.

McCarthy's Packers were living the dream, just one win shy of an NFC championship.

"I hit Donald with a snowball. I did," Favre said. "When I kind of packed it up and threw it, it got kind of hard, like a golf ball. So I kind of threw it at his back or his butt or something. I'm thinking, 'You don't want to puncture an eye or something.' He turns around, packs one and hits me in the face. Good thing it hit my face mask, it might have hit my tooth or something."

In all, the Packers couldn't have had much more fun in the snow. "Yeah, that was awesome," Favre said. "I've been hoping for that for 17 years. I was watching the weather all day and it's a shame, I'm like, 'Just give us one of those big snow games.' I wanted to play where you couldn't see the field and the snowplow comes out. It keeps getting worse and worse."

Things only seemed to be getting better for McCarthy and his Packers, though.

One day later, the top-seeded Dallas Cowboys lost on their home field to the fifth-seeded New York Giants. Instead of traveling to Dallas for the NFC Championship, the Packers would now be hosting the Giants.

"Very excited," McCarthy said. "I'm just excited about having the game here at Lambeau Field.

"To have the NFC Championship game at Lambeau Field I think is just wonderful for the Green Bay community, for our fans, especially after our fans' performance yesterday. Just to bring the game here is really the excitement that we're all feeling right now."

McCarthy's team was just one game away from the Super Bowl. They'd be facing a Giants team they routed in Week 2, 35-13. And the game would be played at Lambeau Field, where the Packers were 8-1 in 2007.

"The Super Bowl is the ultimate goal," said veteran cornerback Charles Woodson, who played for Oakland when the Raiders lost Super Bowl XXXVII to Tampa Bay. "I'm always thinking about the Super Bowl — what I could've done different on different plays in that game. I'm just looking forward to another opportunity to win the game.

"We feel good about our opportunity. It's just a matter of us taking advantage of it. We've got a chance. That's all we're worried about. We've got an opportunity to play in the championship game."

It was a place not even the most diehard Packer fan could have predicted five months earlier. And the most important game of McCarthy's career was now coming.

From McCarthy's first day on the job, he talked about the Super Bowl. Now, his team was just 60 minutes away. "I've been talking about the Super Bowl since the first day I stood up here," McCarthy said. "So the first overlay I ever put up in front of our team was to win the Super Bowl, and the toughest challenge we'll have as a team is the handling of success. And that's something I put in front of them as a reminder every so often when it needs to be addressed.

"This is always the goal. It will always be the goal as long as I'm the coach here. It's part of coaching the Green Bay Packers. The standard has been set, the history is in place, and it's our responsibility to make sure we get that done."

8

Heartbreak Hotel

11 years since an NFC Championship game
ed in Green Bay. That frigid afternoon in 1996 will always be remembered as one of the greatest days in franchise history. The Packers beat Carolina, 30-13, that day and erased three decades of futility. While the Packers would go on and win Super Bowl XXXI, many players from that team have always insisted the NFC Championship was even more rewarding.

"That was the game that showed we had arrived," former Packers general manager Ron Wolf said. "I'll never forget it. Playing in our stadium in front of our fans and going up to the podium to accept that (NFC Championship) trophy. That was some kind of experience."

Now McCarthy was hoping for similar results in the biggest game of his life. The Giants were an even more unlikely participant in the NFC title game than Green Bay was. New York finished second in the NFC East, was a wild-card team, and had pulled off impressive road wins at Tampa Bay and top-seeded Dallas to reach the conference's championship game.

The Giants were seven-point underdog in Dallas. But Eli Manning threw two touchdowns, and the Giants defense stymied the high-powered Cowboys offense in a 21-17 win. "I'm so proud of our players," New York coach Tom Coughlin said. "They really rose up."Amazingly, the Giants brought a 9-1 road record to Green Bay. New York went 7-1 away from home during the regular season, then won its two playoff road games. So venturing into hostile territory wasn't something that bothered them. "Oh, you have to respect the fact that they went into Dallas and they went into Tampa Bay in a playoff atmosphere and won those games," McCarthy said of the Giants' playoff success. "So it's a credit to their players, their coaching staff, the ability to focus and get over the hurdles that road games do present to you, and that's why they're playing in the NFC Championship game. It's going to be two very good football teams battling to go to the Super Bowl."

McCarthy was doing all he could to keep his young team in check. But it certainly wasn't easy. The national media flooded Green Bay, and random players went from being ignored to having television cameras and tape recorders in their faces much of the time. "It's pretty crazy," reserve cornerback and special teams ace Jarrett Bush said. "A lot of us aren't used to it."

Green Bay's top players held press conferences in the media auditorium. This football-crazed city was abuzz, and the players couldn't escape the excitement. Through it all, McCarthy was trying to maintain a certain sense of normalcy, as hard as that was.

"The football part of it has really been the same," McCarthy said two days before kickoff. "The week has really flowed. I'm sure the excitement will build here tonight and tomorrow.

"But it's been a normal week with the benefit of the extra day, which has been helpful because you do have the extra responsibility as far as with the media and the administrative things that surround this type of game. But it's been a pretty normal week for me."

When the game finally arrived, there was nothing normal about it. Temperature at kickoff was 1 below zero with a wind chill of minus 23, making it the second-coldest night in Lambeau Field history and the third coldest in NFL history. During the legendary Ice Bowl played on December 31, 1967, it was minus 13 at kickoff and minus 46 with the wind chill.

At the start of the second quarter, it was 2 below zero with a wind chill of minus 21. That went to minus 3 and minus 20 at the start of the third quarter and minus 3 and minus 24 at the start of the fourth. It was so cold, Giants wide receiver

Amani Toomer said his lungs downright ached. Packers punter Jon Ryan said kicking a football was more like punting a rock. And Coughlin's cheeks were the color of a fire hydrant.

"It was cold," Manning said. "Me and (wideouts) Amani and Plaxico (Burress) came out about two hours before the game to do our warm-up, and we only got through about a quarter of it, and we said, 'Hey, we've got to go in.' My left hand was numb. My receivers, they didn't have any hand warmers, they were done. I said, 'Hey, I can throw. Let's take it in. We're good.' "

The problem for McCarthy and the Packers was that the visitors handled the elements better than the hosts. Packers quarterback Brett Favre — who made a living by thriving in the cold most of his career — played progressively worse as the temperatures dipped. Green Bay had no running game to speak of. And Giants wideout Plaxico Burress made Packers cornerback Al Harris his personal whipping boy.

Somehow the Packers forced overtime. But after the Packers won the coin toss, Favre badly underthrew a pass to Donald Driver, and Giants cornerback Corey Webster intercepted Favre's floater. Four plays later, New York kicker Lawrence Tynes drilled a 47-yard field goal for a 23-20 win that sent his team to the Super Bowl.

That quickly, the season came to a screeching halt for McCarthy and his surprising team. "It's horrible. Just horrible," Packers defensive tackle Ryan Pickett said. "I've been through this before and it's hard. You've just got to take it and learn, though, I guess. Hopefully, we can learn a lot from this.

"Maybe we keep this pain and get us motivated and use this as momentum. I think we will just by looking in everybody's eyes. Everybody's hurting. And it's a feeling you don't want to have again. It's brutal, just brutal."

There were several aspects of the game that were brutal to Packer Nation. Green Bay entered as a 7.5-point favorite, but the Giants took the fight to the Packers for much of the night. The worst matchup came between Harris and Burress, which was as one sided as they come. Burress hauled in 11 passes —

almost all while working against Harris — for 154 yards. Nine of Burress' catches went for first downs and he abused Harris on almost every type of pattern possible, with the "back-shoulder" route the most successful.

"We watched film all week, and just watching everything that he did, and we just pretty much played to his weaknesses tonight," Burress said of Harris. "He pretty much played a bump-and-run and we took advantage of it.

"We really didn't think — at the line of scrimmage he was hard to get off the line, hard to beat, and he doesn't really have great speed. If we got the ball up high, throw it back shorter, we can make the play downfield."

Burress had huge catches of 32, 21, 18, 18 and 14 yards — all against Harris. Burress had seven receptions for 105 yards in the first half alone as the Giants built a level of confidence, then continued to haunt Harris throughout the second half, as well.

The 6-foot-5 Burress had a four-inch height advantage on Harris. He also had better speed than Harris and ran several routes to perfection that left the Packer cornerback in his tracks.

Harris' performance was probably the worst by a Packer corner since Ahmad Carroll was wearing green and gold. And unfortunately for the Packers, it came during their biggest game in a decade.

"We knew they were going to be throwing that back shoulder, underthrown balls," Harris said. "(Burress) is their guy. But, hey, he made some good catches. Hats off to him. I have a lot of respect for the gentleman. I think he played well and they did a good job."

Meanwhile, McCarthy couldn't get his offense on track. In Green Bay's previous 10 games, it had averaged 31.6 points. The Packers had also scored 31 points or more in eight of those 10 games. But Green Bay never could get going against the Giants. The Packers ran for a season-low 28 yards, while the Giants went for 134. Despite the cold, McCarthy never gave his ground attack a chance and ran the ball on just 28.6% of his 49 offensive plays.

"I thought they played good run defense," McCarthy said of the Giants. "We didn't do a very good job of knocking them off the ball, and I was not really committed to the running game today."

Grant had rushed for 1,130 yards in his previous 11 games, including 201 the previous week against Seattle. Against the Giants and their terrific front four, though, Grant had just 29 yards in 13 carries.

One reason for the paltry production was a lack of opportunity. McCarthy felt he could take advantage of a suspect New York secondary, even if the weather didn't cooperate. And the Packers' percentage of run plays was their second-fewest of the year, trailing only their Week 3 total of 22.4% against San Diego.

"That's not disappointing," Grant said of his limited touches. "It's disappointing that we lost. They did a good job of clogging it up, so we had to go to some different areas."

That area was the right arm of Favre, who had played like the league's MVP for much of the season. In the bitter cold, though, Favre couldn't get it done against the Giants. Despite the brutal conditions, Favre played under control most of the way. He threw a 90-yard touchdown pass to Donald Driver early in the second quarter to give Green Bay a 7-6 lead. Midway through the third quarter, Favre fired a 12-yard TD pass to Donald Lee that put the Packers in front, 17-13.

But as the game progressed, Favre began reverting to many of the bad habits that plagued him during his latter years in Green Bay. On the final play of the third quarter, Favre threw a bomb for James Jones into triple coverage and was lucky the pass wasn't intercepted.

Just two plays later, Favre scrambled left and bought himself plenty of time on a play that lasted nearly eight seconds. Finally, Favre made an awful throw into coverage downfield that was intercepted by cornerback R.W. McQuarters.

Favre's most damaging pass, though, came in overtime when Driver ran a 15-yard out pattern. Favre's throw needed to be to the outside, but he missed badly and floated his pass to the inside, where Webster was able to make an easy interception.

"I just didn't throw it outside enough," Favre said. "It was what we call a shake route. Donald had slipped him more like an out route, which was fine. I just didn't get it out far enough. It's too bad."

Driver's release on the play wasn't great. But his route was solid. This blunder was on Favre. "I knew that Donald Driver was one of the key guys on their team, so I kind of figured that they would be looking to go to him," Webster said. "I had a good jam on him at the line of scrimmage, and then I was able to jump the route a little bit."

Four plays later, Giants kicker Lawrence Tynes lined up for a difficult 47-yard field goal. Not only was Tynes kicking in lousy conditions, he had missed his previous two attempts — a 36-yarder at the end of regulation following a bad snap, and a 43-yarder with 6:49 to go.

But with two minutes, 35 seconds elapsed from overtime, Tynes sent the Packers and their frostbitten crowd home in heartbreak. Just like that, a magical year for McCarthy's group was over.

"Right now I'm disappointed we didn't win the game," Packers general manager Ted Thompson said afterward. "I'm disappointed for our team because I really liked the guys on this team and I liked the way they were accountable to each other, played hard and did things a lot of people didn't expect, but we expected. It'll take some time to sit back and do all that, but I am very proud of these guys."

Favre agreed with his general manager. "In some ways, it was a surprise to a lot of people we were in this game," Favre said. "Unfortunately, the last thing you remember usually is a game like tonight. For me, the last play. But there have been so many great achievements that will stand out."

Favre was right about that.

Green Bay went 13-3 during the regular season, a five-game jump from 2006. The Packers then won their first playoff game since 2003 and reached the NFC Championship game for the first time in a decade.

Along the way, the 38-year-old Favre had one of the best seasons of his magnificent career. Favre completed a career-high 66.5% of his passes, threw 28 touchdowns versus 15 interceptions, and posted a passer rating of 95.7 — the third-highest of his career. Favre, who threw 47 interceptions during 2005-06, played much smarter in 2007 and limited his risk-taking. But Favre also made an enormous number of spectacular plays and helped Green Bay tie a franchise record for victories in a season.

Grant was a revelation and gave the Packers a running back they could trust. And while the defense needed some tweaking, it still ranked 11th overall.

"This group of players was a fun group to coach, it was a fun run we were on," McCarthy said. "We won a lot of football games, won a lot of them in big fashion, won some tight ones, too. But just the culture that's been created. I feel very good about the program, the direction of our program that is in place. So do the players.

"They feel they're treated extremely well, the communication and all the key elements of being successful are in place. There has been so much positive about how the year went along, but everybody to a man is disappointed the way it ended. So we have a lot of positive energy, a lot of positive experiences to tap into as we move forward."

Still, the loss was a brutal pill to swallow. McCarthy's team had done so many good things for five months. But in a matter of four hours, many of those positives were forgotten.

"We made a lot of progress as a football team," McCarthy said. "We were able to win a lot of games. We put ourselves in position for home-field advantage in the NFC Championship game. But we didn't finish the race. That's the lesson we need to learn. It's a tough lesson, especially in front of our home crowd. It's disappointing, it's going to take some time to move on from this, but this is a lesson we will learn from. And we will move on and continue to grow."

Safety Nick Collins agreed. "Getting to this stage is hard, unbelievably hard," he said. "And that's what makes this so hard. We had our opportunities to make plays and we didn't. We had our chances and we didn't take advantage of them.

"But this group of guys, I throw my hat off to them. Everybody had doubts about us at the beginning of the season, and we ended up one step away from the Super Bowl. And I think we'll have another chance next year." That was the prevailing thought with the offseason suddenly at hand.

Green Bay was the youngest team in football in 2007 and had come within an eyelash of the Super Bowl. But McCarthy knew that approaching the top was actually much easier than staying there.

"Our challenge to improve on 13-3 is much bigger than the challenge that we encountered this year, in my opinion," McCarthy said. "Because a lot of people outside of our locker room really didn't think we would be that good. We were a team that improved week to week and grew up as the season went forward. But we have a whole different set of challenges."

McCarthy's last sentence turned out to be incredibly prophetic. At the time, he simply had no idea what those challenges were going to be. Over the next few months, he would find out the hard way.

9

A Bitter Divorce

Mike McCarthy was walking into his daughter Alexandra's basketball banquet in early March 2008, when his cell phone rang. As McCarthy answered, little did he know the path of the Green Bay Packers was about to change for the foreseeable future.

Quarterback Brett Favre was on the other end, informing McCarthy he was retiring. For the time being, anyhow. "He informed me it was time for him to hang up the cleats, as he referred to it," McCarthy said of Favre. "It was really very similar to the conversations we've had the last four weeks.

"I was surprised ... when he told me, no question. I had to remove myself from where I was standing, because I was taken back. But it's something he's given a lot of thought."

McCarthy and Favre talked again later that night. But Favre's mind was made up. He was calling it quits. After 17 NFL seasons — 16 in Green Bay — arguably the greatest Packer in team history was done.

"I've given everything I possibly can give to this organization, to the game of football, and I don't think I've got anything left to give, and that's it," Favre said. "I know I can play, but I don't think I want to. And that's really what it comes down to. Fishing for different answers and what-ifs and will he come back and things like that, what matters is it's been a great career for me, and it's over." Despite the disappointing end to the 2007 season, this was a cruel pill for Packers fans everywhere to swallow.

Although Favre was now 38, he enjoyed one of the best years of his certain Hall of Fame career. Favre guided the Packers within a game of the Super Bowl and finished second in the

MVP voting. Favre's final season in Green Bay was a memorable one, as well. After two straight subpar years, Favre bounced back with a stellar season in which he posted the third-highest passer rating (95.7), the highest completion percentage (66.5%) and the third-most passing yards of his career (4,155).

Favre exited Green Bay with the NFL's all-time record for wins (160), touchdown passes (442), passing yards (61,655) and completions (5,377). At the time, Favre was the only player to ever win three MVPs, and his 275 consecutive starts (including playoffs) remains a record for quarterbacks.

But Favre was mentally and physically exhausted. And he said his commitment simply wasn't what it once was and what it needed to be. "I'm not up to the challenge anymore," Favre said. "I can play, but I'm not up to the challenge. You can't just show up and play for three hours on Sunday. If you could, there'd be a lot more people doing it, and they'd be doing it for a lot longer. I have way too much pride, I expect a lot out of myself, and if I cannot do those things 100 percent, then I can't play.

"I'm not going to sit here like other players maybe have said in the past and say that I won't miss it, because I will. But I just don't think I can give anything else, aside from the three hours on Sundays, and in football you can't do that. It's a total commitment, and up to this point I have been totally committed."

To many, Packers general manager Ted Thompson was the villain in this decision. Favre had been contemplating retirement every offseason since 2002. And when McCarthy was hired in January 2006, he and Thompson established a plan. McCarthy would stay in contact with Favre, calling roughly once a week. McCarthy would then keep Thompson in the loop, and occasionally Thompson would touch base, as well.

Multiple reports during this particular offseason said Favre was bothered that Thompson didn't keep in greater contact. Then it was learned Favre wanted to add Randy Moss when the wide receiver became a free agent, something the Packers didn't do.

Bus Cook, Favre's agent, said, "I know (Favre) wants to play one more year. I do not know how much conversation there was (between Favre and the Packers), and I don't think anyone forced him to make that decision. But I don't know that anyone tried to talk him out of it."

Scott Favre, Brett's brother, told WTMJ-TV in Milwaukee, "I think they could have maybe done more or let Brett know how much they needed him, or what they were going to do, or ask him questions on what he thought about what they can do. I don't think they communicated enough."

McCarthy, though, insisted that was all hogwash. "He was clearly wanted back," McCarthy said. "How could you not want Brett Favre's career to continue? Clearly one of the greatest or the greatest football player to ever step on the field."

Regardless of why Favre left, his departure was a blow to McCarthy and his team — at least in the short term. McCarthy had been Favre's quarterback coach in 1999. But the last two years were different. The pair had grown closer. They talked year round. They became more than just player and coach.

"I was fortunate to be his position coach and his head coach," McCarthy said. "He's a tremendous player. He was a joy to coach, day in and day out. Unique personality, the way he could affect people, the way he can walk into a room, the effect he had on the room, regardless of the age or the type of people in that room. Clearly one of the most unique individuals I've had the opportunity to work with.

"He's very unique. He brings great energy to the workplace. He's very consistent in his approach. Personality, like I've said earlier. He's an excellent teammate. There's going to be a lot of things I'll miss about Brett Favre."

McCarthy and Favre had worked together to bring a title to Green Bay. McCarthy now knew if the Packers were going to be world champions again, it wouldn't be with Brett Favre under center. Considering Favre was the only quarterback to start a game in Green Bay since September 27, 1992, that was a scary proposition.

"Personally, I think all of us would have loved to see Brett Favre ride out on top," McCarthy said. "I think everybody to a man in the locker room and probably throughout the organization, I can't speak for everybody, but it definitely would have been a great way for him to end his tremendous career, no doubt about it." As McCarthy left Lambeau Field that day, he knew things were about to dramatically change.

Aaron Rodgers, a laid-back, intelligent and levelheaded 24-year-old from Chico, California, had waited his turn the past three seasons. Rodgers sat, watched and learned behind Favre. Now, the former first round draft pick and University of California product faced the daunting task of replacing the iconic Favre.

"I'm not Brett Favre," Rodgers said. "If (fans) want me to be the next Brett Favre, I'm not going to be him. I'm Aaron Rodgers. That's who I am. I'm going to be the best quarterback I can be. He did it his way and I'm going to do it my way, and hopefully I can be successful."

The 6-foot-2, 223-pound Rodgers was preparing as though he'd be Favre's backup for a fourth straight year. But on the day the news of Favre's decision broke, Rodgers received eight phone calls by 7 a.m. The attention didn't stop. That quickly, Rodgers went from obscurity to the spotlight.

"I'm always going to be compared to Brett, obviously," said Rodgers, who played collegiately at Cal. "I think I just need to be my own quarterback, be my own man.

"And I think the most important thing on Tuesday (when Favre retired) to me was the texts I got from my teammates — just the encouragement. I've always felt like they believe in me just because they see my work ethic. But just to have that reinforced by some of the text messages and calls I got was pretty special."

Rodgers was expected to be a top-10 pick back in 2005, when he plummeted on draft day. Thompson finally threw Rodgers a net when he took him with the 24th overall selection and thought all along he got a steal. In Rodgers' first three seasons, he played in only seven games and threw just 59 passes (completing 35). He also missed six games in 2006 with a broken foot and four in 2007 with a hamstring injury.

In that time, though, Rodgers became far more comfortable with the NFL game, something he showed during a stellar performance in Dallas during the 2007 campaign. Rodgers also bonded with several teammates, earned the respect of the locker room, and tried becoming a leader.

"I like the fact that he has come into a situation that is difficult, and he has taken on those responsibilities," Thompson said the weekend after Favre's retirement. "The fans haven't seen him, but he goes out to practice every day, he's very well received by his teammates, he and Brett got along well, he understood his role.

"That's a difficult thing to do for a young man who wants to play. So I think he's positioned himself as a leader even though he wasn't playing, and I think he's positioned himself to be a leader going forward."

Rodgers had improved immensely under the tutelage of McCarthy and quarterbacks coach Tom Clements. Much of his progress came during the offseason at McCarthy's quarterbacks school.

In their two years together, McCarthy also helped Rodgers lower his release point. When Rodgers arrived in Green Bay in the spring of 2005, he had a mechanical throwing motion and was releasing the ball from the ear hole of his helmet.

The previous coaching staff, led by head coach Mike Sherman and offensive coordinator Tom Rossley, left Rodgers' release point alone. Not McCarthy. Instead, McCarthy gradually lowered Rodgers' carriage. Suddenly Rodgers' throwing motion began to look more natural and effortless.

"I think quarterbacks, the techniques for quarterbacks is no different than any other position," McCarthy said of Rodgers. "You're always trying to improve, you're always trying to get better. The way we do it in our quarterback school, we address areas of fundamentals that we feel are a must, that we feel we need to address and try to fix immediately. Then there are things we're conscious of that you see the particular quarterback may have a tendency to do once in a while.

"In Aaron Rodgers' particular situation, he had a very high ball carriage, which I felt there was a stiffness to the way he carried the ball. It wasn't as natural, because he is a very good athlete, and it's something you didn't see, in my opinion, in his earlier days, how good of an athlete he was. I think it's something that we've adjusted and he's very natural with it. Every quarterback that I've ever coached, you're always looking to improve their mechanics."

Those adjustments—and Rodgers' burning desire to succeed and prove his many naysayers wrong—were major reasons he had improved dramatically during the 2006 and 2007 seasons. And it's why McCarthy felt the Packers wouldn't fall off the NFL map with Rodgers under center instead of Favre.

"I have zero concerns about Aaron Rodgers," McCarthy said shortly after Favre retired. "I think his time is now. He's ready to go, and he will have another offseason to prepare for that. We need to make sure that we're ready for the whole quarterback position, and that is our focus."

For his part, Rodgers understood that very few quarterbacks who follow a legend ever enjoyed success. But Rodgers grew up idolizing the San Francisco 49ers, where Steve Young became an MVP and Super Bowl winner after replacing four-time Super Bowl champion Joe Montana. And Rodgers was cautiously optimistic his story could be similar.

"I'm in a good situation, I've got a great team around me," Rodgers said. "A lot of people have been focusing on what I'm going to do. It's what the team is going to do, really. I'm an important part of that and I know my role. I need to play well, and I'm not really going to have a grace period, either.

"The expectations that people are going to have are very high. The expectations I have of myself are very high as well. I've definitely been told there haven't been a lot of guys following a legend play well. Hopefully I'll have like a Steve Young kind of experience here."

It was under that backdrop that McCarthy began his third offseason in Green Bay. His legendary quarterback was now gone. His new quarterback was itching to go but had played almost no meaningful football during his three years in the National Football League. And McCarthy's team that fell one game shy of the Super Bowl was anxious for redemption.

During organized team activities that offseason, McCarthy — and the rest of the Packers — raved about Rodgers. He was sharp, accurate and crisp. He was poised, confident and composed. While Rodgers still had proven nothing on Sundays, his teammates were starting to believe.

"It's becoming a catch phrase, but we're all excited," former left guard Daryn Colledge said. "Everyone misses Brett. Everyone loves Brett and his humor and all that. But we're such a young team that I think there's just a ton of excitement out there right now. There's kind of a buzz right now and we want to prove everybody wrong.

"We don't want to be that team that was 13-3 and then doesn't make the playoffs. We want to build a dynasty. We want to do it with Aaron. I think he's going to bring a whole different dynamic than Brett. He's the kind of guy that most guys will definitely go to battle for."

Wideout Donald Driver played nine seasons with Favre and admitted he missed him dearly. But Driver was like many others, expressing excitement, not concern. "It's always going to feel different because you're so used to having (Favre) around the locker room," Driver said. "But I think the biggest thing is you get to a point where you feel used to it.

"The thing is, (Rodgers) has an opportunity. Be A-Rod and I think he knows that. And I think that's all that matters. As long as he knows he can play this game, he'll be able to play for a long time. And we all think he can play the game."

Green Bay was also bringing back 22 of 24 starters in 2008, meaning Rodgers was walking into an ideal situation for any young quarterback. "It feels great," Rodgers said. "I've taken the No. 1 reps in practice throughout the last three years, but to know that I'm the guy going into the season is pretty exciting, because guys are starting to rally around my leadership style and the way I do things. Like I said, I've been waiting for this experience, this opportunity, my whole life, so it's pretty exciting.

"I've been setting myself up mentally for this for a while," Rodgers continued. "It's exciting, it really is, to know that I'm going to get first shot, that I'm the guy, and really my own destiny is in my hands. If I play well, everything is going to take care of itself."

Rodgers lost some points with the fan base when he told *Sports Illustrated*, "I don't feel I need to sell myself to the fans. They need to get on board now or keep their mouths shut."

Rodgers later backtracked and told the *Milwaukee Journal Sentinel*. "I do care deeply about the fans, and I think anybody who has been to training camp sees I'm a lot of times the last one out signing autographs, sees I care about the fans, I care about their opinions," Rodgers said. "Everybody wants the fans to care for them and to pull for them and I am no different.

"The biggest disappointment in this whole thing is if anybody is offended by the stuff I say, because I think that my track record pretty much speaks for itself in the way I feel about the fans. I don't want the wrong message to come out of this."

On the field, Rodgers was winning points with his coaches and teammates. The months of May and June are often referred to as "underwear football." The practices are padless and players are in shorts. So getting a firm grasp on a player can be tough.

But as the offseason progressed, McCarthy began to believe more and more that his team would be just fine with Rodgers. "I like a lot of things about him," McCarthy said of Rodgers. "I like the combination of his mental and physical makeup. Replacing Brett Favre wouldn't be easy for anybody, regardless of their size, speed, mental capacity. It's important for Aaron to stay focused on things he can control, and that's a big part of my responsibility and the coaching staff and we'll continue to do that."

They did throughout the spring, and as the Packers got ready for their version of summer vacation—a five-week window in late June and July—confidence again resonated through the building. "It's Super Bowl for me every day," McCarthy exclaimed after his team's final practice. "I don't operate that way as far as trying to build up a bunch of what I would refer to as false confidence. As far as our roster, with the names on the board, the talent level on our depth-chart board, it's the best that it has looked since I've been here, especially at this time of year. The amount of work that we were able to get done from March until today has been the most productive that we've been able to get done in my three years.

"What does that lead to? We're trying to win every game, so I don't believe in predictions. I don't really get caught up in them. Once again, we're trying to win every single football game, and this team has a team that has the ability to be something special, and we felt that way coming off our offseason last year. We felt good about the direction we were going.

"I think our challenges are going to be a lot different this year. The obstacles that we're going to have to get over are going to be a lot different. We just have to go out week in and week out and find ways to win games. That will be our focus."

If only it were that simple.

On June 20 — the final day of offseason practices — Favre called McCarthy and told his coach he still had an "itch" to play and wanted back in. "When he picked up the phone again after he dropped it, he said, 'Oh God, Brett. You're putting us in a tight spot,'" Favre later said of his conversation with McCarthy. "He said, 'Brett, playing here is not an option.' Those were his exact, exact words."

McCarthy was about to enjoy some much-needed downtime. He was going to visit his daughter, Alex, in Texas. McCarthy and new wife, Jessica, were also set to move into their new home. But with Favre-a-Palooza beginning, the summer of 2008 was not going to be a vacation for McCarthy.

Instead, it was Favre versus Ted Thompson.

Favre versus Aaron Rodgers.

Favre versus the Green Bay Packers.

The saga became THE sports story of 2008. And McCarthy faced challenges that were entirely new to him.

On July 8 of that summer, Favre met with McCarthy and Thompson and told them both he wanted back in. Neither man seemed interested. McCarthy had made significant adjustments to his offense tailored toward Rodgers' strengths. McCarthy didn't want to set a precedent in which a player could miss the entire offseason program, then show up for training camp and play — something Favre was now trying to do. And perhaps more than anything, both McCarthy and Thompson wanted to finally see what they had in Rodgers. Rodgers had been patient. And if Green Bay sent him back to the bench, odds are he would have asked for a chance to play elsewhere.

On July 11, Favre asked the Packers for his release so he could play with another NFL team. The Packers believed Favre wanted to return to the NFC North with either Minnesota or Chicago and denied his request.

"The finality of his decision to retire was accepted by the organization," the Packers said in a team statement. "At that point, the Green Bay Packers made the commitment to move forward with our football team."

On July 14, Favre told "Fox News" that he wanted to play for a team other than the Packers. That led to a "Bring Back Brett" rally outside Lambeau Field organized by brothers Erick and Adam Rolfson of Pewaukee. Hundreds attended and showed their support for Favre. Polls across the state also showed the majority of fans wanted to allow Favre "back in."

"I know if I was a fan, on the outside looking in, you don't have all the facts, you're not privy to all the conversations," McCarthy said. "I just hope they respect the fact that we're going about this in a positive manner, with the Packers organization's best interests at hand. It's really as simple as that.

"They can disagree. That's OK. I'm not going to sit here and say I've made every decision that's been correct. I'm fine with that. But the disagreeable part of it, when you deal with an organization or a group trying to move forward, that's what holds you back. I respect their passion, I respect everything about our fans. There's nothing like them. But my father told me a long time ago that not everybody is going to like you. Get over it. That's life."

Favre also told "Fox News" that Thompson had lied to him several times, and he didn't feel like he could trust the Packers' general manager. Favre said Thompson promised to re-sign either guard Mike Wahle or Marco Rivero after the 2004 season, then didn't. Favre said that Thompson assured him we would interview Steve Mariucci for the head coaching job that eventually went to McCarthy in 2006, but didn't. And when Randy Moss was available in 2007, Favre lobbied hard, but Thompson denied the quarterback had pushed for the trade.

"Ted and I, I thought, have always had a good relationship," Favre said. "We don't talk a whole lot. We don't go out and eat and shoot the bull. But on three different occasions — I don't want to say 'lied,' I think that's kind of a harsh word, but I think 'untruth' or whatever is better."

As the summer dragged on, the soap opera thickened. On July 17, the Packers accused the Vikings of tampering, something that was never proven. Favre did not show up for the start of training camp on July 27, but two days later faxed his official request for reinstatement to the NFL.

As camp opened, McCarthy had chaos on his hands. The national media flooded Green Bay, and the only topic in Wisconsin anyone talked about was Favre. During McCarthy's season-opening press conference, the first 29 questions were about the Favre saga. In all, McCarthy took 50 Favre-related questions during the press conference. At one point, an exasperated McCarthy said, "I can anticipate we are going to do this for a while here."

Then he added, "Aaron Rodgers is the starting quarterback for the Green Bay Packers. That has been stated over and over again. I hope we can finally understand that. That's where we are as an organization; that's where we are as head coach of the Green Bay Packers. I don't know how else to answer your question."

Rodgers also faced an endless stream of questions, and almost none of them was about his on-field play. "I don't need people to feel sorry for me," Rodgers said. "Playing quarterback is a tough job, and there's a lot of scrutiny that goes along with that. You get too much blame a lot of times, you get too much credit a lot of times. And you just have to stay balanced and stay even-keeled.

"The last three years and this offseason have made me the person I am today, and I wouldn't have changed it for anything."

On July 30, Packers president Mark Murphy flew to Mississippi and offered Favre a lucrative marketing deal — 10 years and $20 million — to stay retired. Favre rejected the offer, then flew to Green Bay on July 31.

Two nights later, during the Packers' annual "Family Night" scrimmage at Lambeau Field, Rodgers heard a mixture of boos and cheers when he was introduced. "Yeah, I take it personally," Rodgers said. "But like I said, it's not the first time and it won't be the last time."

With Favre's shadow looming large, Rodgers struggled that night, missing six straight passes at one point and throwing an interception to safety Aaron Rouse.

One day later, NFL commissioner Roger Goodell reinstated Favre and Green Bay's quarterback situation was murkier than ever. "There have been no promises," McCarthy insisted. "Once again, there has been indecision throughout Brett's path back here to Green Bay. It's important for us to sit down, communicate. There are some things that we need to go through and then once again, from that information that comes out of that conversation will be used to move forward in the decision we'll make for our football team. That's where we are."

The Favre mess became too huge for Packers' public relations director Jeff Blumb and his staff to handle. So Green Bay hired former White House spokesman Ari Fleischer as a public relations consultant for the duration of training camp.

"I think any time you have an opportunity to tap into someone that's been successful at his particular job and the keys he can give you," McCarthy said of bringing Fleischer in. "He's just very clear. He has a message, and he's very clear about it. He doesn't dangle in the middle ground. He's either this way or that way as far as his message, and I thought he did a great job with our team and the message he gave our team."

While the Favre drama lingered, many Packers were getting worn out. Green Bay was coming off a 14-win season and a trip to the NFC Championship game. But the oodles of media members that descended on Green Bay had little interest in what was happening on the field. Instead, it was all Favre, all the time. And some players admitted it was hard not to feel slighted.

August 2, 2008, Green Bay, WI. Green Bay Packers quarterback Aaron Rodgers and head coach Mike McCarthy talk during a training camp workout at Clarke Hinkle Field in Green Bay, WI. (photo by Jeff Hanisch-US PRESSWIRE)

"It does bother me a little bit because of the quality of football team we have," said center Scott Wells. "We came off an outstanding year last year and we're looking to build on that and we've got a lot of the same players returning.

"Our team's not going to be determined by one player. It's a little frustrating."

Wideout Greg Jennings agreed with Wells. "I'm amazed at how much the media has turned this into a circus," Jennings said. "You guys make more of this than we do. We really, honestly, could care less. Aaron (Rodgers) is more than capable of taking this team the distance as well as Brett. Whichever one we have, the pieces are in place for either one. This is a good football team.

"A team is a team, and it's not just one individual player or a couple guys that make up the team. Especially with our team here. We had guys step up last year, and we're trying to do the same thing now and move forward."

McCarthy's challenges were immense. Not only did he — and the rest of the Packers' brass — have to figure out how to best defuse the Favre situation, McCarthy also had to keep his team focused, on task, and get them ready for the 2008 campaign.

"It's a challenge any time there's a tension put on your football team that has nothing to do with performance," McCarthy said. "And that's where we need to keep our focus."

Deep down, though, McCarthy knew focus would be virtually impossible if both Favre and Rodgers were on the roster in 2008. Favre, one of the top players in NFL history, had plenty of good football left in that golden arm. Favre felt that 16 years of high-level play earned him the right to change his mind on retirement and keep his job. Rodgers, who was groomed the entire offseason to take the reigns, was ready for his opportunity. And if Rodgers didn't get it, Green Bay's quarterback of tomorrow was likely gone.

McCarthy had to figure this out—and soon—or risk everything that was built his first 30 months on the job. So on August 4, 2008, McCarthy and Favre gathered for undoubtedly the most important meeting of McCarthy's Green Bay tenure.

The two began their pow-wow at 6 p.m., and it didn't end for six hours. The two took a break at one point for pizza. Thompson and Favre also talked for about an hour. McCarthy and Favre even talked again the next morning for another hour. When it was over, all were in agreement that Favre would keep playing. He just wouldn't do it in Green Bay.

"I thought it was an extremely healthy conversation. I would probably classify it as a conversation that had everything you wanted to say, everything you wanted to ask went on in it," McCarthy said. "I thought it was a conversation that was brutally honest. We agreed to disagree. We stood on opposite sides of the fence on a number of issues, and I respect the way he feels.

"But the one thing that I was looking for out of that conversation was whether he was ready and committed to play football for the Green Bay Packers. And his answer frankly throughout the conversation was his mindset, based on the things that happened throughout this whole course, that's not where he was. So with that, we didn't really move ahead.

"We talked about all of the different options … but the essence of the whole thing was I had a list of questions for him to answer those questions. I had questions that I felt were important for him to answer. I had questions for him from the locker room, from his teammates, and he did a great job. I thought it was a very respectful conversation. The feedback was back and forth. But once again, his feeling was, I don't want to speak for him, but based on where he is, the path that it took to get to this part, he wasn't in the right mindset to play here."

McCarthy and Favre went back and forth on what had transpired since March and how they found themselves in this current position. They covered many of the same issues multiple times. McCarthy told Favre he could compete for his old spot. And according to McCarthy, Favre had no problem with that.

But it never came to that. At the end of the day, the relationship between Favre and the Packers had been damaged beyond repair. McCarthy wasn't sure Favre would ever get past what had taken place since March. And deep down, McCarthy was terrified of what that could do to his football team.

"I'm not doing the P.R. thing anymore," McCarthy said. "I'm coaching the football team. The football team has moved forward, OK? The train has left the station, whatever analogy you want. He needs to jump on the train and let's go, or if we can't get past all of the things that have happened, I need to keep the train moving, and he respects that. He understands that.

"When I started the meeting my whole intent was, 'Was he coming into the locker room to play for the Green Bay Packers, and where is your mind at?' That was the first question I asked him, and we could never get back to that point where he was comfortable. It's very personal for him, and understandably so. I have had a very up-front seat throughout this whole process; he has been right in the middle of it. It's emotional for him, very personal. I don't want to be redundant; I don't want to speak for Brett. I respect the way he feels, but he is in a tough spot."

To be honest, both sides were in a brutal spot. So on August 5, Favre went home to Mississippi as the Packers tried to trade him. And one day later, Favre was sent to the New York Jets for a third-round draft choice. Thompson also had a comparable offer from Tampa Bay, but he undoubtedly wanted Favre out of the NFC.

Thompson was the first to admit he was extremely uncomfortable being known as the guy who traded Favre. "I don't think anybody would be comfortable with that," Thompson said. "It is, in many ways, sad that this is where it came to. At the end of the day though, I think all parties involved felt like it was the best solution to a very difficult situation."

While the situation was extremely difficult, McCarthy won some points for how he handled things. "Mike has been solid as a rock through this whole process, and really I think one of the main reasons that we finally have had closure to this situation was the difficult and honest and frank conversations that Mike had with Brett," Packers president Mark Murphy said. "I have also been very impressed with the way Mike has handled this matter with the team. He has kept the team together, and that has not been easy, and he has handled it as a real pro.

"I know as an organization we have taken hits, and it has split our fans, but it is important as we look to the future that we come together. I am very confident in the future of this organization and we will come through this process, a very difficult process, as a stronger, more unified organization. We're anxious to move forward and focus on the field with a goal of delivering a successful 2008 season to our fans."

So were McCarthy and his team. After weeks of speculation, guesswork and hypotheticals, Favre was gone. Rodgers was officially the quarterback. The 2008 season could begin.

"A sense of relief? You could say in a lot of ways," McCarthy said. "I'm about press-conferenced out, number one. That's something, it's a responsibility, I understand, but it was something that the situation needed to be resolved, and it was nice to get to a finality of that. But I'm relieved that we're talking about football, our football team, and that's what the focus needs to be on."

10

From the Penthouse to the Outhouse

The rest of that summer was disjointed to say the least. McCarthy had shortened the number of training camp practices and liked the pace at which his team practiced. On the flip side, there was an inconsistency and the Packers never established the flow their head coach wanted.

"Your team is never where you want it to be," McCarthy said shortly before the 2008 opener. "It's a football team that has an opportunity to be a good football team. We have some targets we still need to hit. It's my responsibility and the coaches' responsibility to get our team ready, and I have all the confidence in the world that we will do that. But we still have work to do."

To many, the Packers remained the class of the NFC North. Green Bay lost just two starters from its 14-4 team in 2007 — Favre and defensive tackle Corey Williams. And if Rodgers could play at a high level, most believed the Packers would again contend with the NFC's big boys.

"Nothing changes," wideout Donald Driver said. "We don't do anything different than we've been doing when Brett was here. The play calling is going to stay the same. Cadence is going to stay the same. Nothing different. You just see a different face and we all move on. And I think that's the big thing with us."

McCarthy was part of a coaching staff in San Francisco in April 2005 that passed on Rodgers. Instead they made Alex Smith the No. 1 overall pick, while Rodgers slid all the way to No. 24.

In the three years since, Smith had struggled immensely with the 49ers, throwing 31 interceptions and just 19 touchdowns. Rodgers, on the other hand, was getting his first chance on the big stage. While Rodgers remained a mystery to most, McCarthy had witnessed the day-to-day growth first hand. And with the Packers set to begin the year against Minnesota—arguably their No. 1 rival—McCarthy liked where his team stood at quarterback.

"I think it is important for (Rodgers) to focus on playing quarterback, and I think he has done a great job of that," McCarthy said. "I think he has done everything right as far as his focus, how he has handled every step of the way to get through this process. I think his play has reflected that, and that is ultimately what he will be judged by. We can't control the outside pressures. It is a part of our business, but I think he has done a very good job of managing it."

The Packers went just 1-3 that preseason, but Rodgers had a passer rating of 103.6. As well as Rodgers was performing on the field, McCarthy was even more impressed with how he had handled things off the field.

While the circus surrounding Favre took on its own life at the outset of camp, Rodgers was as steady and consistent as any of the Packers brass could have hoped. Rodgers fielded a daily stream of Favre questions but never said anything outlandish to throw gas on the fire. Instead he practiced hard, studied harder, and never blinked.

"I think he grew up," McCarthy said of Rodgers. "I think we all grew up a little bit during that situation. I think he did a very good job of handling a challenge, handling a situation that there really wasn't a script for and was unprecedented. I think it is definitely something he can learn from."

Rodgers was given an awfully big stage to show what he had learned — a Monday night game against the hated Vikings. For months, the Packers had intended to retire Favre's No. 4 at this game. Instead, it was up to Rodgers and his teammates to make the night a party. And that's exactly what they did.

Rodgers certainly didn't make anyone forget Favre during his first NFL start. But he was efficient, accurate and managed the game well as the Packers notched a 24-19 win at Lambeau Field in the season-opener for both teams.

Rodgers finished the night 18 of 22 for 178 yards, threw for a touchdown, ran for another, and posted a passer rating of 115.5. He also rushed for 35 yards and wasn't sacked a single time.

"It feels great," Rodgers said afterward. "You've got to remind yourself it's just one win, but it was a big one. I think the talk this week was a lot about the Vikings, and I don't think enough about the kind of team that we had. So we definitely wanted to play well tonight and I think we did."

Rodgers did his part on a night where all eyes were directed at him. Rodgers became the first quarterback other than Favre to start a game for Green Bay since Don Majkowski on September 20, 1992. Following Favre's messy divorce from the Packers, Rodgers immediately found himself under more pressure and scrutiny than any NFL player in years.

Making things even more uncomfortable for Rodgers was the fact that Favre had excelled in his victorious New York Jets debut with a passer rating of 126.0. But Rodgers never blinked.

McCarthy's game plan leaned on the conservative side. Rodgers was told to keep his passes short and simple and to take relatively few risks. The Packers also used a high percentage of maximum protection packages to slow Minnesota's vaunted pass rush.

"I thought Aaron Rodgers played well," McCarthy said. "Number one, I thought he managed the game … I thought he did a good job managing the game without taking chances. Playing with the play call and taking what the defense gave you and so forth. So I was pleased with his performance."

McCarthy liked how his team played the following week in Detroit, as well. The Lions rallied back from an early 21-0 deficit and took a 25-24 lead midway through the fourth quarter.

But Rodgers, who threw touchdown passes on three of Green Bay's first four possessions, answered with a 60-yard pass to Greg Jennings. That set up a 39-yard go-ahead field goal by Mason Crosby that gave the Packers a 27-25 lead. From there, Green Bay never looked back, getting defensive touchdowns from both Nick Collins and Charles Woodson in the final three minutes and rolling to a 48-25 win.

"The thing we've always focused on is winning football games," McCarthy said. "We had a big home opener against the Vikings on 'Monday Night Football.' I'm not naïve to everything circling around it. I thought our guys did a great job preparing for that game and doing what we needed to do to win that game.

"We did a lot of good things in this football game — I mean we won by over three touchdowns. But you could tell, just the feeling in the locker room, that we made some big mistakes, and those are the things we need to eliminate as we move forward. It's an excellent win. Winning is all that matters, and that's our focus. But there are a lot of things in this game that we can build off and learn from."

The Packers were 2-0, sitting atop the NFC North and looking just fine for picking Rodgers instead of Favre. Over the next few weeks, though, that would all change.

The Packers faced a "measuring stick" game the following week when they hosted Dallas on a Sunday night. The previous year, the Cowboys had drubbed the Packers, 38-27, in Texas in a game that eventually determined the NFC's No. 1 seed in the playoffs. Although this game was in Green Bay, the result was eerily similar.

The Packers—a team that McCarthy insisted would be built on defense—allowed a whopping 453 yards. Dallas had 217 of those yards on the ground, the most allowed by the Packers in nearly two years. McCarthy's high-powered offense was also rather pedestrian, totaling just seven first downs and 186 total yards through three quarters.

In the end, the Cowboys made a statement with their 27-16 victory. The Packers, meanwhile, had failed their first big test of the post-Favre era. "The reality is that it's the third game of the season," McCarthy said. "It was a big game. It was a great measuring stick for our football team, and I'll tell you exactly what I told them. The Dallas Cowboys are further ahead than we are right now. That's the facts and that's Week 3. How far ahead, time will answer that question."

Not all of the Packers were buying that, though. "We just couldn't make a play when we had to and Dallas did," left guard Daryn Colledge said. "Does that make them a better team? Maybe tonight it does. But it's a long season. This was just Week 3. I think we'd all like to see them again."

The way the Packers were headed, though, that wasn't going to happen. One week later, a Tampa Bay team quarterbacked by Brian Griese downed the Packers, 30-21. Bucs running back Ernest Graham, a rather mediocre player, haunted the Packers with 111 rushing yards and a touchdown.

Rodgers was inconsistent, throwing his first three interceptions of the year before leaving the game late with a shoulder injury. "Offensively we were poor today," McCarthy said after his team fell to 2-2. "(We) didn't run the ball very well. I thought they got after us up front with the running back and the run-blocking unit not in sync. We need to get that corrected. That's two weeks in a row. We need to do a better job there.

"We just made a number of the same mistakes that we made the first three weeks — that's four weeks now. When you have penalties, turnovers, it's very difficult to win a football game like that. You're playing a good football team, a very good defense in a tough environment. I just felt offensively we clearly didn't do enough to win the game. I thought our defense played outstanding time and time again and gave us a number of opportunities to win this football game, and we didn't take advantage of it."

Things went from bad to worse for Green Bay when its losing streak hit three the following week. Visiting Atlanta, led by rookie quarterback Matt Ryan and bruising running back Michael Turner, downed the Packers, 27-24, in Lambeau Field.

"We're going through a phase that every team goes through," McCarthy said. "That's what we're in right now and it's important for people to step up."

The loss knocked the Packers out of first place in the NFC North for the first time since the final week of 2006. But the Packers insisted they weren't in panic mode. "It's a long season," Packers defensive end Kabeer Gbaja-Biamila said. "I'm not going to panic. We didn't play well, but we've got to get back to work, we've got to get healthy and got to get better. We've been so focused on the end result, but we've got to stay focused on the moment, even focus on every second. There's a long season ahead of us."

Green Bay's defensive line had been hit hard with injury—one reason the Packers ranked near the bottom of the NFL in several key defensive categories. During its three-game losing streak, Green Bay had allowed an average of 28.0 points per game.

Offensively, the Packers were extremely inconsistent. While they were averaging a respectable 20.3 points per game during their slide, 45.9% of those points came in the fourth quarter. That meant the Packers weren't good enough early and were digging holes they couldn't climb out of.

"The thing is, when you lose, things get magnified," defensive end Aaron Kampman said. "And now that we've had three in a row, we've got an electron microscope on us right now. That's perfectly all right because we need to. When you're not winning football games, you should probably have a little closer microscope on you." Which meant all eyes were now planted firmly on McCarthy, who faced the immense challenge of rallying his team out of this mess.

Perhaps the Packers' biggest challenge was getting their defense on track. Green Bay headed to Seattle ranked 26th in total defense, allowing 363.2 yards per game, and 24th in scoring defense (25.6). The Packers were an abysmal 27th against the run (161.4) and 20th in third-down defense.

Minnesota's Adrian Peterson (103), Dallas' Marion Barber (142), Tampa Bay's Graham (111) and Atlanta's Turner (121) had all surpassed 100 yards against the Packers in the first five weeks of the season. But the Packers' defense turned things around against Seattle with an impressive 27-17 win.

Green Bay held the Seahawks to just 177 total yards. That marked the first time since Week 16 in 2006 against Minnesota that the Packers held an opponent under 200 yards.

"Excellent performance from the defense," McCarthy said afterward. "We'll take that every game. It was what we needed, what we needed as a team. We needed to come in here and play very well on defense."

Charles Woodson and Tramon Williams both had interceptions. Seattle managed only 13 first downs and the Packers won the time of possession battle by nearly 15 minutes. Green Bay also benefitted from the fact that the Seahawks were down to third string quarterback Charlie Frye.

Seahawks Pro Bowl quarterback Matt Hasselbeck was out with a knee injury, and backup Seneca Wallace was benched with a bad calf. So the Packers caught an enormous break when Frye had to play. "I mean shoot, losing is hard," McCarthy said. "We haven't won a game in a month. It was important for us to come up here — we knew it was going to be a big challenge because of the territory you're walking into here — and it was important to win this game, no doubt."

The Packers were back to the .500 mark. Plenty of problems remained, but there was optimism that they were back on track as high-powered Indianapolis and quarterback Peyton Manning came to Lambeau Field. Manning, who would go on to win his third MVP award that season, had to be licking his chops beforehand. The Packers were down two starting defensive backs — cornerback Al Harris and safety Atari Bigby — and appeared to be vulnerable in the back end. But for the second time in 2008, Green Bay returned two interceptions for touchdowns, and they trampled the Colts, 34-14.

Aaron Rouse's 99-yard interception return for a touchdown tied the Packers record. Safety Nick Collins also picked off Manning and brought it back 62 yards for a score. "I thought our defense was excellent today along with the crowd,"

McCarthy said. "When you play great defense and have the crowd at Lambeau Field, that's what it looks like right there.

"That's what we'll continue to talk about as a football team, the importance A) of winning home games but the importance of B) utilizing Lambeau Field as a home-field advantage. I thought it was a great victory for our team. I thought our defense was huge today."

Rodgers, who played a third straight game with a sprained right shoulder, was also terrific. Rodgers completed 21 of 28 passes for 186 yards and a touchdown despite 30-mph wind gusts at Lambeau Field. The win vaulted Green Bay to 4-3 heading to its bye week and put them back in the running in the NFC North.

"There was no doubt we needed to be 4-3 going into this bye," Rodgers said. "You know, it's been a situation where guys have stepped up in the absence of guys that have been injured, and guys that have been injured have been playing well through the pain. This is going to be a great week for us to just relax and get healthy."

The Packers had a chance to make an enormous statement when they traveled to unbeaten Tennessee after their bye week. The Titans entered the game 7-0 and had an average margin of victory of 13.3 points per game.

Earlier in the week, Rodgers had signed a contract extension through the 2014 season. He then had a chance to lead Green Bay to a victory late in the contest.

With the game tied at 16, Rodgers drove the Packers to the Titans' 45-yard line with just under two minutes left. But the Packers stalled and the game went to overtime. There, Tennessee won the coin toss, marched deep into Packers' territory, and won it, 19-16, when kicker Rob Bironas drilled a 41-yard field goal.

Tennessee won its 11th straight regular-season game, while the Packers remained mired in mediocrity at 4-4.

"We didn't perform well enough at the end to win the game," McCarthy said. "I thought it was a hard-fought football game, and they were able to move the ball in their two-minute drill."

To a man, the Packers felt like they'd let one slip away against one of the NFL's giants. Rodgers had thrown for 314 yards, including 136 and a touchdown to Donald Driver. The Packers outgained the Titans, 390-347, but lost the turnover battle, 2-0.

"We just didn't play how we wanted to play today," Packers wideout Greg Jennings said. "Hats off to them, they got one that we felt we should have got. That is the way it goes sometimes. When you have close games, it is all about finishing and we weren't able to finish. You can't let a game like this slip away."

Unfortunately for McCarthy and the Packers, this was just the beginning. Green Bay went to Minnesota the following week for a critical game with the Vikings. Both teams entered at 4-4, one game behind division leading Chicago (5-3). A win and the Packers were right back in the playoff picture. A loss and they'd slip to third in the mediocre NFC North.

McCarthy, like the rest of his team, wasn't happy with Green Bay's lot in life. "We're 4-4 for a reason," McCarthy said. "We haven't made plays in critical times of football games. We've been competitive in every outing this year. We've had opportunities to win those games. We did not. So it's important for us to continue to build off the positives that we have accomplished. There's a lot of positive things about our football team.

"I really like this team. I like the way they work. They give you everything they have on Sundays. Effort is never an issue. Frankly, we don't need to talk about it much anymore. But it's the details. We have to win the close, tight games. We haven't done that this year."

McCarthy was a perfect 5-0 against the Vikings and head coach Brad Childress, though. And everyone in Packer Nation was optimistic that they could make it 6-0 in this make-or-break game. "We've had some positive outcomes against the Vikings in our past experiences," McCarthy said. "It's really a one-game-at-a-time approach. This game I'm sure is going to be different than the others."

It was, largely because the Packers had no answers for Adrian Peterson — football's best running back. Peterson ran for 192 yards and scored the game-winning touchdown with just more than two minutes left as the Vikings rallied for a 28-27 victory. Packers kicker Mason Crosby had a chance to play hero, but his 52-yard field goal in the closing moments was just wide right.

"I just felt like as a football team, they fought like crazy like they always do," McCarthy said. "They give great effort, keep fighting to give one another a chance to win the game. In the end, we had that chance and didn't get it done."

That was a consistent theme in what was becoming an incredibly disappointing season. During the 2007 campaign, when things were remarkably rosy in Packerland and Favre was under center, Green Bay owned close games. In regular-season contests decided by fewer than 10 points, the Packers were 5-1 — a huge reason they went 13-3 and notched the NFC's No. 2 seed.

With Rodgers running things in 2008 as a first-time starter, the worm had completely turned. Following Green Bay's loss at Minnesota, the Packers were 1-4 in games decided by single digits. Green Bay's inability to close was a huge reason it was now 4-5 and in third place in the NFC North.

"The critical situations that we haven't been able to overcome, it's the National Football League," McCarthy said. "You can break it down to explosive gains, negative plays, the different things that go on, and the factor hasn't fallen on our side.

"We have to continue to work, continue to make those critical plays at critical times, and we haven't done that. We have five losses, and you can point to specific plays in every single one of those games. We need to turn some of those around in our favor."

Having a three-time MVP like Favre certainly helped the Packers in nailbiters in 2007. During his 16 seasons in Green

Bay, Favre rallied the Packers to fourth quarter, come-from-behind wins 40 times. Through nine games, Rodgers had done it just once with a Week 2 win in Detroit.

It wasn't just Rodgers who was failing late, though. Green Bay's defense, special teams and some questionable coaching decisions helped spell doom, as well. "We just need to play the way we're capable of playing," Rodgers said. "The season is definitely not over by any stretch of the imagination. We're very confident, both sides of the ball and special teams. We just need to get back to doing the things we're capable of doing."

Despite the Packers' disappointing 4-5 record, they were still alive thanks to the porous division where they resided. Chicago and Minnesota led the division at 5-4, the worst record for any first-place team in football. In all, the NFC North had just a .389 winning percentage, which ranked sixth among the NFL's eight divisions.

"It's still wide open," cornerback Charles Woodson said. "But we've got to do our part."

The Packers did just that the following week, playing inspired football in a 37-3 destruction of Chicago. The Packers dominated in the trenches, as Ryan Grant ran for a season-high 145 yards and Green Bay had a season-best 200 rushing yards. When Minnesota lost to Tampa Bay that same day, the Packers, Bears and Vikings were all tied atop the division at 5-5.

"This is November football and this is how you have to do it," McCarthy said. "I thought the run blocking unit, in particular the offensive line, time and time again we were able to get the movement up front and get back to the second level. That was big."

One week earlier, Tennessee managed just 20 rushing yards and averaged 0.69 yards per carry against the Bears' terrific run defense. With the Packers toting the NFL's 23rd-ranked rushing attack to Lambeau Field, few expected Green Bay to get healthy against the Bears' fourth-rated rush defense. Shockingly, though, that's what happened.

"They have a very good front seven, they play downhill, but we wanted to get them on their heels and make them adjust to what we had to do," Grant said. "I feel like Coach did a great job of balancing, making sure that they really didn't know what we were doing.

"I felt like throughout the whole game, they were really kind of confused on different things, and that's a testament to guys playing football, playing hard, guys were real vocal the whole time, and that's what you want. It feeds throughout the whole team."

The NFL season is a tremendous grind. From the grueling month that is training camp to the week-to-week pressures of the regular season, players are physically and mentally exhausted at different points in this eight-month marathon. The 2008 season had been a series of challenges for the Packers, and to be frank, they'd failed more than they ever anticipated. But through 10 games, Green Bay was right where it was when the year began. Tied atop the division.

The 5-5 record wasn't ideal. But Green Bay still had a chance to make something of a largely disappointing year. "It's really a six-game season," McCarthy said.

The first step of the journey took McCarthy back to New Orleans, where he had spent five years as the Saints' offensive coordinator earlier in the decade. And while McCarthy's offenses in New Orleans performed at a high level, they never played like this.

Saints quarterback Drew Brees threw for 323 yards and four touchdowns as New Orleans routed Green Bay, 51-29. The Saints tied a team record with 51 points, the third-highest point output in "Monday Night Football" history.

Green Bay's secondary entered the game ranked third in the NFL, allowing 176.3 passing yards per game. But Brees and the Saints carved up the Packers. Rodgers, meanwhile, couldn't keep up and threw three interceptions.

"Give credit to the Saints and the play of their quarterback," McCarthy said. "He was on fire coming into the game, and we didn't cool him off any. It was disappointing. I don't really have much to say about our defense. They played excellent on offense."

Little did the Packers know at the time, but when they left the Louisiana Superdome that night, their season was about to implode. One week later, the Packers led visiting Carolina, 31-28, in the final minutes. But the Panthers got a 45-yard kickoff return, then Jake Delhomme and Steve Smith hooked up on a 54-yard pass-and-catch to the Packers' 1-yard line. One play later, DeAngelo Williams ran up the middle for his fourth touchdown of the game — one that gave the Panthers a 35-31 win.

"We've just come up short so many times this year," Rodgers said. "We're not going to make excuses. We've had the opportunity in just about every one of those games. You look at the games we've lost, we've lost with opportunities to win in the last minutes. Make a play and win in the last minutes. We haven't done that."

Green Bay was now 5-7 and suddenly two games behind NFC North-leading Minnesota. "We've been way too inconsistent," Rodgers said. "I mean, definitely underachieving at times. The inconsistency is the biggest disappointment, I think."

Green Bay's season was back on life support as it welcomed the lowly Houston Texans (5-7) to town. Oddsmakers made the Packers a seven-point favorite, and with a kickoff temperature of 3 degrees, most figured Green Bay would get back on track against their visitors from the South.

Wrong.

Texans quarterback Matt Schaub had missed the previous week with a knee injury. But Schaub returned to shred Green Bay's secondary, throwing for a career-best 414 yards and two touchdowns. Schaub also drove Houston into field-goal range, and Kris Brown drilled a 40-yarder as time expired to give Houston a 24-21 win.

Green Bay had lost three straight games. It was now 5-8 and three games behind suddenly hot Minnesota. For all practical purposes, the Packers' first season without Favre was over with three games left.

"I'm frustrated," McCarthy said. "I'm very frustrated on the way particularly today's game unfolded. It's a little bit of a picture of how our season has gone. We had a number of opportunities, and we didn't cash in on them. We had some breakdowns and unfortunately that's why we're sitting here again with a loss. We need to win a game around here."

Amazingly, Green Bay's pattern of close losses and fourth quarter collapses continued the following week in Jacksonville. And for the third straight week, the Packers blew a game in the final minutes. Green Bay led, 13-7, heading to the fourth quarter, and 16-14 after a Mason Crosby field goal with just more than five minutes left. But like so many Packers games in 2008, Green Bay had no answers in the closing moments.

Jaguars quarterback David Garrard hooked up with Dennis Northcutt for a 41-yard gain. Maurice Jones-Drew then scored from two yards out with 1:56 left to give the Jaguars a 20-16 come-from-behind win.

Not only did Jacksonville snap a four-game losing streak, it also ended a four-game home losing streak. The Packers lost their fourth straight, fell to 5-9 and were eliminated from the playoffs.

"It's tough. We have a lot of players on this team that work so hard," wideout James Jones said. "When you get to this point and know for sure you're not going to the playoffs, then it hurts. There's a lot of pride in this room. You can't put your finger on one thing. The main thing is to keep working and build some momentum going into next year."

McCarthy felt like he was watching a bad movie — over and over and over. And someone had hidden his remote control. "This game has a lot of similarities from the games we have played as of late," McCarthy said. "There's no doubt about it. The bottom line is the outcome, and we didn't make enough plays to win the game. No one is happy where we are. We had high expectations and those expectations have changed."

Remarkably, the song remained the same the next week in Chicago when the Packers dropped a 20-17 decision in overtime to the Bears.

Crosby, the Packers kicker, had a 38-yard potential game-winning field goal blocked by Chicago's Alex Brown with 18 seconds left. Bears kicker Robbie Gould then drilled a 38-yard field goal early in overtime and the Bears prevailed.

The Packers fell to 0-7 in games decided by four points or less and 5-10 overall. Christmas remained three days away, and it was safe to say, this wasn't going to be a very happy holiday for the Packers.

"I do not see pressure as a problem for our football team in the fourth quarter," McCarthy insisted. "You look at the number of things that have gone right and the things that have not gone right. I wouldn't say it's individuals out there pressing or doing things outside of the scheme or doing things that are totally different than the way we operate. We've had some execution issues in some spots, and we've had some breaks go the other way. We've had opportunities to win games and we haven't converted them."

McCarthy would never go on the record and say the Packers missed Favre. But some of his players did. The previous season, when Green Bay was 13-3 in the regular season, the team mounted stirring late-game wins against Philadelphia, San Diego, Denver and Kansas City. Now, with Rodgers calling the shots, the Packers couldn't do anything right in close games.

"Yeah, I miss Favre. I'm not going to lie about it," linebacker Brady Poppinga said. "You know, you miss playing with a guy like Favre, man. He's a passionate, competitive guy. And any time a guy like that leaves, you're going to miss him. He's a legend, man. What are you talking about? Of course we miss him."

Favre was the master of late-game comebacks. Now, that element was missing inside the Packers' huddle. "The biggest difference between last year and this year is the games that were tight in the end, we found a way last season," center Scott Wells said. "This year, we haven't found a way, but that's a lot more than just Aaron. At the end of the game, we're just not getting it done. And it's not any one thing or one player that's causing that. We're just not doing it. That's the biggest thing."

The Packers' year had been a colossal disappointment. About the only way it could get worse was by losing their season finale to a Detroit Lions team that came to Lambeau Field with an 0-15 record.

Detroit was trying to avoid becoming the NFL's first winless team since 1976, when Tampa Bay went 0-14. All week long, Green Bay's players heard about the humiliation a loss would bring. "Human nature would say it's in the back of your mind," Poppinga said. "No one wants to be the first team to lose to someone. I think it's in the back of your mind."

It quickly went to the forefront of everyone's mind, when the lowly Lions tied the game at 14 early in the third quarter. And after the Packers regained a 24-14 advantage, Detroit pulled within three points with just 7 ½ minutes left.

Green Bay's fans — frustrated by the long year and another rough performance — let the boos reign down on the home team. "To me, that's tough love," Wells said. "I can understand the frustration there. But at the same time, they were cheering us as soon as we got the ball back."

That's because on Green Bay's very next play, Rodgers and Donald Driver hooked up on a 71-yard touchdown. And when Packers safety Nick Collins intercepted Lions quarterback Dan Orlovsky on their next possession, Green Bay finally had things under control.

Green Bay closed the year with a 31-21 win and snapped a five-game losing streak — its longest since 1990. The win certainly didn't make up for what had transpired the past four months, but it sure beat the alternative.

"It's like I told the other guys, I was like, 'It feels good to get this win,' " cornerback Tramon Williams said. "It was a lot of pressure relieved off a lot of guys. It feels good.

"Even though we're not going to the playoffs and such, just getting a chance to go into the offseason and feeling good, building from it, coming back ready to go. You don't want to go into the offseason with six straight losses. You don't know how it's going to affect guys, coming back from the offseason. It's just great to get that win."

Green Bay finished seven games worse in 2008 than 2007, the greatest one-season drop-off in victories in franchise history. And the 2008 Packers became just the 12th Green Bay team to have double-digit defeats. The ultimate slap in the face would have been a loss to the lowly Lions. That's why Green Bay headed to the offseason somewhat happy.

"Winning is the goal," Packers coach Mike McCarthy said. "And any time you have an opportunity to win and beat a division opponent, those are all aspects of your program you can point to and build off of. This is the way you want to start the (next) season. It's short-term. It's definitely something positive we can point to."

Overall, though, McCarthy was the first to admit this was unacceptable. And he was quick to point to himself. "Well, 6-10. My name is on the front door," McCarthy said. "It's not what we were looking for. It's not what we prepared for. I'm not satisfied, and I'll start from the top down.

"I don't think anybody in the Green Bay Packers organization is flippant about what just happened here. I'm the head coach. I was given an opportunity to coach a group of men, and we won six games. I clearly understand the responsibilities in the great organization I am working at. It is not acceptable. I'm not satisfied.

"There are reasons why we are here. We need to correct them as we move forward, and that's the facts. I'm not going to comment on past seasons and so forth, but that's the reality of where we are. We need to do a better job."

Many of McCarthy's staff wouldn't get that chance. One day after the season ended, McCarthy fired defensive coordinator Bob Sanders and seven other members of his coaching staff.

McCarthy also fired defensive ends coach Carl Hairston, defensive tackles coach Robert Nunn, secondary coach Kurt

Schottenheimer and nickel package/cornerbacks coach Lionel Washington from the defensive side of the ball. Strength and conditioning coach Rock Gullickson and offensive quality coach Ty Knott were both let go, as well. Later, special teams coordinator Mike Stock was pushed into retirement.

"What it came down to was I just didn't feel we were headed in the right direction on the defensive side of the ball," McCarthy said. "It was really an evaluation of our last three years. It was a three-year process, and I felt that a number of things that occurred in Year 1 showed up again in Year 3. So those were some of the factors that put me in that decision."

The Packers defense returned 10 starters from 2007, when they ranked 11th in total yards and sixth in total points. And when the year began, Green Bay's players—and even McCarthy himself—talked openly about building the post-Brett Favre Packers around their defense.

But that never materialized. Instead, the bottom fell out, and the Packers finished the year ranked 22nd in points allowed and 20th in total defense. Green Bay finished 26th in rushing defense and 26th in rushing yards per carry.

"I take responsibility for everything," Sanders said 24 hours after Green Bay's 6-10 season had ended. "It's my responsibility. Certainly I know what this (4-3) scheme can do. At times, I didn't get the job done."

Most head coaches get one chance—at the most—to clean out their staffs. If there needs to be a second time, the head coach is exiting, as well. McCarthy knew this was his one "get out of jail" free card.

"I mean, how much more pressure can you have?" McCarthy said when asked if the pressure had just been intensified. "My view of how I attack the job is going to stay the same.

"I think I bring passion, energy, work ethic to the job every day and I have one goal in mind. I'll do everything in my power to bring home the next championship, and that's the way I view it. That will never change. Unfortunately you have to make some tough decisions, and that was part of the last two weeks. Trust me, it was very difficult."

Two weeks later, McCarthy made arguably the most important hire of his career when he brought in Dom Capers to try to rescue the defense. Capers spent nine years as an NFL head coach—four in Carolina and five in Houston. He was also a defensive coordinator three other times during his terrific career. By hiring Capers to run the defense, not only was he switching coordinators. McCarthy was also changing defensive schemes — dumping the 4-3 he used his first three years in Green Bay and moving to a 3-4.

Some saw McCarthy's move as an act of desperation, one that saved his own job for the time being. "I don't agree with it," McCarthy said when presented that theory. "It was an evaluation period that went on, and I felt it was in the best interest of our program to make changes."

Desperation or not, McCarthy certainly got a high-end coach. Capers led Carolina to the NFC Championship game in 1996, one the Panthers lost in Green Bay. He was also named the NFL's Assistant Coach of the Year twice when he was a defensive coordinator. Now Capers was being asked to save Green Bay's defense — and perhaps McCarthy's job, as well.

"I think it was a matter of fit," Capers said of coming to Green Bay. "I felt very good about the interview here. It made an impression on me in terms of the way the interview was handled. I just felt comfortable in terms of I know the tradition that is here.

"You always are evaluating the team, the options and what you think can be done there. I had a good feel about it. There are a lot of things, no matter how many pluses and minuses you put down, there is always going to be a gut instinct there of what you feel is going to be the best marriage."

The McCarthy-Capers marriage had to work. If it didn't, the entire staff would soon be looking for work elsewhere.

11

2009: Bouncing Back

Never let them see you sweat. During Ted Thompson's stint as the Green Bay Packers general manager, this was his mantra. When dealing with a press corps that had its fair share of tigers, Thompson had been almost Buddha-like. No matter how edgy or probing a question may be, Thompson's tone, body language and approach never varied. Some wondered if the man ever blinked, let alone perspired.

But just four weeks before the 2009 season opened, a bead or two of sweat almost certainly formed on Thompson's brow. The same went for Packers head coach Mike McCarthy.

That was the day former Green Bay legend Brett Favre signed with Minnesota, the Packers' most hated rival. Thompson and McCarthy were already on the hot seat following the Packers' dismal 6-10 season in 2008. Now, with Favre in the division seeking revenge on the team that sent him packing one summer earlier, that seat went from hot to scalding.

"You're a fool if you don't realize this is a business and take note of what's going on around you," Packers linebacker Aaron Kampman said. "We all know it's a large year around here, an important year. That's probably an understatement. Big year for everyone here, yes."

Just 19 months ago, Thompson and McCarthy had been living large. The general manager had overhauled the depleted roster that former coach and general manager Mike Sherman left behind. McCarthy brought renewed energy and imagination to a team that desperately needed both. And Thompson and McCarthy received a lion's share of the credit when the Packers went 13-3 and reached the 2007 NFC title game.

Fast forward to 2009, when the natives were restless and jobs were on the line. Green Bay's seven game slide in 2008 was the greatest in team history. It also tied lowly Detroit for the league's biggest drop. If the losing wasn't bad enough, the organization took a major public relations hit from the Favre fiasco, one that eventually led to the future Hall of Fame quarterback being traded to the New York Jets. While many fans sided with Packers management, the Favre loyalists came out in full force, as well. That led to something many never believed possible: a divided fan base. It all added up to a bleak year in Green Bay, which led to a make-or-break 2009 for many in the organization.

"A guy or a team can go from being the talk of the NFL to being ripped like crazy," linebacker A.J. Hawk said. "It's just a crazy sport how it works. Obviously going 6-10 last year and how we did it, that doesn't sit well with anyone in here. This is a high pressure job for everybody. Everyone's always getting evaluated, coaches, players, everybody. And I'm sure this year is huge for a lot of us."

Starting with Thompson.

Thompson trained under Ron Wolf in Green Bay for eight years in the 1990s. In Thompson's first four years on the job, though, he didn't have the same level of success as his legendary mentor. From 2005-08, the Packers went 31-33 (.484) and reached the playoffs only once. Green Bay's magical 2007 season was the only year it was above .500.

"It doesn't sound very good when you put it that way," Thompson said. "Yeah, it's a tough league. Especially last year, we were disappointed in the record last year. We felt like it should have been better, and that's my responsibility, so we're going to try to do better."

Thompson had never been popular among the fan base because he guards every morsel of information as if he's working for national security. In a city where the fans own the team, running a covert operation—especially when you're not winning—doesn't fly.

Thompson also paid little attention to free agency, instead choosing to build through the draft, then resign his own players. And while Thompson's drafts were largely successful, they weren't enough to consistently get the Packers over the hump.

Packers president Mark Murphy supported Thompson and McCarthy throughout the Favre ordeal and the 2008 campaign. But former president Bob Harlan hired Thompson, and if the Packers stumbled again in 2009 and the Vikings soared, many anticipated that Murphy would make some changes.

"I think in the NFL every year's a big year," Murphy said. "You obviously saw last year how quickly things can change. But I have confidence in both of them, and I think they made the changes and did what they needed to do to turn things around and make sure we have a successful year this year."

Just two seasons ago, McCarthy was the runner-up to New England's Bill Belichick in the *Associated Press* coach of the year voting. McCarthy was given a five-year, $20 million contract extension after the 2007 campaign, then proceeded to have his worst coaching season.

"I'll tell you this: I always refer to it as the lessons of 2008," McCarthy said. "It gets me up every day. It still burns my gut."

McCarthy cleaned house on his staff after the 2008 season. He then hired Dom Capers to rescue a defense that gave up more points than any other Packers team in 22 years. It was a remarkably bold move, with Capers implementing a 3-4 defense that was brand new to almost everyone. If the transition was slow and the desired results weren't immediate, McCarthy's job would certainly be on the line.

"I don't view it that way," McCarthy said. "I'm thankful to be here today talking to you, if you can believe that. I'm serious. I have the best job in professional sports. I'm excited to coach these guys. I'm just excited that I am up here in 2009 ready to go."

There were plenty of reasons for excitement.

The 2008 Packers did something that was fantastically rare. They outscored their opponents by 39 points, yet somehow managed to go 6-10. In the previous decade, 30 teams finished a season 6-10, and their average point differential was minus 51.03. Of those, only the Jacksonville Jaguars in 2001 (+8) and 2002 (+13) finished ahead of their opponents in net points.

"That is crazy when you think about it," tight end Donald Lee said. "Just crazy."

It was also a big reason why the Packers didn't feel their 6-10 record was a true indication of who they were. As 2009 approached, there were five major reasons McCarthy believed the Packers would be one of football's most improved teams. They included:

1. **Aaron Rodgers.** The Packers quarterback was solid statistically in 2008, his first year as a starter. But Rodgers failed to deliver with the game on the line.

   Green Bay went 0-7 in games decided by four points or less, and Rodgers' inability to produce late-game magic was a major reason. The Packers believed Rodgers had Pro Bowl ability but needed to play with greater consistency at the end of games for that to happen.

   "He has improved every year from our first year together, so I think he is very consistent there," McCarthy said of Rodgers. "But the biggest change I see is just really the interaction and the way he treats (his teammates) and the way his teammates treat him. You are definitely seeing his leadership ability moving forward."

2. **Ryan Grant.** The Packers running back missed the start of training camp in 2008 due to a contract dispute, suffered a hamstring injury shortly after arriving, and was a shell of his 2007 self. Sure, Grant ran for 1,203 yards, but he averaged a pedestrian 3.9 yards per carry.

   "There were a lot of factors that went into that (3.9)," Grant said. "This will be a much better year."

3. **The 3-4 Defense.** In 2008, Green Bay gave up its most points in a season since 1986. Out went Bob Sanders and his somewhat predictable 4-3 scheme. In came Dom Capers and his 3-4 defense.

The Packers then used first-round draft picks on line-backer Clay Matthews and nose tackle B.J. Raji, two players tailor-made to fit the 3-4.

"It's just a lot of change, the way the meetings are conducted, the way we practice, the volume of the scheme, the different types of pressures," McCarthy said of switching to the 3-4. "I think we're off to an excellent start."

4. **Healthy and Happy.** Green Bay's preferred starters missed 44 games due to injury in 2008. In 2007, when the Packers reached the NFC Championship game, their starters missed just 10 games.

   "Those things usually even out," said defensive end Cullen Jenkins, who missed 12 games with a pectoral injury in 2008. "Hopefully that happens for us."

5. **No more Favre craziness.** The Packers' summer of 2008 will go down as the most drama-filled in team history. After Brett Favre announced he wanted back in, the team's quarterbacking picture became hazy, players picked sides, and tiny Green Bay became a media circus. In 2009, the focus was strictly on football, and everyone associated with the team knew what a positive that was.

   "Well, distractions are part of our business," McCarthy said. "Sometimes you see them coming, sometimes you don't. Sometimes they come in different forms and fashions. I think last year is an outstanding opportunity to look back on and learn from, and that's really how we've addressed it as a football team."

Green Bay opened the 2009 campaign by hosting Chicago on "Sunday Night Football." And everyone—from the coaches to the players to the janitors—inside 1265 Lombardi Avenue couldn't wait to turn the page from 2008 to 2009.

"Well, 6-10 is over," McCarthy said. "You don't get to carry what you did last year forward, whether you are coming off a successful season or an unsuccessful season. Every team is generated every single year. We clearly identified that back in the spring.

"One thing about the NFL, you either improve or you go backward. I think our team has improved since last year. It starts in the offseason program. How we played in those preseason games is evident of where we are as a football team. We get 16 opportunities. We're going to line up. We're excited about our first one against the Chicago Bears."

The Bears made one of the NFL's biggest offseason moves when they acquired quarterback Jay Cutler from Denver for a pair of first-round draft picks, a third rounder and quarterback Kyle Orton. Cutler's arrival gave the Bears, who lacked top-end quarterback play for more than a generation, real hope at contending for a title.

In the season-opener, though, the Packers got the best of Chicago and Cutler. Green Bay intercepted Cutler four times, the highest total of his career and the most by a Green Bay team since December 31, 2006. Cutler finished with a shoddy passer rating of 43.2, the second-worst of his career. And the Packers' mastery of the Bears signal caller was a major reason they prevailed, 21-15.

"With Jay, you're going to get some good throws from him," Packers cornerback Tramon Williams said. "But you're also going to get those throws, those errant throws. That's the way he plays the game. He's a gunslinger, and you live and die by it."

However, despite Cutler's struggles — and the stellar play of Green Bay's defense — the Packers trailed 15-13 late in the game. Then, for the first time in his Green Bay career, Rodgers came up big at crunch time.

Rodgers hit wideout Greg Jennings with a 50-yard touchdown pass with 1:11 left, allowing the Packers to escape victorious. "I don't think I ever lost confidence in myself or my abilities (in 2008), but when you have some struggles and you make some throws you want back late in games, it's good to start a season out and be in a situation where you're called upon and expected to perform late in the game," Rodgers said afterward. "To be able to, in crunch time when it was needed, to come up with a big throw and get (the ball to) our playmaker

Greg (Jennings) was very important for myself and also for our team."

Green Bay had just three second-half points when it began its final drive on its own 28-yard line. Four plays later, the Packers faced a third-and-one from midfield. McCarthy called for a run with Ryan Grant, but when Jennings lined up in the wrong spot, the Packers had to call timeout.

"It was my fault," Jennings said. "I actually designed that, to line up on the wrong side of the field so that we could go for the gold. And it got it done for us."

After the timeout, the Bears were expecting run and brought an eighth man into the box with safety Al Afalava. Rodgers ran a play-action pass, and his first option was to tight end Donald Lee on a wheel route.

Rodgers looked right to Lee, which held safety Kevin Payne in place. Jennings, who lined up on the far left, raced past cornerback Nathan Vasher.

Rodgers, who was sacked four times and hit nine others, had terrific protection on this play and lofted a perfect pass. Jennings caught it in stride at the 14 and waltzed in with one of the biggest plays of his — and Rodgers' — career.

"I just told the guys, 'Hey, just give me one drive,' " Rodgers said of the game-winning march. "Up front, I went to the linemen and said, 'Hey, let's just protect this one drive. Give me some time, and we're going to go down and score.'"

That provided a terrific start to the 2009 season. But the next two months were just the opposite. One week later, Rodgers was sacked six times — many of them his own fault after holding the ball too long. And the heavily favored Packers lost at home to Cincinnati, 31-24.

Green Bay improved to 2-1 with an easy 36-17 win over St. Louis the following week. Considering the Rams had lost 30 of their past 35 games, though, no one was doing backflips.

The Packers' biggest test of the young season — and perhaps of the McCarthy era — came in Week 4. Green Bay traveled to Minnesota to meet Favre and the 3-0 Vikings.

The previous week, Favre had fired a 32-yard touchdown to receiver Greg Lewis with two seconds left, giving Minnesota a miraculous 27-24 win over San Francisco.

"I think he still throws the ball with good velocity," McCarthy said. "I think it was clearly evident just on the last throw of the San Francisco game. It was an excellent throw and a great catch. I think he still has good feet. He's always had great command of the line of scrimmage, just the way he has handled that aspect of it. I think he looks sharp."

Without question, this ranked among the most anticipated Packers games ever. Favre and the Packers had one of the messiest divorces in league history. Green Bay thought they'd seen the last of Favre when they shipped him out of the conference to the New York Jets.

But Favre retired again after the 2008 season, and the Jets released him in April 2009. Four months later, Favre joined the Vikings — sending Packer Nation into an uproar.

"I'm sure that there are some people who are disappointed or upset," Favre said. "Sixteen years I spent there, I know how personal the Packers are to the fans, the state of Wisconsin. I'm very, very aware of that, and that's the beauty of that organization, and will always be.

"You can't find an empty seat in a town, where you can go to New York and L.A. and you can't fill the seats at times. So it's a special place, and I know people take a lot of ownership in that, and that's fine, that's great. Once again, that's what makes it such a wonderful place to play and watch a game.

"But my intentions are not to do anything else but to play and hopefully lead this team to a championship, as the other teams and players feel across this league. I've said this 100 times, and I'll say it again, that you can't take the 16 years away that I spent there. It was outstanding. So if there are people disappointed and have picked sides, I'm not surprised by it, but you can't take that away. So it is what it is. But I can't control that."

A few nights later, though, Favre and the Vikings certainly controlled the Packers. Favre outplayed Rodgers. Minnesota's

Brad Childress outcoached McCarthy. And Favre "stuck it" to Thompson, the man who chose Rodgers over Favre in the summer of 2007.

Vikings 30, Packers 23.

Favre 1, Packers 0.

"I just did what I was expected to do today," Favre said afterward. And how. Favre orchestrated four drives that went deep into Green Bay territory. And on all four, Favre's Vikings left with touchdowns.

"I didn't think he would do that," Packers cornerback Charles Woodson said. "I thought we would play better.

"I give him a lot of credit. Apparently he got his wish, and he stuck it to us pretty good. A lot of it is on us, but I give him credit."

Rodgers and the Packers weren't nearly as successful in Viking territory. On three different occasions, Rodgers led Green Bay into scoring range. Rodgers fumbled once, threw an interception, and the Packers were also stopped on downs. Three trips. Zero points.

"To have three possessions where you are in their territory and come away with zero points ... two of them were directly related to mistakes by myself, it's disappointing," Rodgers said.

Rodgers' final numbers probably made fantasy football owners happy. He threw for a career-high 384 yards and a pair of touchdowns and had a passer rating of 110.6. But Rodgers was also sacked eight times, including 4.5 by Vikings defensive end Jared Allen.

On paper, Rodgers' statistics were comparable to those of Favre (271 yards, 3 TDs, 135.3 passer rating). The difference, though, was Favre and the Vikings made the most of their chances, while Rodgers and the Packers couldn't.

"You can't have it," McCarthy said of the turnovers. "The two turnovers we had, particularly with the sack-fumble, took points off the board, and the second, the interception, should never have happened. Just the timing and the fit between the quarterback and the receiver is something we cannot let happen there. They took points off the board."

Some argued that McCarthy was his own worst enemy on one failed trip to the red zone. The Packers trailed, 28-14, late in the third quarter and marched to the Vikings' 5-yard line. After Ryan Grant ran for four yards on first down, fullback John Kuhn was stopped for no gain and a Rodgers pass to Jermichael Finley gained nothing.

There were still 17 minutes left in the game, but after a timeout, McCarthy bypassed the field goal and tried for the TD. Instead, Rodgers faced heavy pressure, threw off balance for Donald Lee, and the tight end dropped what should have been a touchdown.

"I'm playing to win," McCarthy said. "I thought it was a good play. Frankly the third-down call bothers me more than anything. They're in a goal-line defense, we're in a goal-line offense and it's a tempo play and the ball was held up by the referee or whatever happened, and frankly I didn't have time to change the play because of the 40-second clock. Liked the fourth-down call, wish I had the third-down call back."

The Packers wished they could have had the entire 60 minutes back. Favre had exacted revenge on Thompson — and his former team. And Green Bay (2-2) was two games behind the Vikings (4-0) just one month into the season.

"One game is not going to define my career, good or bad," Favre said. "It's sweet, but it has nothing to do with revenge. What I've done in my career speaks for itself. And we have to play them again."

McCarthy faced an immense challenge following the loss in Minnesota. Green Bay was again the youngest team in football. Rodgers had yet to win a meaningful football game. Overall, the Packers' collective psyche was extremely fragile.

Green Bay was entering one of the easiest stretches of its schedule. And McCarthy knew his team couldn't afford a hiccup.

They didn't.

Green Bay shut out Detroit for the first time since 1946, blanking the Lions, 26-0. The Packers then held the punchless Cleveland Browns to a paltry 139 total yards and an average of just 2.7 yards per play in a 31-3 victory.

Green Bay had allowed just three points in its last two games, something the franchise hadn't accomplished since Weeks 6-7 of the 1966 season. "We've got a chance to be a really good defense when it's all said and done," linebacker Nick Barnett said. "It was a new defense for everybody and that always means you've got a chance to get better and better as you go. Right now, I think that's what's happening."

But could it happen against Favre and the Vikings? That answer was a resounding 'No.'

Thanks to a scheduling oddity, Green Bay and Minnesota were set to meet just 27 days after their first encounter. Only this time, Favre returned to Lambeau Field, the place he'd given Green Bay fans 16 years' worth of mostly terrific memories. This time, the memories were painful for Packer Nation.

Favre was surgeon-like, carving up Green Bay's secondary with remarkable precision and accuracy and leading the Vikings to a critical 38-26 win. Favre threw four touchdown passes for the 21st time in his career, which tied him with Dan Marino for the most in NFL history, and posted a lights-out passer rating of 128.6.

"Am I pleased with the way these two games have turned out? Absolutely," Favre said. "It had nothing to do with trying to prove myself to anyone. I still have a passion for it. It's a little bit tougher to get up and bounce back, but my arm feels great.

"My mind is in a good place, the team has welcomed me in, and really all the other stuff doesn't matter. I know it makes for a good story. But I'm glad it's over, I'm glad we won both, but I'm not going to sit here and throw any daggers."

In the two games against Green Bay, Favre went 41 of 59 for 515 yards, threw seven touchdowns and no interceptions for a passer rating of 135.9. Most importantly, Minnesota improved to 7-1 and swept the season series against the Packers (4-3).

"We talked a little bit about not doing too much," Vikings coach Brad Childress said. "You have a tendency to do too much sometimes, and I thought he did just about what he needed to do. He didn't get too creative or try to rig anything up. I just thought he kept it in body, didn't get out of body."

Favre exited the visiting tunnel and ran onto the field at 2:27 p.m. for warm-ups, and roughly 75% of the crowd booed. Although the stadium had more purple in it than perhaps ever before, the overwhelming majority of shirts and signs were anti-Favre. A plane even circled Lambeau Field before the game with a banner that read, "Retire 4 Good."

The booing continued at a frenzied pace throughout the game, as the regular-season record crowd of 71,213 let Favre know what they thought of their one-time hero wearing purple. But McCarthy and Capers were never able to figure out Favre and give the Green Bay faithful anything to cheer about.

Afterward, Favre raised both arms to the sky before being hugged by several former teammates, as well as McCarthy and Jerry Parins, the Packers' longtime director of security. Favre made his way to a tiny media room, one much different than the palatial auditorium he used to share his thoughts in.

Roughly 20 cameras—twice as many as the 2007 NFC Championship game—and perhaps 75 reporters were waiting. Wearing a sweater, jeans and tennis shoes, Favre said the win "ranks high." And while Favre admitted he was nervous, he handled his emotions "better than the first game" against his former team.

Favre also said he understood where Packer fans — most of whom had picked sides in his messy split from Thompson and the organization — were coming from. "Packer fans cheer for the Packers first," Favre said. "I know that. But I hope that everyone in the stadium watching tonight said, 'I sure hate those jokers on the other side, but he does play the way he's always played.'"

Meanwhile, McCarthy had a laundry list of issues. Defensive end Cullen Jenkins questioned the 3-4 defense afterward. Rodgers again failed to win a big game. And Green Bay's special teams were a mess. "We're 4-3. We're 4-3 for good reason," McCarthy said. "I think we have not handled two prime-time games very well. I'm confident that we'll learn from these experiences. I thought we would have learned more from the first game up there to this one. We had some repeated mistakes; that's frustrating and something that we take with full accountability as coaches.

"There are so many more positives to our football team in my view than the negatives, but the thing I don't like is that the valley between our positives and our negatives is too big right now. The way we play at an extremely high level ... our bad plays need to be closer to our good plays is the point I am making. Our good plays need to overshadow our bad plays, but we've just got a little too big of a valley right now."

Months later, many Packers admitted the home loss to Minnesota stuck with them for days. Favre's face haunted them. Doubt crept in. "That game was a tough one to get past," Packers nose tackle Ryan Pickett said. "That stayed with us a lot longer than most games ever would."

Now, as the Packers prepared to travel to Tampa Bay—the league's lone winless team at 0-7—their focus was not where it needed to be. And what followed was the most embarrassing loss of the McCarthy era.

Green Bay went to Tampa Bay as a 10-point favorite but allowed the Buccaneers to hang around. By early in the fourth quarter, though, the Packers had taken a 12-yard touchdown run from Rodgers and built a 28-17 lead.

Shockingly, the Bucs answered right back. Rookie quarterback Josh Freeman, who had struggled throughout his first NFL start, threw a touchdown pass to tight end Kellen Winslow to make it 28-23.

Freeman threw another TD pass to rookie seventh-round draft pick Sammie Stroughter with just more than four minutes left to give Tampa Bay a 31-28 lead — its first of the game.

Then with Rodgers trying to lead the Packers back, he was intercepted by safety Tanard Jackson in the final minute. Instead of going to the ground, Jackson weaved 35 yards for a final TD and a stunning 38-28 Tampa Bay win. This was about as low as it gets.

"Low point? It doesn't feel good," McCarthy said. "It never feels good when you lose. This one definitely hurts. It'll definitely rank up in there, but it's still one loss. I'm not trying to downplay it.

"I'm disappointed in the way we played today, disappointed in the way we didn't sustain momentum in the game, because that's something we've done now two weeks in a row. That's something we need to look at. We've got some recurring problems that we have not cleaned up yet, so that's definitely cause for concern as we move forward."

It was the midway point of what was supposed to be a season of redemption in Green Bay. Instead, the Packers were 4-4, had lost two straight, and were going nowhere fast.

Rodgers, who was sacked six times in the loss to Tampa Bay, had been dumped a total of 37 times in the first eight games of the year — the most in the NFL. Part of that was due to an offensive line that lacked stability. But a bigger part was the indecisiveness of Rodgers, who was holding the ball too long and playing as though he was terrified to make a mistake.

The protection issues had forced McCarthy to shorten his playbook and keep more blockers in to protect Rodgers. But even that wasn't working. "It has to stop," McCarthy said of the horrific number of sacks. "You can't sit here and keep taking sacks. I'm sure you're tired of asking the question; I'm tired of talking about it. That's a reflection of coaching and playing. It's something that's been coached, something that's been trained, and it keeps showing up on Sundays.

"You look at Tampa Bay's quotes all week, that's all they talked about was sacking the quarterback, and it happened again today. It has to end. We cannot continue to have the numbers that we have in the sacks. The other part of it, too, I thought he had plenty of time to throw."

The next day, the Packers had a come-to-Jesus moment. It was one that would go on to define their season — and perhaps the futures of McCarthy and Thompson.

After the offensive players watched film of their loss to Tampa Bay, the veteran leaders took turns speaking. And there was an honesty and frankness that could either rally a team or divide it even further.

"There were some deep-seeded emotions in that room that needed to get out, that guys were holding in," Rodgers said. "It was great. There were a lot of harsh words said, but at the end of the day we moved on together.

"A lot of times when there is strife on a team, it can get out in the wrong way—guys talking in the media on their own or behind the scenes—but we sat in the room as an offense and said, 'What are the main issues here?' Myself, Donald (Driver) and different guys spoke up and we got our issues on the table and moved forward as a team. It wasn't a divided locker room. We stayed together, talked about our problems and moved forward together."

No one was more blunt than wide receiver Donald Driver, who had been in Green Bay longer than any other Packer. "If we don't win — and I mean now — they are going to fire all of our (butts) at the end of the season," Driver told the *Milwaukee Journal Sentinel*. "I'm serious."

McCarthy knew that Driver was dead on. "Our message is very clear," McCarthy said. "The head coach has to coach better, the coaches have to coach better, the players have to play better, and we have to win games. That's our focus."

Seven days after a loss to then-winless Tampa Bay, the heat on this Packer management team was at an all-time high. McCarthy and Thompson were lambasted in several media outlets through the week. And as the Packers prepared to meet Dallas on a Sunday night, many fans around Lambeau Field donned buttons that read "Fire McCarthy" and "Fire Thompson."

Under that backdrop, the Packers took the field as three-point underdogs. In the 24 games since Brett Favre had been gone, Green Bay's biggest win as an underdog came October 19, 2008, when Indianapolis was favored by 2.5.

But the Packers surprised the oddsmakers and many of the 70,894 paying customers by topping Dallas, 17-7.

Dallas came to town leading the NFC East (6-2), had won four straight games, and was packed with confidence. The

Cowboys left with a season low in rushing yards (61) and total yards (278).

"We were sitting at 4-4 and coming off some tough losses," said cornerback Charles Woodson, who led the defense with two forced fumbles, an interception and a sack. "Now, you've got to win games. We definitely felt like we had to get this game."

A major knock on the Packers since their 2007 season ended in the NFC Championship game was that they couldn't beat quality opponents. Prior to its win over Dallas, Green Bay was 10-14 in the past 14 months and had defeated only two teams with a winning record. While this victory wasn't always pretty, it was probably the most impressive—and certainly the most necessary — of the post-Favre era.

"We said all week, if we want this season to turn out the way we think it should, we have to make a run and it needs to start this week," fullback John Kuhn said. "This is just a starting point, though. It isn't anything special. We're going to enjoy the win for a day or two, then get right back at it."

Truth is, though, this was special. The Cowboys' offense — led by quarterback Tony Romo, running back Marion Barber and wideout Miles Austin — had been one of football's finest all season, ranking fifth in points per game (27.1) and third in total offense (404.5).

Green Bay's defense, meanwhile, ranked a mediocre 17th in points allowed (21.5). But take away games with bottom-feeders Detroit, St. Louis and Cleveland, and the Packers were allowing a whopping 30.4 points per game.

On paper, this looked like a mismatch for the powerful Cowboys. Instead, it was a mismatch the other way. "We knew our backs were against the wall and we came out swinging, and I think we caught them in the chin a little bit," said Packers linebacker Nick Barnett, who had eight tackles and two of Green Bay's five sacks. "I felt like guys were out there playing with a lot of energy and enthusiasm."

The question now was whether these inconsistent Packers could use the victory as a springboard to something greater, or would they simply fade away quietly like they did in 2008.

"Well, it was important for us to get back on track," McCarthy said. "You know, especially after the past two weeks. We had some excellent performances across the board, especially against a very good Dallas football team and a hot team and a powerful offense. We had a whole lot of respect for those guys coming in here. I was very proud of our defense."

Much to the delight of McCarthy — and Packer Nation — the fun was just beginning. One week later, tailback Ryan Grant erupted for 129 yards and a touchdown as the Packers toppled San Francisco, 30-24. The 49ers entered the game ranked first in yards per carry allowed (3.3) and second in yards per game allowed (69.3).

But Grant averaged a whopping 6.1 yards per run, and the Packers' 158 rushing yards was their second-highest total of 2009.

"When we can run the ball like that, it really balances the offense, controls the clock, and controls the ball," Grant said. "That's big for us, big for our running game.

"When the weather turns around here, running the ball is important. You want to be able to hit that stride, start getting more comfortable and get your legs underneath you. I feel that. I've always felt like I'm the type of guy who can do that."

The only downside was Green Bay lost defensive end Aaron Kampman and cornerback Al Harris to season-ending knee injuries. Both players would never play another down for the Packers.

"Injuries have kind of fallen upon us," Mike McCarthy said. "It's unfortunate; you don't want to see any of your players get hurt, but it's part of our job. That's really a big part of a coach's responsibility to overcome these types of situations and navigate through your medical phase of and aspect of your football team."

But the Packers were hot now, and the injuries didn't slow them in the least bit. Green Bay clobbered Detroit, 34-12, on

Thanksgiving to stretch its winning streak to three games. Rodgers threw three touchdowns, and the Packers intercepted Lions rookie quarterback Matthew Stafford four times — including two by Woodson.

On Woodson's second pick, he went 38 yards for a touchdown, then struck the Heisman pose in the endzone. "I don't know who is playing better football than Charles Woodson around the National Football League," a glowing McCarthy said afterward. "He had a huge day for us.

"His level of play is the highest I've been around as far as productivity for a defensive player. The ability to anticipate, recognize, the versatility of playing a number of different positions, he's productive, tough, instinctive. He's playing at an extremely high level for us."

That was certainly true.

Woodson, who signed a seven-year, $52 million free agent deal with the Packers before the 2006 season, never wanted to play in Green Bay. But when the Packers were the only ones to come bidding, Woodson had little choice but to accept their offer.

Woodson and McCarthy butted heads throughout the summer of 2006. But somewhere during that season, the two began to peacefully coexist, and Woodson has been one of football's elite corners since.

Now, with Capers in charge, Woodson was playing some of the best football of his life. "He has the combination you look for," Packers defensive coordinator Dom Capers said of Woodson. "He has the size and physical tools to play the position. The thing I like is that he's a smart player. Not only does he have good football instinct, but he understands the game. He gives you the flexibility where you can move him around."

Woodson lined up on No. 1 wideouts like Cincinnati's Chad Ochocinco, Detroit's Calvin Johnson and Baltimore's Derrick Mason and stymied them all. He also shut down standout tight ends like Dallas' Jason Witten, Chicago's Greg Olsen and Tampa Bay's Kellen Winslow.

Woodson was lining up at cornerback, safety, linebacker and playing from the slot. He even played on the line of scrimmage in a package the Packers call "Bear."

"He's a Hall of Fame player and that's just how he's playing. Like a Hall of Famer," said Packers cornerbacks coach Joe Whitt Jr. "I tell my other guys, 'Don't look at Woodson now. He has the ability to do some things other guys just can't do.' And he's doing them."

While Woodson was at the forefront of Green Bay's defensive revival, he was getting plenty of help. Sure, it took some time for everyone to feel comfortable with Capers' 3-4 scheme. But now Green Bay was rolling.

One week later, the Packers whipped the Baltimore Ravens, 27-14. And again, Green Bay's defense led the way.

The Packers intercepted Ravens quarterback Joe Flacco three times and sacked him three more. Baltimore standout running back Ray Rice was also limited to 54 rushing yards.

"There are a lot of positive aspects and variables of our football team," McCarthy said. "The most important thing is those positive things, we need them to show up every week and we need to continue to improve. I think youth plays into that. I think we had some injuries that play into that, so with those factors involved, I think we have an opportunity to get better. I think we can play better.

"I think our defense has hit their stride. I think our offense hasn't hit their stride for four quarters, and I think the same thing for special teams. Then you do that one game, then you've got to do that two games. That's really how we approach things."

Rodgers was starting to hit his stride, as well. Since the Dallas game three weeks earlier, Rodgers had thrown eight touchdowns and two interceptions. The offensive line had come together. And the Packers were beginning to figure things out on both sides of the ball.

"He's in a groove," McCarthy said of Rodgers. "The pass protection consistency definitely helps you. Because when things aren't going well and you are getting hit and you think you might have to come out more often than you need to and things like that. But I think he's trusting his feet, he's trusting the pocket, and he's being smart."

Green Bay stayed red hot, rolling past host Chicago, 21-14, the following week. Grant led the way with 137 rushing yards on 20 carries, his second-highest total of the year.

Grant ripped off a 62-yard touchdown run on Green Bay's first play from scrimmage to stake his team to an early 7-0 lead. Grant later scored the go-ahead touchdown with 12 minutes, 42 seconds left to propel the Packers to their first season sweep of the Bears since 2003.

"It was great to see Ryan get on the second level and finish the run," McCarthy said. "You can't start the game any better than that. He's a tough, hard-nosed runner. He's very consistent."

Not only had the Packers (9-4) won their fifth-straight game, they eliminated Chicago (5-8) from the playoff picture. "This is special. Trust me, I know what my division record is: 17-7, 4-4 against the Bears," McCarthy said afterward. "I'm definitely in tune with where we are in our program. This is an important game. It's an important game for each organization. It's a very important game for the cities. There are a lot of people that put a lot into this game. It's a very, very important game for our fans, and I'm sure they're excited. Trust me, we feel very good about the victory today."

The Packers were as hot as anyone in football. During Green Bay's five-game winning streak, its average margin of victory was 11.6 points per game. McCarthy's offense was rolling. Capers' defense was surging.

What better time for a homecoming?

McCarthy was born and raised in Pittsburgh. The Steelers were his team, and much of his family remained die-hard Pittsburgh fans. Now McCarthy was bringing his Packers to Pittsburgh's Heinz Field to battle the defending Super Bowl champion Steelers. Pittsburgh had lost five straight games and was 6-7 overall. But the game was huge for both McCarthy and those close to him.

"It's very special to go home," McCarthy said. "Make no bones about that. But it is a business trip. You probably have about two or three hours to have dinner with your family. But it's a great opportunity for our football team. I have a lot of pride in my football team, and to take them back to Pittsburgh and to compete against the world champions. That's the way I'm viewing the game, I know that's the way our team is viewing the game.

"This is a great opportunity for us to get to 10 wins, and they are still the champion until acknowledged otherwise. We're looking for a competitive atmosphere over there at Heinz Field, and I'm really looking forward personally."

McCarthy grew up watching the Steelers win four world championships thanks largely to a ferocious defense. Joe Greene. Jack Ham. Jack Lambert. L.C. Greenwood. Mel Blount. Mike Wagner.

Those Steelers defenses were loaded with Pro Bowlers all over the field. Today's Pittsburgh team — led by nose tackle Casey Hampton, linebackers LaMarr Woodley and James Harrison, and safety Troy Polamalu — wasn't any different.

When it came to the Steelers, everything started and ended with defense. "That's the way it always was in Pittsburgh," McCarthy said. "You play great defense, and that was always the bottom line to winning championships. I know being a Pittsburgh native during the '70s, their formula has not changed. They had great defenses in the '70s; it was the backbone of their championship years, and they really never changed it.

"I know my history as an offensive coach, but clearly when I became a head coach, I did not want to be known as a former quarterback coach that was a head coach. It definitely starts with defense. That's always been my vision, and we feel like we've made strides toward that this year definitely. I think that's just part of growing up in western Pennsylvania."

While both teams entered with high-end defenses, this game was all about offense. And the two teams combined to play one of the most memorable games of 2009.

Green Bay took a 36-30 lead with 2:06 left when Rodgers hit James Jones for a 24-yard TD. But that left the Steelers with too much time.

On the game's final play, Pittsburgh quarterback Ben Roethlisberger fired a 19-yard TD pass to rookie Mike Wallace in the front left corner of the end zone, with Josh Bell in coverage. That pass and catch gave the Steelers a dramatic 37-36 win and snapped Green Bay's five-game winning streak.

Roethlisberger established a new Pittsburgh franchise record with 503 passing yards, and he became just the third quarterback in NFL history to top 500 yards while throwing for three TDs and no interceptions. That overshadowed a terrific night by Rodgers, who threw for 383 yards and three TDs.

"All losses are difficult," said McCarthy, noting this one was even more so. "Losses in December are probably a little more important. This was a game we had a lot of confidence coming into. We knew we were going to have to score some points today on the offensive side of it. I don't think we thought it would go that way as far as their aggressiveness and the passing game against our defense.

"We came up one play short and it will be corrected tomorrow. I'm sure there will be a number of opportunities where we could've probably made one play. I think this is classic December football. It came down to the last play of the game, and we didn't get it done."

The loss continued a disturbing trend for Green Bay's defense. The Packers had done a terrific job against many of the league's bottom-feeders at quarterback. But when Green Bay faced elite competition, it was melting down.

The Packers had faced four quarterbacks with top-10 passer ratings: Minnesota's Favre twice, Roethlisberger and Dallas' Romo. In those four games, the quarterbacks combined to complete 94 of 144 passes for 1,269 yards, 11 touchdowns and one interception. That's a whopping passer rating of 115.8.

In Green Bay's 10 games against non-top 10 quarterbacks, its defensive passer rating was a stellar 55.1. Those quarterbacks had gone a combined 162 for 327 (49.5%) for 1,844 yards, 16 touchdowns and 22 interceptions.

Clearly the Packers were building an impressive résumé against the dregs of society but were outclassed against the NFL's brightest stars.

"I guess you can look at it that way," cornerback Tramon Williams said. "I think we've got a lot of talent back there, though."

The end of the regular season was both predictable and encouraging. The Packers hammered a Seattle Seahawks team going nowhere fast, 48-10. The running back trio of Grant, Brandon Jackson and Ahman Green combined for five touchdowns.

"Running the ball is crucial this time of year, especially when it's getting cold outside," center Scott Wells said. "You want to be able to have a two-dimensional attack going into the playoffs.

"I think it's a great feeling to be able to go out there and have a well-balanced attack. You don't want to be having question marks about one part of your offense."

The Packers (10-5) won for the sixth time in seven games and clinched their first playoff berth in the post-Favre era. Green Bay couldn't catch NFC North champion Minnesota and knew it would be a wild-card team. But that was just fine with McCarthy & Co.

"It feels great," McCarthy said. "Our focus all along was to get to the 10 wins, and fortunately with 10 wins, we're in the playoffs today. That's always the first step. As we talk as a football team, our goal of winning the world championship is right in front of us. And that's all you can ask for, is opportunities.

"You have to get into the playoffs to accomplish that. We're going to be a road warrior mentality as we plan for that, but let's be honest: we still have work ahead of us. We're excited about qualifying for the playoffs, but you know we need to continue to play the way we're playing. I'm excited about the momentum and the progress we've made as a football team, and we still have an opportunity to improve."

Green Bay closed the year with a 33-7 rout of defending NFC Champion Arizona in the desert. The game was largely meaningless, with the Packers locked into the No. 5 seed in the playoffs and Arizona set as the No. 4 seed. That meant the two teams would meet again one week later in an NFC wild-card game.

Despite knowing the game held no true meaning, McCarthy played his starters most of the way. Arizona head coach Ken Whisenhunt kept his in the game roughly a quarter. "I'm not going to stand here and act like I have all of the answers," McCarthy said afterward. "But I have the pulse of my football team. Our football team needed to stay on course. We set a path.

"We had some bumps in the road at 4-4. We continued to improve each week and won some football games along the way. I thought it was important to take this last opportunity to make sure that we were playing the best we possibly could coming out of the regular season."

With the playoffs at hand, McCarthy's Packers were as dangerous as anybody in football, having won seven of eight games. Meanwhile, the top two teams in the NFC were struggling.

New Orleans, which had started the year 13-0, dropped three straight to finish the regular season. And second-seeded Minnesota stumbled to the finish line, as well, going 2-3 in its final five games.

McCarthy's Packers, meanwhile, were playing their best football of the season. "I think so," linebacker Nick Barnett said when asked whether the Packers were dangerous. "I like where we are as far as our confidence level, our momentum.

"We're in the dance and by no means is that our final goal. We're trying to get to the big dance, and I'm trying to get the cha-cha slide on."

The Packers certainly had that slide going since losing at lowly Tampa Bay in Week 9 and falling to 4-4. In the eight games since, Green Bay outscored its opponents by an average of 31.8-15.6 per game.

The Packers scored at least 27 points in six of their final eight games and eclipsed the 30-point barrier five times. Defensively, Green Bay held six of its last eight foes to 14 points or fewer.

"It's an impressive body of work the second half of the season," Mike McCarthy said. "That's the truth, that's the reality, and that has been acknowledged. Also, it's our responsibility as coaches to keep driving this football team. They're fun to coach. They still have a lot of work in front of them. I still see the opportunity to improve. ... We've been playing really good football here the second half of the season."

Green Bay finished the regular season ranked No. 2 in total defense (284.4) and sixth in total offense (379.1). What remained to be seen is whether those numbers were padded against one of football's easier schedules. Green Bay's opponents finished the year with just a .471 winning percentage.

"I guess that's something we'll just have to find out," Packers safety Nick Collins said. "I think we're playing good football and can play with anybody around. There's a lot of good teams, and you have to be playing your best at the end to have a chance. We're not playing our best, but we're getting closer."

The Packers entered the postseason with one of football's more dangerous and multidimensional offenses. Rodgers had a passer rating of 103.2, which was just behind Bart Starr's franchise record of 105.0 set in 1966. Rodgers' passer rating was above 100.0 in 10 of the past 14 games, and his touchdown-to-interception ratio of 30-7 was off the charts.

After a slow start, Greg Jennings emerged, while tight end Jermichael Finley finished the year with a bang. Running back Ryan Grant also had six touchdowns in his last four games.

At the heart of it all, though, was an offensive line stabilized by the return of right tackle Mark Tauscher. After a slow start, that unit was playing the type of football you can win with in January.

"We're doing a lot of good things right now, and we want to be sure not to take our foot off the gas," said left guard Daryn

Colledge. "Playoffs are playoffs, and you can throw the records out once we get to that. So I think everything's wide open once we get to that."

Green Bay's greatest questions remained on the defensive side of the ball. Oh sure, they dominated several of the NFL's doormats during the regular season. But when the Packers faced high-end offenses, they struggled.

Green Bay had issues in the secondary, where nickel-and-dime backs Jarrett Bush and Josh Bell were picked on often. The Packers also struggled against tight ends, and teams with good ones made them a huge part of any game plan.

"There's still a lot of things to work on and we know that," Barnett said. "But it makes us more hungry to go in there and work on that kind of stuff."

The Packers were looking to recent history for both motivation and confidence. In the last four seasons, both Pittsburgh (2005 playoffs) and the New York Giants (2007) were wild-card teams that won three road games, as well as the Super Bowl.

Could Green Bay do the same in the apparent wide-open NFC? They'd soon find out with a return trip to Arizona. "I feel very good about our football team," McCarthy said. "It's like anything you're trying to build as far as the vision, the plan. I like the way our football team looks right now. I like the energy they're playing with, I like the way they prepare, and I like the way they're focused, and we'll be totally in tune with the fact that playoff football is different.

"We have a group of men that experienced this two years ago. We have a group of men that have not experienced it. Through our week of preparation, I'm looking for a focused, disciplined week of preparation, and we're getting ready to go play Arizona. We're playing an opponent on the road, they're the defending NFC champions, they've won their division. There's definitely some challenge of playing a little bit uphill, and that's the mindset we're taking into this game."

12
Doomed in the Desert

Aaron Rodgers dropped to pass, which seemingly was good news for the Packers. Rodgers had been brilliant for most of Green Bay's wild-card game at Arizona. He had thrown for 423 yards and four touchdowns. Rodgers also led the Packers to seven straight scoring drives — six touchdowns and a field goal — as the Packers rallied from a 21-point deficit and forced overtime tied at 45.

Now, Green Bay won the coin toss to start overtime, and its high-flying offense was headed back to finish off the Cardinals once and for all. Just one problem: Arizona's defense made a play for one of the few times all day. On a third-and-six from deep in Green Bay's end, Rodgers took a three-step drop. Arizona blitzed nickel back Michael Adams from the right slot.

Adams arrived in 3.5 seconds, which was more than enough time for Rodgers to deliver the ball to somebody, anybody. Instead, Adams hit Rodgers, the ball came free, linebacker Karlos Dansby picked it out of midair and returned the fumble 17 yards for a game-winning touchdown.

Arizona 51, Green Bay 45.

McCarthy fell to his knees, stunned over what had transpired. That fast, the scalding-hot Packers were done.

"This is just going to make myself and these guys want it that much more," Rodgers said of the loss to Arizona. "It might not look like we came that close, but we still feel like we were close to achieving all the goals we set forth at the beginning of the season."

The Packers seemed poised to keep chasing their dreams as one of the NFL's wildest postseason games ever unfolded. The teams combined for more than 1,000 yards and just two punts. While Rodgers was terrific, Arizona's Kurt Warner was even better — throwing five touchdowns and completing 29 of 33 passes (87.9%).

"It was just one of those games where I felt great," Warner said. "I felt like I was seeing everything well and it accumulates to 51 points."

The defense that McCarthy and Capers watched grow up in 2009 vanished at the most critical moment. That allowed Arizona to build leads of 17-0 and 31-10.

Rodgers made a remarkable number of plays, though, in his first playoff start. Early in the third quarter, Rodgers fired a six-yard TD to Greg Jennings and an 11-yard scoring strike to Jordy Nelson with three minutes left to pull the Packers within 31-24.

After the Cardinals answered back, Rodgers engineered scoring drives of 80 and 67 yards to tie the game at 38. It was the first time the game had been tied since the opening minutes. Warner responded with a 17-yard TD pass to Steve Breaston to put the Cardinals back ahead, 45-38. But Rodgers never flinched and threw an 11-yard TD pass to Spencer Havner to force overtime.

"If you had come in this morning and told me our offense would score 45 points," defensive end Cullen Jenkins said, "I'd be like, 'Yeah, we're going to win.'"

When the Packers won the coin toss to start overtime, they had to feel like a win was in the cards. But on the first play of overtime, Rodgers missed a wide-open Jennings on what would have been an 80-yard, game-winning TD.

"I just missed it, unfortunately," Rodgers said. "When I came off the fake, I wished I had just a tad more time. I still felt pretty good about the throw. Unfortunately, it was just a little too far."

Two plays later, Rodgers dropped back against Arizona's strong-fire pressure. There was plenty of time for Rodgers to make a play, but instead he was sacked, fumbled, and Dansby's return ended Green Bay's year.

"We have an opportunity from a time clock to get the ball out," McCarthy said. "It's just like anything; at the end of the day, the quarterback and the people that handle the ball, and it's something that we put a lot of time in from a practice perspective. You have to take care of the football, and we didn't do that as a football team, and it really factored into the outcome of the game."

Replays showed that Adams grabbed Rodgers' facemask on the sack and strip. But no flag was thrown, and the Packers' season was over just like that.

"I think any time you're sitting around waiting on calls to win football games, you're in a mode of excuses," McCarthy said. "The way the game ended, you don't want it to come down to an officiating call. Nobody wants that. You want it to be about player productivity. There was a lot of productivity in that football game, especially from an offensive standpoint. But I'm not going to sit here and try to discredit Arizona's victory by no means, because it really doesn't do any good.

"We need to learn from the experience. That's the difference between winning and losing in the playoffs, and that's where we have to make sure we go as a football team, that we're not in that position. And that's the way I view it. We're never going to count on the officials to win a football game."

The hangover from this loss promised to be a lengthy one. But when the Packers moved past that, their collective spirits were certain to rise. Green Bay rallied from a miserable start to the season. The Packers were as good as any team in football over the second half of the year. And for the first time since Favre left town, Green Bay seemed to have its confidence back.

McCarthy wasn't fully ready to label the year a success, though. "I'll say what I say every year," he said. "There's only one team, in my view, that has success, and that's the team that wins the Super Bowl. That's the ultimate success. One team shares that.

"But I think you do have different levels of success. I think we've had some successes. There's definitely a lot of opportunities we can learn from. I look at the type of games we played in during the course of the year. We played in more big games this year than we did last year, and the youth of our team will definitely learn from that. We have the playoff experience with the youth of our team that we can carry forward. We'll learn from that. We have improved in a number of areas, so we've had some successes. But there's only one team that can say it had a successful year when the season's over."

Green Bay was one of football's youngest teams in 2009. Rodgers was just 26 years old and on track for a stellar career. And the defense figured to be better in the second year of Capers' 3-4 scheme.

"We've got a lot of young guys and a lot of young guys that can play," said cornerback Charles Woodson. "Those guys, they're only going to get better, so having playoff situations just seasons them a little bit more. Hopefully this year is just the start. We'll see."

Woodson knew better than anyone that tomorrow provides no guarantees. He was on three straight playoff teams in Oakland, including one that reached Super Bowl XXXVII. The next three years, though, those Raiders were a combined 13-35.

"When I first got to Oakland and (Jon) Gruden was there, we were just building, and you could feel the growth in the team," Woodson said. "We got ourselves to the championship game, then the playoffs, then the Super Bowl. You felt like from there, it was going to continue, but we proved you never know.

"The thing is, we should continue to get better, but other teams are going to get better, too. So we all have to keep driving, or it can go backward."

The Packers had gone backward after their trip to the 2007 NFC Championship game, going 6-10 the next season. The task now was to make sure that slippage didn't happen this time.

"We definitely have a good team and a good foundation," Jenkins said. "But you never know what the future holds as far as injuries and things like that. We had a good team last year, but we had some unfortunate stuff. So you can never predict that stuff. It's always tough to say. But we are set up pretty well."

It did appear as if these Packers could have some staying power. And that McCarthy's talk of winning a Super Bowl was more than just lip service.

The key, of course, was Rodgers, who was just entering the prime of his career. Rodgers' numbers were eye-popping in 2009 and he was terrific while rallying the Packers back against the Cardinals. But his greatest flaw — holding onto the ball far too long — was evident again in the playoff loss. Not only did Rodgers bear at least some responsibility for all five sacks that day, his fumble that led to the Cardinals' game-winning TD could have been avoided had he gotten rid of the ball faster.

"Aaron had done a good job throughout the game extending plays and making plays, and that time he extended a play and it didn't work out," McCarthy said. "That's the plus and minus of having the ability to extend some plays."

Rodgers still hadn't reached the level of the NFL's great quarterbacks, but he was getting closer. And if he continued his ascension, Green Bay's future was as bright as any team in football.

"I think Aaron has had a very good year," McCarthy said. "I don't think there's (any) doubt about that. When you go win it all, I think that's when you start talking about great seasons. But he was definitely a very bright positive for our football team, both on the field and in the locker room, and we feel very good about that as an organization. I definitely felt that he had a very, very good year."

The Packers possessed a lot more pieces, too. The pass catching group led by wideout Greg Jennings and tight end Jermichael Finley was mostly young and gifted. The offensive line improved throughout the season.

And while Green Bay's defense struggled against elite offenses, it had made strides. "Our goal will never change," McCarthy said. "You guys probably think I'm nuts when I sit up here and say it every year; that's just the way we go about our business. But the reality of it is, expectations are 'what are we going to get done in the offseason program?' Every year is different, every football team is different. You need to rebuild, reload, restructure.

"We have a good foundation. We have a program, a blueprint that works, but we need to improve it because we did not get past the first round, and that is something that we'll identify with and so forth. No. 1, we need to have a very good offseason program. We've got a lot of younger players that need to take full advantage of individual improvement opportunities in March, April and May.

"That's the way I view it. You've got to build it. You've got to stack those successes. We have some successes and some experience from this past year that we'll be able to carry over that we did not have last year, so I'm confident that will help us. But the goal will never change here."

McCarthy and the Packers appeared to be closing in on their ultimate goal. As a wild and wacky 2009 season came to a close, most of the dominoes were in place.

"I think every guy up here feels like we've got a bright future," cornerback Tramon Williams said. "I think some special things are going to happen around here."

Little did Williams know how prophetic he would soon be.

13

Winning Time

It was February 1996. The Green Bay Packers had just completed an 11-5 regular season that included an NFC Central Division crown and a trip to the NFC Championship game. Those Packers ranked seventh in the NFL in offense and 14th in defense.

General manager Ron Wolf and head coach Mike Holmgren were both a little more than four years into their jobs of turning around a moribund franchise. Wolf was 57 years old and Holmgren was 48. Quarterback Brett Favre was just 26, entering his sixth NFL season and coming off an MVP season.

Now fast forward to 2010.

Again the Packers were coming off an 11-5 regular season, although this one didn't include a divisional title and featured a first round playoff loss. The 2009 Packers, though, ranked sixth in total offense and second in total defense.

General manager Ted Thompson was 57—the same age as Wolf — and had just completed his fifth year on the job. Like Holmgren, McCarthy was 46 and had just wrapped up his fourth year. And quarterback Aaron Rodgers—like Favre—was 26 years old and beginning his sixth NFL season.

As Green Bay prepared for the 2010 season, the parallels between these Packers and the 1996 bunch were downright eerie. "That is crazy," Packers wideout Jordy Nelson said.

"I know you guys can do a lot with stats, but that one is pretty wild."

But there was also one enormous difference. Back in 1996, Wolf sensed just how close his team was to a world championship. So the Packers general manager used free agency to sign defensive tackle Santana Dotson, kick returner Desmond Howard, wideout Don Beebe, left tackle Bruce Wilkerson and linebacker Ron Cox, then also traded for safety Eugene Robinson. That group all played huge roles the following season as the Packers won their first Super Bowl in 29 years.

Thompson had six months to improve his roster after the Packers' 51-45 overtime loss to Arizona in the NFC wild-card round. Aside from the NFL Draft in April, though, Thompson stood pat. He didn't sign a free agent. There were no trades. For the most part, it was crickets. And with such little activity, many wondered whether Thompson could get this team over the hump, as his mentor Wolf did 14 years ago?

"You have to make a decision as a general manager: Do you want to win championships or do you want to win games?" said former safety LeRoy Butler, who made four Pro Bowls during his 12-year Packer career. "Ted's going to win games because of Aaron (Rodgers) and because he drafts well. But unless he changes his philosophy when it comes to free agency, it's going to be hard to win championships.

"Right now, the gap between Minnesota and the Packers is huge if Brett (Favre) comes back. How are the Packers going to close that gap by just drafting a bunch of young guys? The thing is, Ted doesn't believe in getting a 30-year-old veteran to help you do that. He wants to fill his holes with young guys."

Following the 1995 season, one in which the Packers fell at Dallas, 38-27, in the NFC Championship game, Green

Bay knew just how close it was to greatness. And Butler still fondly remembers the flight home that day.

"Coach (Mike) Holmgren stood up and thanked everybody for the season and all that," Butler said. "Then he said he thinks he knows the strategy to beat the Cowboys and the 49ers and teams like that. We all started getting pretty excited."

That strategy was to find veteran help to complement a roster that was close to a title. And while free agency can be a hit-or-miss proposition, almost everything Wolf touched that offseason turned to gold.

Dotson was a 15-game starter at right defensive tackle and was second on the team with 5.5 sacks. Robinson led the Packers with six interceptions and fit perfectly in back with Butler. Howard shattered the NFL record for punt return yardage in a single season with 870. Then Howard had a memorable postseason, highlighted by his 244 all-purpose yards in Super Bowl XXXI, which earned him MVP honors. Wilkerson stepped in at left tackle when rookie John Michels and veteran Gary Brown both flopped. Beebe had 11 catches and 220 yards during a regular-season win over the 49ers that helped give the Packers homefield advantage throughout the postseason. And Cox was the Packers' No. 4 linebacker, who then started in the NFC Championship game and the Super Bowl after middle linebacker George Koonce tore his ACL.

"I remember in the locker room after the Dallas game, a lot of us were crying," said Robert Brooks, a wideout with Green Bay from 1992-98. "I was crying, Reggie (White) was crying, Leroy (Butler) was crying. Just a whole bunch of us because we knew how close we were, and we almost felt shameful that we hadn't got it done.

"But then that offseason, Ron Wolf did a lot of great things. We had a lot of the pieces in place already, and then he went and filled in all the gaps. And when we returned for training camp, we knew. We knew we were about to have a special year." They did, rolling to a 13-3 regular season and defeating New England, 32-21, in Super Bowl XXXI.

Compare that to the 2010 offseason, where Thompson was as quiet as a field mouse. To Thompson's credit, he re-signed unrestricted free agents Chad Clifton and Mark Tauscher. But he also let free agent Aaron Kampman get away and didn't bring in a single veteran.

Instead, Thompson elected to fill the holes on his roster with draft picks that most didn't think could become major contributors until at least 2011.

"Oh no, I disagree," Thompson said of the premise that his draft picks wouldn't be impact players immediately. "I think we got guys that can come in and make an impact."

Butler, like many others throughout Packer Nation, wasn't buying that argument. "I just think that everybody has a pretty short window in this sport, maybe like three years," Butler said. "And when you get your chance, you have to go for it. What have the Packers done to show you they're going for it.

"I know with our team, we mixed some veterans in with our other guys, but Ted just keeps sticking with those young guys. And the only way they're ever going to get over the top is to hit home runs in the draft."

Brooks had a slightly different take than Butler. "I know we added some veterans to help us get over the hump," Brooks said. "But if you've got players who can step in and play, it doesn't matter if they're rookies or if they've been around a long time. Me personally, I'm really excited about this Packers team coming up."

So were the Packers themselves. In fact, after that April's draft, McCarthy gushed, "We're a better football team in 2010 today than we have been in the past, in my opinion … I really like the way our football team looks on paper."

The question remained, though: Did Thompson do enough to catch teams like Minnesota and New Orleans in his own conference?

As Butler noted, the window for success in the NFL is small. For example, the Packers went 37-11 from 1995-97, played in three NFC title games, two Super Bowls and won one world championship. Favre was also at the height of his brilliance, winning three MVPs in that time.

Then, free agency, coaching changes, age and injury took a toll. And it took until 2007 before the Packers reached another NFC title game.

The window for the current Packers appeared to be right now. Rodgers was entering his sixth year in the league, and his combination of physical skills and knowledge of the offense were nearing their peak. McCarthy's stamp was all over this team. And barring anything unforeseen, Green Bay was bringing back 21 of 22 preferred starters.

Fourteen years ago, Wolf determined that players like George Teague, John Jurkovic, Fred Strickland, Harry Galbreath and Anthony Morgan—all starters in 1995—weren't good enough to be part of a Super Bowl roster. Wolf then replaced each and every one during an aggressive offseason.

Thompson did just the opposite and brought back virtually the same team in 2010 that he had the previous season. His hope was there would be enough improvement from within to catch the league's elite teams.

Which way was right? "I'll still take Ron's way because it's proven," Butler said. "Ted should have learned last year that you can't go into the playoffs with Jarrett Bush as your third corner. Your big move in free agency can't be Frank Walker.

"I'll give Ted a decent grade because his formula has worked as far as turning it around from 6-10 (in 2008). But how do you get to 13-3 now? That's the big question."

McCarthy had no doubts about Thompson. The pair had decided years earlier that the best path to greatness was to draft well, develop those players, then sign the ones you like best when they hit free agency. Thompson had won points for a string of successful drafts. And McCarthy had proven himself as one of football's best offensive minds, a coach who made his players better, and a stellar leader of men.

"Our job as coaches is to take the individual and maximize his ability, create opportunities for him to be successful, and make sure our systems—offensively, defensively and our special teams—have the wide range and the flexibility to take advantage of any individual that we bring in here," McCarthy said. "That's my viewpoint, and it has been since the day I became head coach here."

Despite Green Bay's quiet offseason, optimism was contagious throughout the Packers organization. Green Bay's terrific young talent was a year older and better. The Packers were now operating in Capers' defense for a second year. Then, of course, there was Rodgers, who was coming off a Pro Bowl season and undoubtedly trending upward.

When the Packers concluded their offseason program in late June, McCarthy lightened the mood by holding a home-run hitting contest. Rookie offensive tackle Bryan Bulaga won the event, and for his efforts was presented a broken-down Saturn SL as the grand prize.

"Baseball, that's my game right there," Bulaga said that day. "I've played all my life. A nice, easy, steady swing, put the bat on the ball and watch it go."

While many chuckled at Bulaga's new vehicle, the message on the car was no laughing matter. On the driver's side, it read "To Super Bowl—Dallas."

"I stand up here every year, and maybe you laughed at me in the past four years, I have no idea, but it is no different from my viewpoint. I have every intention and belief that we have the capability of winning the Super Bowl," McCarthy said. "Every decision that we make toward our football team, toward our program, toward our environment is always trying to improve our football team. Whether it is adding depth, redoing our facilities, anything to try to find a way to keep building toward winning that Super Bowl here in Green Bay. That is definitely our goal."

Later that summer, Rodgers and several of his teammates showed up at the annual Welcome Back Packers Luncheon wearing cowboy hats and bolo ties. By all accounts, the stunt was Rodgers' idea.

The message was crystal clear: Green Bay's goal was to finish the season in Arlington, Texas, home of Super Bowl XLV. "I definitely think we're positioned to do that," veteran wideout Donald Driver said. "Super Bowl's the goal and I don't think we're going to be shy about saying it."

Bold. Brash. Bombastic. It was clear this is how the 2010 Packers were going to operate.

While McCarthy shared the confidence of his players, it was also his job to temper enthusiasm and keep heads level. Remember, this group still hadn't won a thing since Favre left town. No divisional titles. No playoff victories. And a 17-16 overall record.

Sports Illustrated and several other national pundits picked Green Bay to win the Super Bowl. That was certainly the goal. The next step, though, was figuring out how to get there.

"I just had our team meeting and we talked about winning the Super Bowl," McCarthy said. "We talked about where it is played at and the relevance of our team meeting room. The only team pictures that are in that room are the team pictures of the world champions of the Green Bay Packers. Everything that we have done throughout the offseason and everything that we'll do starting tomorrow will be taking a step to being the next team up on that wall. That's our goal."

The season opener in Philadelphia was just days away, and after a productive summer, optimism was at a fevered pitch. "We talked about the Super Bowl expectations, we set our goals for the season on the first day of training camp," McCarthy said. "I don't want to disappoint anybody here in the room, but ... we're talking about Philadelphia. I think it's important to set goals, identify with what the media is talking about, and just make sure we're on the same page.

"We're about Philadelphia, whether we're buying cowboys hats ... to me that's not a real big deal. That's not a focus of ours. We're not a flamboyant-type football team. It's by design. I like the confidence of our team, but we're at the starting line. We're zero and zero. We're preparing to win our first game."

Which is exactly what the Packers did.

Philadelphia was a house of horrors for Green Bay for nearly half a century. The Packers hadn't won in Philadelphia since 1962, a string of eight consecutive losses. Some of those defeats — like the 4th-and-26 debacle in the 2003 postseason or the 10-9 loss in Week 2 of the 1997 season — still remained painful.

But the Packers kicked off 2010 in style, with a 27-20 win over the Eagles in a hostile environment. "I thought it was a very gutsy performance on both sides of the field, and we feel very fortunate to come out of here with a win,"

McCarthy said that day. "This is a tough place to play and it's a tough football team to play against."

The Packers built a 20-3 lead, then held on for dear life as Michael Vick — who replaced an injured Kevin Kolb — led the Eagles back. But Rodgers threw two touchdowns, and linebacker Clay Matthews had a monstrous game with three sacks.

The bad news was Green Bay lost two players to season-ending injuries: running back Ryan Grant damaged ligaments in his ankle and defensive tackle Justin Harrell tore his ACL. Defensive end Cullen Jenkins also broke his left hand in the first quarter but returned in a huge cast later that game, largely because the Packers had just two healthy defensive linemen remaining.

Unfortunately for the Packers, this was just the start of an injury-filled season like few others in team history. "Injuries are part of the game, very unfortunate," McCarthy said. "There is definitely a personal side any time something happens to one of your members of your football team. Specific to Ryan Grant, Ryan Grant is exactly the type of individual you want on your team and in your program, the way he goes about his business. He is a hard-working, tough guy, no-nonsense, no-excuse individual, and he is a very good teammate. So the personal angle of Ryan's injury is definitely difficult."

The Packers followed that with a 34-7 thrashing of Buffalo and improved to 2-0. Matthews had three more sacks, pushing his total to six through just two games. "He's almost unblockable," Packers defensive end Ryan Pickett said of Matthews. "Certainly not with just one guy. What he's doing is off the charts."

Rodgers was also sharp, throwing for two TDs and running for a third. The Packers led, 13-7, at halftime, but rolled in the second half.

"I thought frankly we were flat and sloppy in the second quarter," McCarthy said. "And we just kind of re-started our engine at halftime and played the way we were supposed to play."

The next month, though, was one of the most frustrating of the McCarthy era. Green Bay was a favorite in four straight games but went a dismal 1-3 in that stretch.

The slide began with a 20-17 loss in Chicago during a game the Packers were in control of most of the night. But the Packers couldn't overcome one of their sloppiest games under McCarthy.

Green Bay set a franchise record with 18 penalties, including a late pass interference penalty on rookie safety Morgan Burnett that set up the game-winning field goal by Bears kicker Robbie Gould. Packers wideout James Jones had a costly fumble with just more than two minutes left that gave the Bears the ball back with the game tied at 17.

In all, it was a forgettable night, as Chicago improved to 3-0 and the Packers at 2-1 fell into second place in the division. "We'll take a look at the film, but (18) penalties, that doesn't cut it," McCarthy said. "You can't play football like that."

Green Bay bounced back with a 28-26 win over Detroit. But the Lions scored the game's final 12 points to nearly emerge victorious. Green Bay's offense didn't score in the second half, and there wasn't much celebrating after this mediocre showing.

"We're not playing championship football right now," Packers tight end Donald Lee said. "I'd agree with that. But there's a lot of season left."

Green Bay, which had talked openly and loudly about winning a Super Bowl just a few short months ago, now had a laundry list of problems.

The injury to Grant left the Packers with the pedestrian platoon of Brandon Jackson and John Kuhn, and neither was getting it done.

Green Bay's special teams bordered on laughable. Kick returner Jordy Nelson lost a pair of fumbles against the Lions. Just one week earlier, Chicago's Devin Hester returned a punt for a touchdown and kicker Mason Crosby had a field goal blocked.

"Didn't like it," McCarthy said of his special teams. "Didn't like the two turnovers, I can tell you that."

And the defense was struggling, allowing 331 yards to Lions journeyman quarterback Shaun Hill. "Yeah, I was a little surprised they were able to throw for so many yards," safety Nick Collins said of the Lions. "They did a good job, but we definitely weren't as sharp as we could be."

To top things off, safety Morgan Burnett and linebacker Nick Barnett were both lost with season-ending injuries — Burnett with a torn ACL and Barnett with a right wrist injury. Suddenly, one of football's deepest teams was becoming razor thin. The Packers were 3-1, but as McCarthy said, "Don't feel like it, does it?"

Still, it felt a lot better than 3-3 — which is where the Packers were sitting two weeks later.

First, Green Bay laid an egg in Washington D.C. and dropped a 16-13 stinker in overtime to Donovan McNabb and the Redskins. The Packers were in control throughout, building leads of 10-0 and 13-3 early in the fourth quarter. Washington eventually tied things, 13-13. Then Packers kicker Mason Crosby's game-winning field goal from 53 yards out hit the upright with one second left. In overtime, Redskins safety LaRon Landry intercepted Rodgers, and Graham Gano knocked home a 33-yard game-winning field goal.

"There is no 'woe is me' here," McCarthy said. "This is the National Football League. It's a dynamic business."

As tough as the loss was, Green Bay's injury situation was becoming even more painful. Tight end Jermichael Finley was lost for the remainder of the season due to a knee injury. Rodgers suffered a concussion, although he wouldn't miss any time. And a hamstring injury to Matthews sidelined him the following week.

McCarthy didn't want a pity party, though. "I think this is an excellent opportunity for us to show what we are about," McCarthy said. "I know there is probably doubt outside the room."

There was — and it only intensified the following week. Green Bay's defense, playing without four "preferred" starters, gave a gutsy effort. But the Packers offense struggled and the Packers lost their second straight overtime game, 23-20.

Green Bay's season-long struggles on third down continued, as it converted just three of 13. Rodgers was sacked five times and had a mediocre passer rating of 84.5. And the running game produced just 76 yards in 21 carries (3.6).

"I would not say we are in rhythm on offense right now," McCarthy said. "I thought we had a number of favorable third downs and we had opportunities where our defense was on the field, I thought they were hanging in there, bend do not break, keep them out of the end zone.

"And we had opportunities to get out in front of that game. And third down has been an issue two weeks in a row. So, we need to do a better job on third down on offense."

The Packers were reeling, and Brett Favre was coming back to town. One year earlier, Favre and the Vikings drilled Green Bay, 38-26, at Lambeau Field. And the Packers admitted afterward they didn't handle the big stage very well.

"I'd say there was a little nervousness, a little anxiousness," Jenkins said of facing Favre. "There was a lot of hype and a lot of anxiousness. It might have affected us a little bit."

This time, both teams were struggling. The Packers had lost two straight and were a disappointing .500, while Minnesota was 2-3.

Green Bay knew if it had any hopes of reaching its 2010 goals, beating the Vikings was a virtual must. And that meant slaying Favre. "We can't have another loss," linebacker Desmond Bishop said.

To the delight of Packer Nation, they didn't.

Favre and the Vikings trailed, 28-24, in the game's closing moments. But the Old Gunslinger drove Minnesota to Green Bay's 20-yard line where the Vikings faced fourth down.

On what was the final snap Favre ever took at Lambeau Field, he dropped to pass and immediately fell to the turf. For a brief second, shades of Steve Young and Terrell Owens had to sweep through all of Packer Nation.

Favre got up, bought some time with his 41-year-old feet, and fired left for Randy Moss, a player who had haunted the Packers for more than a decade. Really, everything was perfectly aligned for the Hollywood ending Favre longed for. Only this time, the Packers rewrote the finish.

Packers cornerback Tramon Williams and linebacker Desmond Bishop had solid coverage on Moss. Favre's pass sailed a tad high and Moss mistimed his jump. And when Favre's final throw landed incomplete, Green Bay had escaped with a 28-24 win. The Packers—and their extremely nervous fans—could all exhale.

"I'm thinking we've got to find a way to stop one of the greatest ever," Packers linebacker A.J. Hawk said when asked what he was thinking on the final play. "That's what he does. He comes back on a big stage like that, last drive of the game. That's what Brett does. He throws touchdowns to win games."

It actually appeared as though Favre had led the Vikings to a dramatic win three plays earlier when he hit Percy Harvin with an apparent 35-yard TD. A booth review, though, showed Harvin's second foot was out of bounds negating the touchdown.

"Just relief," Nick Collins said of Green Bay's temporary reprieve. "Just really happy for a second, but you got to go back to work."

The Packers work against Favre all night was first-rate. Green Bay intercepted Favre three times — including a 32-yard "pick six" from Bishop. Favre's passer rating was just 50.4, and afterward, his own coach took him to task.

"It goes back to taking care of the football," Brad Childress said of Favre. "You can't throw it to them. You have to play within the confines of our system. Sometimes it is OK to punt the football. You can't have seven points going the other way, not in a game like this with a high-powered team."

One year earlier, the Packers didn't lead for a single second of their two losses to the Vikings. This time, Rodgers led the Packers to touchdowns on two of their first three drives as they got off to a solid start.

After Minnesota had taken a 17-14 halftime lead, Rodgers led a third-quarter TD drive that he capped with a 14-yard scoring pass to Greg Jennings. From there, the Packers never trailed again and survived the frenetic finish.

"We knew it was going to be a grinder, character, gut-it-out type of performance, and our guys stepped up big,"

McCarthy said. "I was very, very proud of those guys today. We had individuals that had been playing in some tough spots. We had a number of individuals that overcame things during the course of the week to get out there and play, and that's a good team win right there."

Green Bay was now 4-3, back on track, and in the middle of the playoff hunt once again.

One week later, the Packers traveled to the New York Jets, led by the NFL's loudest — and largest — head coach, Rex Ryan. The Jets entered with the NFL's best record, but Green Bay's defense was sublime in a 9-0 blanking of New York. The Packers won the turnover battle, 3-0, and notched their first road shutout since 1991.

"It's an excellent road win," McCarthy said. "We've been fighting through a tough spot, and I'm very proud of what we were able to accomplish here today."

Earlier in the week, the Packers had placed three more key defensive players on the season-ending injured reserve: linebacker Brady Poppinga with a reinjured knee, linebacker Brad Jones with a reinjured shoulder and defensive end Mike Neal with an injured shoulder. In came nose tackle Howard Green, and linebackers Erik Walden and Matt Wilhelm — players who had been on the street just days earlier. But the Packers never flinched, and played one of their best defensive games in years.

"It's a credit to our players, and I'll tell you what, it's a credit to our defensive staff," McCarthy said. "We played our defense, they played at a high level. That's the way we play defense."

Green Bay stayed hot with a 45-7 thumping of Dallas. After struggling to get on track for much of the season, Green Bay's offense finally resembled the unit most expected it to be. The Packers rolled up 415 yards of total offense, their second-highest total of the season. Green Bay also had a season-high 26 first downs and converted a season-best 66.7% of its third downs (10 of 15).

"We did a lot of good things," said Packers offensive coordinator Joe Philbin, who's the head coach in Miami today. "Sounder football than we've played. We've had no giveaways now for two weeks in a row. That's a real plus. Our guys performed better, played better, executed better."

The Packers entered the Dallas game ranked 16th in total offense, 22nd in rushing offense and 10th in passing offense. In 2009, Green Bay had finished sixth in total offense, 14th in rushing yards and seventh in passing offense. Not only were the Packers down in all three of those categories, they were also scoring 23.0 points per game after averaging 28.8 a year ago.

But nothing made teams feel better about themselves than a visit from Dallas. The Cowboys dropped their fifth straight game, fell to 1-7, and fired head coach Wade Phillips the next day.

Rodgers threw for 289 yards and three touchdowns, completed 79.4% of his passes, and had a 131.5 passer rating, the third-highest total of his career. Wideout James Jones set career highs in catches (eight) and yards (123). And the Packers ran for 138 yards, their second-highest total of the year.

"(The Packers) whipped us about every way you could whip somebody," Phillips said on his way out the door. "They're a good football team playing at home, and they played well and we didn't play well at all. That's the way the game went."

The Packers reached the bye week with a 6-3 record, having won three straight games and leading Chicago (5-3) by one-half game. "I would definitely say the last three weeks ... the players and the coaches have stayed the course," McCarthy said. "Nobody blinked. I think it says a lot about the volume of character in our locker room.

"The leaders that continue ... the development of the leaders in our locker room. I'm very pleased with the growth we've had the last few weeks. It's about winning games, don't get me wrong. I think this team is improving week to week, and I think that says a lot about the individuals in that locker room."

Green Bay continued trending upward after its bye week, with a stunning 31-3 destruction of Minnesota. Over the previous three games, the Packers had allowed just 10 total points, their fewest since November 10-24, 1974, when they also allowed 10.

The Packers had been so dominant defensively that McCarthy deferred and kicked off after his team won the opening coin toss against Minnesota.

"I've never deferred a coin toss in my career here, and there are a number of factors that go into making that decision," McCarthy said. "We're playing excellent defense, we're playing outstanding adversity defense, and that's why we wanted to get up and get started with our defense ... and get on the field and get going. I've been very pleased with the job the defense has done, particularly the last four or five weeks."

Green Bay held Favre to a miserable 17-of-38 performance with no touchdowns and an interception. Rodgers, meanwhile, was red hot, going 22-of-31 for 301 yards and four touchdowns, including three to Greg Jennings.

The McCarthy-Rodgers tandem improved to 2-2 against Favre. "This has got me at a loss for words," Favre said afterward. "Disappointing would be an understatement."

The next day, Minnesota fired head coach Brad Childress, marking the second straight week a team fired its coach after getting blown out by the Packers.

"We've got a foot on the gas, hands on the wheel and we're looking straight ahead," McCarthy said.

Next up was a trip to Atlanta, which had the NFC's best record at 8-2. With a win, the Packers could take over the conference's top seed. Instead, Atlanta's Matt Bryant drilled a 47-yard field goal with nine seconds left to lift the Falcons to a 20-17 win. Green Bay fell to 7-4, and its four losses had all been by a field goal.

"We need to do a better job of making one more play than the other team in these close games," McCarthy said.

The teams appeared headed for overtime after Rodgers hit Jordy Nelson with a 10-yard TD pass to tie the game, 17-17, with 56 seconds left.

But Atlanta's Eric Weems broke loose on the ensuing kickoff, was tackled by the facemask, and the Falcons began on the Packers' 49-yard line. Four short passes from Atlanta quarterback Matt Ryan set Bryant up with the game-winning kick.

"It was a big NFC game," McCarthy said. "At 7-4, we still have a lot of football in front of us, but we need to get this next one, because now we're into December football. There are no redos or 'Hey, we can get 'em next week.'

"We've been playing good football, and we did a lot of positive things, a lot of positive play from a number of different players. You have to play big at the adverse times in the game."

Green Bay bounced back with a 34-16 win over San Francisco in a game filled with subplots. Back in April 2005, McCarthy was the offensive coordinator in San Francisco when the 49ers selected Alex Smith with the No. 1 pick in the draft. Rodgers, who was one of the players the 49ers were giving consideration to, shockingly fell to No. 24, where the Packers gobbled him up.

San Francisco general manager Scott McCloughan and head coach Mike Nolan, the organization's primary decision makers, decided Rodgers was too cocky and settled for too many checkdowns in a programmed offense at Cal, so San Francisco chose Smith.

One year later, McCarthy was coaching Rodgers. And with McCarthy's guidance and knowledge of quarterbacks, Rodgers was developing into one of football's elite players.

"I think it's about opportunity and it's about performance and production, and he's answered the bell," McCarthy said of Rodgers.

Smith, meanwhile, was thrown into the fire from Day 1, and in 2005 was asked to lead a dreadful offense that was coordinated by McCarthy. In his rookie season, Smith threw one touchdown pass, 11 interceptions and had a miserable passer rating of 40.8. Smith improved gradually over the next two years and had somewhat of a breakout season in 2009 with 18 TDs and 12 picks. But Smith struggled immensely at the start of the 2010 season, feuded publicly with head coach Mike Singletary, and was usurped that season by undersized Troy Smith.

"I think every player, particularly quarterbacks, the path that you're put on has a lot to do with your success," McCarthy said. "There's a lot of factors that go into developing a quarterback. Obviously they both had unique ability to even be considered to be part of the conversation of being the No. 1 pick in the National Football League."

Green Bay already knew it had the right quarterback, but this game only reinforced it. Rodgers threw three touchdowns — two to Jennings and a memorable 61-yarder to Donald Driver. Troy Smith, meanwhile, completed just 40% of his passes.

On Driver's TD, he lined up in the right slot, found a hole in San Francisco's zone, and hauled in a Rodgers strike at the 49ers' 38. Driver spun away from safety Reggie Smith at the 30, then ducked under a tackle attempt by safety Dashon Goldon at the 22.

Cornerback Nate Clements had an angle on Driver, but Driver simply shoved him out of the way at the 10. Three 49ers finally corralled Driver at the four, but he dragged them into the right corner of the end zone for an improbable 61-yard TD and a 21-13 Green Bay lead.

The Packers rolled from there. "He's Hercules," Philbin said of the 35-year-old Driver. "It was a great run. You've got to give him a lot of credit. They couldn't drag him down, and I'm real pleased about it."

It was Driver's first touchdown since Week 4, and a rebuttal for those saying he'd lost a step—or more. "My whole thing is that sometimes you don't want to be denied," Driver said. "This week … last month you could say everybody was just writing me off, saying I was done. My thing is, I felt like I had to prove something.

"Every year I've been playing in this league it seems like I have to prove something … and I'm OK with that because it just makes me who I am. Today was one of those things. I saw the ball, made the catch, and I wasn't going to be denied going to the end zone. Whatever I had to do. When I saw it, I wasn't going to go down."

One week later, though, the one player Green Bay couldn't have go down did. And they suffered an embarrassing 7-3 loss against lowly Detroit.

Late in the second quarter, Rodgers left a scoreless game with a concussion. Green Bay's offense was struggling with Rodgers and became lost without him.

The Packers led, 3-0, midway through the fourth quarter when Lions third-string quarterback Drew Stanton engineered an 80-yard touchdown drive. The Packers reached the Lions' 31-yard line late in the fourth quarter, but backup quarterback Matt Flynn couldn't finish the deal.

Lions 7, Packers 3.

Suddenly, Green Bay was 8-5 and fighting for its playoff life. "We have to find a way to get it done and get these close games done," Packers linebacker A.J. Hawk said. "A loss is a loss no matter what, whether you lose by 30 or you lose by three. You just have to figure out a way to win, and we haven't done that."

Now they'd have to do it in New England, against football's best team. Bill Belichick. Tom Brady. This was football's elite pair, winners of three Super Bowls and owners of an 11-2 record in 2010.

McCarthy knew all week the odds of Rodgers playing were slim. Instead, McCarthy would turn things over to Flynn, the gutsy third-year pro who struggled a week earlier in Detroit.

He also knew this was a time his team needed to be built back up, not torn down. During McCarthy's Wednesday meeting with the media, he was being queried about the Patriots' dominance. At that moment he let rip the blast that could wind up on his tombstone someday. "We're nobody's underdog," McCarthy insisted. "We have all the confidence in our abilities. We've had challenges throughout the season. We've stepped up to those challenges, and we feel the same way going into this game."

McCarthy continued: "This is a great opportunity. We're playing a very good New England football team, a very well-coached football team that's playing at a very high level. We're excited about this opportunity. It's a great stage, and ... this is a very important game for us. Everybody understands where we are as far as the circumstances around the playoffs and what's ahead."

Even though McCarthy's team was battered and bruised, he believed they could play with anybody. And by the kickoff, the Packers felt the same way.

If ever there was a good loss, this was it. Sure, the Packers suffered a disheartening 31-27 setback. But the good outweighed the bad. And on that Sunday night in Foxborough, Massachusetts, Green Bay reversed the path of its season.

Flynn played like an All-Pro, throwing three touchdown passes and for 251 yards. New England, which led the NFL in scoring in 2010, managed just 249 total yards.

What eventually doomed the Packers was a Flynn interception that New England's Kyle Arrington returned for a score, and some brutal special teams play that allowed Patriots offensive lineman Dan Connolly to return a kickoff 71 yards.

McCarthy insisted there were no moral victories — and repeated his new pet phrase. "I don't care what you guys think," he said. "We came here to win. We're nobody's underdog."

But the reality was that this loss got the Packers believing again. If Green Bay could outplay the NFL's best team, and do it without Rodgers, anything was possible.

"I think that's exactly how we started to feel," defensive end Ryan Pickett said. "I mean, to go into their house without A-Rod and really play better than they did, that was something to build on."

Left guard Daryn Colledge added, "You never want to say a loss is what turned your season around, but I think that's fair. If there was anybody that didn't believe we could do great things, almost beating New England without our quarterback should have changed their minds."

Rodgers was back the following week, and oh, what a return it was. In one of the biggest games of Rodgers' three years as a starter, he had arguably his finest performance. Rodgers threw for a career-high 404 yards, tied a personal-best with four touchdown passes, and posted the third-highest passer rating of his career (139.9).

Rodgers, who hadn't won many big games during his first 45 regular-season starts in Green Bay, certainly came up huge in No. 46. The result was a stunning 45-17 rout of the New York Giants that had the Packers back in control of their playoff destiny. The Packers (9-6) moved into sixth place in the NFC playoff race. The Giants (9-6) fell into seventh place.

"It was fun," Rodgers said. "I had a good week of preparation this week. I think that's kind of where it started. I felt good throwing the ball all week, liked the game plan, liked the things we were trying to do, and once we were into the game, I liked the rhythm that Mike (McCarthy) had our offense in."

Following his second concussion of the season, Rodgers switched to a new helmet that had additional padding. The goal was to lower the risk of another concussion, but because Rodgers' face was jammed into the helmet, he took a lot of grief.

"Guys definitely gave me a hard time about the way it looked," Rodgers said. "I'm not really so worried about how I look in it. I'm just a little more worried about how I play in it."

There was no need to worry. The Giants entered the game allowing just 188.4 passing yards per contest and holding opposing quarterbacks to a 74.9 rating. But Rodgers threw for more than double that total and nearly doubled that passer rating. Green Bay's 515 total yards were also the most of the Rodgers era.

"He played very well," Giants coach Tom Coughlin said of Rodgers. "I thought they were very efficient with their scheme. I thought his accuracy was outstanding and he had good control of what they were trying to do. We never stopped the run to really get them out of that type of game."

Despite not playing for two weeks, Rodgers was anything but groggy. He was razor sharp with his passes, made plays with his feet, and frustrated a defense that entered the game ranked No. 3 in the NFL in total yards.

The Packers liked their match-ups of Jennings against cornerback Corey Webster and also thought they could take advantage of safeties Kenny Phillips and Antrel Rolle. When Green Bay's offensive line took the fight to the Giants' sensational front four, Rodgers had time to pick on that secondary.

Green Bay also intercepted Giants' quarterback Eli Manning four times and forced six total turnovers. "I would say it definitely ranks up there as one of our most complete games," McCarthy said. "I love the mindset of this team. These guys step up week in and week out, and we've got a big one here in seven days. It can't get here fast enough."

One game remained, a must win that would save or sink Green Bay's season. The Packers prepared to host bitter rival Chicago, a team with nothing to play for. But really, that didn't matter.

The Bears had wrapped up the NFC North division title, and by kickoff were locked in as the No. 2 seed in the conference. All week long, though, Chicago head coach Lovie Smith insisted he would play his starters. But no one believed him. "We're playing our biggest rival this week," Smith said. "We have an opportunity to do something that's never been done in the NFC North, that's win every game in the division.

"We want to continue to improve going into the playoffs. We sure know we have a bye, but nothing else has changed. We have a typical Wednesday practice today, and we're getting ready to play a very good Green Bay Packer team."

Smith later added, "We're playing to win the game. We plan on playing our guys this week. I don't know what else I need to tell you besides that. That's the plan."

Talk of what the Bears might do dominated most discussions throughout the week. McCarthy, though, called it a "polluted mindset" to worry about the Bears' approach.

"Leave the pollution outside the doors," McCarthy said. "We're focused on beating whoever comes out that gate on Sunday. They are going to have white jerseys on and we're going after them. That's our mindset. We need to get to 10 wins, and we've been focused on that for quite some time. We're in position to accomplish our goal of getting into the playoffs, and that's what we're focused on."

Instead of worrying about the Bears, the Packers focused on themselves. Good thing, too. To the surprise of many, Chicago played its starters the entire game, trying to keep McCarthy's Packers out of the postseason. But Green Bay's defense was sensational, and the Packers posted a 10-3 win, earning the sixth and final playoff spot.

"I think it's important for your team to be noted for great defense," McCarthy said. "That's always been the goal in my tenure here, and I think we definitely have reached that.

"I've always looked at defense as the thermostat. When you have great defense, they keep you in games, week in and week out, and it's the responsibility of the offense to score more points than the opponent. I definitely agree with the fact that great defenses win championships."

It wasn't a stretch to now call this Packers defense a great one. Despite a rash of injuries that landed players such as linebackers Nick Barnett, Brad Jones, Brandon Chillar and Brady Poppinga, defensive linemen Mike Neal and Justin Harrell, and safeties Morgan Burnett, Anthony Smith and Derrick Martin all on injured reserve, this defense hadn't missed a beat.

The Packers finished the year No. 2 in scoring defense, allowing just 15.0 points per game. Pittsburgh ranked No. 1 at 14.5. Green Bay held six of its 16 opponents to single digits. And since the NFL went to a 16-game schedule in 1978, the only year the Packers allowed fewer points was their Super Bowl championship season of 1996 (13.1).

"We take pride in what we do, man," Packers linebacker Erik Walden said. "We feel like we should be mentioned with the top defenses. They always talk about the Ravens and the Steelers and that. But we feel like we need to be mentioned in that category, too. We'd like that respect."

The Packers defense certainly earned some respect against the Bears. Green Bay limited the Chicago to 227 total yards, including just 97 in the second half. Walden had two of Green Bay's sacks on Bears quarterback Jay Cutler. The Packers also intercepted Cutler twice and limited him to a 43.5 passer rating — less than half his season average.

"They kept us out of sync," Cutler said. "We didn't change a lot from last game to this game, and I think they did a really good job of taking away some of our hot reads.

"They did some really good stuff to us. They had a really good game plan with some of their slot blitzes and mixing things up with coverages."

Green Bay also struggled on offense throughout and trailed, 3-0, late in the third quarter. But the Packers scored the game's final 10 points to prevail.

The game winner came when Rodgers hit tight end Donald Lee with a one-yard TD pass with 12:42 left in the game. The play was set up by a 46-yard completion from Rodgers to Pro Bowl wideout Greg Jennings.

Chicago drove to Green Bay's 32-yard line in the closing moments. But Cutler was intercepted by Packers Pro Bowl safety Nick Collins to end things.

"We take a backseat to nobody on defense," Packers nose tackle B.J. Raji said. "We have the players, the scheme and the coaches. It's just a matter of executing, and if we do that, we're tough to beat."

The Packers, Giants and Tampa Bay all finished with 10-6 records, but Green Bay won the tiebreaker based on strength of victory. Few expected much from Green Bay coming from the No. 6 seed. But that didn't matter to these Packers.

They had an invite to the party. Now it was up to them to make it count. Their über-confident head coach believed that's exactly what would happen. "I'm just proud of them," McCarthy said. "We've had a different road we traveled this year, and we've met every challenge. We're at 10 wins and we're one of six teams in the NFC. This is an exciting day for the organization. It's an exciting day for our fans. And we're excited as a football team. I'm very proud of our football team, just everything we've accomplished. Nothing's come easy for us, and we wouldn't want it any other way.

"It's one at a time. We feel very good about our chances. We'll play anybody, anytime, anywhere. That's been our motto and we're well-oiled."

McCarthy was now as confident as any coach in football. His team was about to play the exact same way.

14

Off and Running

The film room was an entertaining place in Green Bay before its wild-card matchup with host Philadelphia. As the Packers defensive personnel watched their Week 1 win over the Eagles, outside linebacker Clay Matthews drew plenty of praise for his three-sack outing that day. Matthews also took some razzing, as well.

You see, when Matthews knocked Eagles quarterback Kevin Kolb out of the game that day, it opened the door for then-backup Michael Vick to play. Vick proceeded to take full advantage and had arguably the best year of his troubled career. Perhaps it was inevitable that Vick would have replaced Kolb at some point that season. But Matthews certainly aided the process. "Mike Vick maybe owes me a thank you or something," Matthews joked.

The way Vick was playing, the Packers would have much rather faced Kolb in the postseason. Kolb suffered a concussion when Matthews sacked him late in the first half of the opener. At the time, Kolb's passer rating was a miserable 56.2 and the Eagles trailed, 13-3.

Vick nearly rallied the Eagles back before they eventually fell, 27-20. But Vick accounted for 278 yards in the second half, and his passer rating of 101.9 was the third-highest against the Packers all season. "Clay had to go and get us Vick," Packers nose tackle B.J. Raji joked.

Stopping Vick was no laughing matter, though. The 2010 season marked the first time since 2006 that Vick had been a full-time starter, and he posted career highs in passing yards (3,018), touchdown passes (21) and passer rating (100.2). Vick, arguably the NFL's best dual threat ever, also ran for nine touchdowns and 676 yards.

"Vick's a tough cookie, man," Packers outside linebacker Erik Walden said. "He can do it all. He's always been able to run, and now he makes all the throws, too. He's a phenomenal player. I ain't never seen anything like him. We got our hands full, but we'll be up to the task."

The Packers admittedly weren't up to the task in Week 1. Green Bay spent the entire week planning for Kolb, then were caught off guard when Vick entered permanently. The Packers had prepared for Vick to operate occasionally out of the Wildcat formation, but they certainly didn't expect him to play 42 snaps.

"I'll say this, it was one of those games where we didn't have a big, extensive game plan for him," Packers defensive coordinator Dom Capers said of Vick. "We were counting on six, eight plays in the game and he played the whole second half. He's an explosive guy. I think he's unlike any other guy in the league in terms of what he can do with that ball in his hands."

Prior to Week 1, Capers had faced Vick just one time. That came in 2003, when Capers was the head coach in Houston and Vick was the quarterback in Atlanta. That was Vick's first game back after fracturing his leg that preseason, and he was quiet with just 76 total yards in part-time duty. Now, much of the Eagles' attack was centered on the dynamic quarterback, while Capers had done a masterful job guiding a defense that finished No. 2 in points allowed.

"When he got in, it was definitely a surprise," Packers standout inside linebacker Desmond Bishop said. "We hadn't game planned for him, but it's going to be a little different this time when we can actually game plan for him. It's definitely going be better this time."

Much to the Packers' delight, it was. Green Bay's defense kept Vick and the high-flying Eagles in check most of the way. Rookie running back James Starks came out of nowhere and ran for 123 yards. And Packers standout cornerback Tramon

Williams picked off Vick in the closing seconds to preserve a 21-16 win.

It was Green Bay's first playoff victory quarterbacked by somebody other than Favre since January 8, 1983, when Lynn Dickey led the Packers past the St. Louis Cardinals. It also marked just the second time in Eagles history it had lost two home games to the same team in the same season.

"You have to win the close games in the playoffs," a giddy McCarthy said afterward. "We knew we were going to come in here and we knew it was going to be a 60-minute fight. We spent so much time on the overtime rules this week, I thought, 'Heck, we might as well go into overtime, too.'

"This is the way it's going to be. We're on the road, you play uphill when you get off the bus, and you have to overcome the atmosphere that you're playing in, particularly the communication challenge, and it feels good."

Afterward, no one was feeling better than Starks — and rightfully so. Starks, a sixth round draft choice from Buffalo, entered the game with just 101 rushing yards in 2010. Starks had played in only three games all year, had 29 carries and averaged a mediocre 3.5 yards per run. He missed the first 11 games of the year as he battled back from a hamstring injury and was inactive as recently as Week 16.

But in one afternoon, Starks etched his name in the Packer history books. Starks' rushing total established a Packers rookie postseason record, breaking the old mark of 88 yards by Travis "The Roadrunner" Williams set in 1967. Starks' output was also the highest by a Green Bay running back all season, topping Brandon Jackson's 115-yard effort against Washington in Week 5.

"James was a difference-maker," McCarthy said of Starks. "He was a difference-maker for us just the way he was running the ball. He's a gifted athlete, he's a longer-levered individual and he falls forward, and I just love running backs that fall forward, especially when they're six foot two."

Rodgers agreed. "The way that James Starks was running the ball tonight was maybe one of the most important factors in this win," Rodgers said. "He ran great and I am so happy for him. He is a great kid, and he has really grown a lot in the past couple weeks. He was big tonight."

Starks certainly wouldn't have been a trendy pick to play hero. He had a coming-out party, of sorts, with a 73-yard effort against San Francisco on December 5. But over the final month of the season, Starks had just 11 carries and was inactive in two of Green Bay's final three games.

While the decrease in Starks' chances surprised many, the young running back blamed it on his practice habits. "I just haven't been practicing well," Starks said. "It's something I've just got to get used to.

"Coming from college to the NFL has been a lot different. Practice tempo is a lot different. Now, coaches harp on that and that's something I have to get better at. The best players pick themselves up. I'm just going to keep practicing and keep getting better."

Starks did exactly that down the stretch, and the Eagles paid the price. Starks ripped off a 27-yard run on his first carry of the day, setting the tone for things to come. Starks ran for 36 yards on that drive, one that ended with a Rodgers touchdown pass to tight end Tom Crabtree. By halftime, Starks had 51 yards on eight carries and Green Bay built a 14-3 lead. Then Starks really cranked it up in the second half.

After the Eagles trimmed the Packers' lead to 14-10 early in the third quarter, Green Bay answered back with an 11-play, 80-yard TD march. Starks had five carries for 32 yards on that drive, including a 19-yard burst off the left tackle.

Starks had 15 carries in the second half alone and accounted for 79.3% of the rushes by Green Bay running backs.

"Yeah, he surprised me a little bit," Eagles defensive tackle Antonio Dixon said of Starks. "But it's the NFL. Anything can happen any week. We just have to learn from it."

Green Bay, which entered the game running the ball just 43.6% of the time, ran it 54.2% against the Eagles. The Packers often operated with a full-house backfield, in which fullbacks Quinn Johnson and John Kuhn led the way for Starks.

"Obviously, that was probably the biggest difference," Eagles safety Kurt Coleman said of Starks. "They just kept running the ball and they ran the ball well. He found a lot of holes and kept on running and got the tough yards."

Starks wasn't the only hero on this day. The Packers' defense kept the ever-dangerous Vick in check. Green Bay sent five rushers or more on 18 plays, and Vick's passer rating was a mediocre 79.9. "I thought Dom really did a great job of sticking to the plan with the coverage and pressure, particularly there in the red area, with the amount of pressure he was able to bring with the red-zone blitz, keeping them out of the end zone," McCarthy said of Capers. "They're an explosive offense, to hold them under 20, we felt very good about that. We would've liked to have some [more] point production on offense, that's always the case, but when we put 21 on the board, we're very confident in our defense that we're going to come out of there with a victory."

Thanks to Williams, the Packers emerged victorious. The Eagles drove to Green Bay's 27-yard line in the final minute, trailing by just five points. Philadelphia lined up four wide receivers and Capers rushed just four.

Vick had plenty of time in the pocket and pump faked once. Vick then threw to the left corner of the end zone, where Williams was one on one with rookie wideout Riley Cooper.

The 6-foot-3 Cooper had a four-inch height advantage on Williams, but Williams was defending his position as well as anyone in football. That's why Vick's decision to go in that direction was curious. Sure enough, Williams got inside position on Cooper, then timed his leap perfectly and intercepted Vick.

Game. Set. Match.

"I feel like I got greedy and took a shot at the end zone," Vick said of his last pass. "I didn't throw the ball I wanted and got picked. It's not the way I wanted to go out, but I went down swinging. I have to learn from it."

Rodgers, on the other hand, won his first playoff game after a steady, disciplined and mistake-free afternoon. He went 18 of 27 for 180 yards, threw three touchdowns, and had a stellar passer rating of 122.5.

"It feels great," Rodgers said of the momentous win. "It is disappointing to lose your last game like we did last year, but there are a lot of resilient guys in the locker room and a lot of guys, like I said last week, who stepped up and who we can expect a lot of things from, a prime example being James Stark. We have had a number of contributions from players who at the beginning of the season were not expected to play big roles for us, so I think that shows what kind of character we have in our locker room."

Rodgers was undoubtedly one of those players. Although this was just his third season as a starter, Rodgers was taking a lot of grief for never winning a playoff game. Now that monkey was off his back — even if McCarthy and the Packers refused to acknowledge that one existed.

"We don't look at it that way, and I think you know that," McCarthy said. "We're just getting started. This is the first round, we've established ourselves as a football team, and we won a big football game here in Philadelphia against a championship-caliber program.

"We have the opportunity to go to Atlanta, and we're excited about playing a No. 1 seed down there. Aaron has got a lot of football left in front of him, he's going to be playing for a long time and I think those conversations should be talked about at the end, in my opinion."

McCarthy was optimistic this was just the start of a memorable playoff run. And he knew much work awaited. Next up was top-seeded Atlanta, a team McCarthy had started preparing for three days before the Eagles game. While that might sound premature to some, it's not when it comes to life in the postseason.

Green Bay had just six days between its games with Philadelphia and Atlanta. And there simply wasn't enough time for McCarthy and his staff to prepare the way they wanted, unless they started early and didn't stop. "For me personally, I'll watch Atlanta on the bus ride and on the plane ride home because tomorrow is our game plan day," McCarthy said. "I think (the Eagles game) is going to have to be one of those ones where after the season is over, you look back on it."

As McCarthy exited Philadelphia on that Sunday night, the Eagles were in his rearview mirror. The Falcons were now on his laptop. And Green Bay's run to glory was picking up steam.

15
Burying the Birds

All eyes were on the quarterbacks. As Green Bay headed to Atlanta for an NFC Divisional playoff game, the Packers' Aaron Rodgers and the Falcons' Matt Ryan were attracting all the attention. And it was easy to see why.

Both quarterbacks were first-round draft choices, although Ryan went 21 picks higher than Rodgers. Each player had been starting for three seasons, and both had reached the postseason twice. Since 2008, Rodgers had thrown for 86 touchdowns, 31 interceptions and more than 12,000 yards. Ryan had 66 TDs, 34 interceptions and slightly more than 10,000 yards. Ryan, on the other hand, was the greater winner. Ryan was 33-13 as a starter (.717), while Rodgers was 27-20 (.574).

Rodgers followed an enormous personality and elite talent in Brett Favre. Ryan did the same when he replaced Michael Vick. Rodgers scored a 35 on the Wonderlic test back in 2005. Ryan had a 32 in 2008. Rodgers ran the 40-yard dash in 4.71 and 4.80 seconds at the NFL Combine, while Ryan timed at 4.89. In May 2008, Ryan signed a six-year, $72 million deal that guaranteed him $34.75 million. Six months later, Rodgers signed a six-year, $65 million deal with $20 million in guarantees.

In many ways, these young quarterbacks were extremely similar. So many believed the quarterback that set himself apart in this game would guide the winning team in this postseason showdown. "The way this league is, it almost always comes down to quarterback play," Packers cornerback Tramon Williams said. "That's never going to change."

Ryan gave the Packers plenty to worry about, having quickly established himself as one of football's top signal callers. It wasn't just the numbers with Ryan. He had also been extremely clutch and was given the nickname "Matty Ice."

In 2010 alone, Ryan led the Falcons to six wins with go-ahead scores in either the fourth quarter or overtime. And for his career, Ryan had already led 12 such drives. One of those drives came in the Falcons' Week 12 win over Green Bay, when Ryan led Atlanta to a field goal in the closing seconds that broke a 17-17 tie.

"I don't know Matt personally, but he seems like a very consistent young man and has been successful, and I'm sure that has a lot to do with it," McCarthy said of Ryan. "He looks like he is the same personality week in and week out, and I think that has a lot to do with his level play. He looks to be a very consistent quarterback."

Rodgers was still trying to prove himself in the clutch. During his three years as a starter, Rodgers was 2-13 in games decided by four points or less. And Green Bay's six losses in 2010 came by a combined 20 points, with all decided by four points or less. Rodgers finished four of those games and missed two others due to a concussion he suffered at Detroit. In the fourth quarters and overtimes of the losses in which Rodgers played, he was 37 of 56 for 402 yards with one touchdown and one interception. That's a mediocre passer rating of 85.6. In all other games, Rodgers was 293 of 446 for 3,720 yards, 30 touchdowns and 10 interceptions. That's a passer rating of 104.7.

"I would say Aaron Rodgers' season is probably as much in line with the season we had as an offense," McCarthy said last week. "We've been a little bit up and down at times. If you just look at our point production, it's reflected in that."

Perhaps. But on this Saturday night in a city affectionately referred to as Hot-lanta, no one was hotter than Rodgers. And McCarthy, for that matter.

Rodgers had a night for the ages, displaying accuracy, arm strength and vision rarely seen. Rodgers completed 31 of 36 passes for 366 yards, three touchdowns, no interceptions and posted a passer rating of 136.8. McCarthy was aggressive, in sync with Rodgers, and ahead of Falcons defensive coordinator Brian VanGorder from the first snap. It all added up to a stunning 48-21 Green Bay victory that sent the Packers back to the NFC Championship game for the second time in McCarthy's five seasons.

McCarthy, who had swung the season with his "Nobody's Underdog" comment one month earlier, wasn't backing down now.

"We're a championship-caliber football team, we talked about that before the Philadelphia game," he said. "We have 16 quarters on our mind, we've completed eight of them, and we have an opportunity to play in four more next week. We feel very good about who we are, the way we played, our brand of football in all three areas, and that's what we're sticking to."

Out of everything that was now going right for Green Bay, the play of Rodgers was certainly the most impressive. Rodgers set Green Bay playoff records for completions (31) and completion percentage (86.1%) and had the second-most yardage in team history (366). In 10 possessions, Rodgers led Green Bay to six touchdowns and two field goals, and the Packers never punted.

Rodgers' performance against Atlanta might have been the best postseason effort ever by a Packers quarterback, and it ranked among the finest in NFL history.

"I thought Aaron Rodgers was excellent today," McCarthy said. "Just the ability to play with a run-and-pass mix throughout the game, particularly the first three quarters and stay in favorable down-and-distance, and he was excellent with his in-the-pocket and out-of-the-pocket performance. He was on fire, he likes playing in domes, and you can see why.

"Just the fact that we were able to control the line of scrimmage, I know our offensive and defensive lines coming into this game felt that they had to respond, clearly [from] the way we played the first time down here in November. So, it starts up front, and with that, Aaron was able to run the offense at a very high level today."

Atlanta's defense wasn't a dominant unit. But it ranked in the middle of most statistical categories and had gotten the better of the Packers earlier in the year.

But this night belonged to Rodgers, McCarthy and a Green Bay offense now operating at peak efficiency. Rodgers fired a six-yard touchdown pass to Jordy Nelson, a 20-yarder to James Jones, and a seven-yard TD to John Kuhn. The most impressive part of Rodgers' day, though, might have been his feet.

On several plays, Falcons Pro Bowl defensive end John Abraham broke free and seemed ready to dump Rodgers. But Rodgers continually escaped, made one big throw after another and even had a seven-yard TD run. "This probably was my best performance — the stage we were on, the importance of this game," Rodgers said. "It was a good night."

It was quite a night for Packers emerging cornerback Tramon Williams, too. One week after notching the game-saving interception in Philadelphia, Williams was even better against the Falcons.

With the game tied at 14 late in the second quarter, Ryan took a shot to the end zone for 6-foot-4 wideout Michael Jenkins. But the 5-foot-11 Williams played the ball better, and when Jenkins lost his footing, Williams went up and picked Ryan off with 2:20 left in the first half.

"I think we have lots of guys on the defense that can make those plays," Williams said. "I think I've just been put in that position the last couple of weeks and made those plays from my teammates. I don't see it as a big deal."

It was a big deal, though. And Williams made a play before halftime that was an even bigger deal.

Green Bay had taken a 21-14 lead, but Atlanta was driving into field-goal range and had reached the Packers' 35.

With just 10 seconds left in the half, Ryan rolled left and threw back across his body for Roddy White. Williams jumped the route, though, made a nifty cut past Ryan at midfield, then sailed to the end zone to make it 28-14.

"I think everything he's done, every good thing that's happened to Tramon on the field, all the plays he's making he deserves," Packers linebacker A.J. Hawk said of Williams. "I've never been around probably a better teammate than a guy like Tramon. He's awesome. I love how he prepares. He does everything right."

The odds of Williams ever being in this spot were immense. Williams turned down a scholarship offer from Louisiana Tech in the fall of 2002 and planned to concentrate solely on academics. But as Williams played intramural football his freshman season and watched game after game on television and from the stands, he got the itch. So in the spring of 2003, Williams went to then-Louisiana Tech coach Jack Bicknell and asked back in. Williams eventually made 23 starts for the Bulldogs but ran a slow 40-yard dash time on his pro day (4.59) and went undrafted in 2006. Williams never quit, though; he joined the Packers' practice squad late in the 2006 season and eventually worked his way into the starting lineup.

Now, in this memorable postseason, Williams was playing better than any cornerback in football. McCarthy often talked about his love of developing players. Williams was now one of his poster children.

"Tramon Williams has clearly played at a Pro Bowl level, there's no question about it," McCarthy said. "To see your big-time players step up in the prime-time games, that's what it's all about. We're a very confident football team, we've definitely hit our groove, we're very, very proud of what we accomplished here today, and we're looking forward to next week. Tramon Williams, he has done it all year. He has been playing at this level all year."

The Packers hadn't played at this level before now. But after whipping the Falcons, they were living up to the preseason hype, when many believed they'd be football's best team.

Twenty-four hours later Chicago defeated Seattle in the second NFC Divisional playoff game of the weekend. And that set up a matchup between the Packers and Bears—football's oldest rivals—for a trip to the Super Bowl.

The Packers were red hot, played a brand of football that was fun to watch, and had wowed national audiences on their way to the NFC Championship game.

The more methodical Bears had a message for the rest of the country, though: Don't forget about us.

"I know Green Bay is the hot team. I know they're kind of the sexy team," Bears cornerback Tim Jennings said. "But we're playing some damn good football right now, too. That's why this is going to be such a great game."

Even as a kid in Greenfield, McCarthy knew all about the Packers-Bears rivalry. Now, he was in the middle of it, with a Super Bowl appearance at stake.

"I think everybody that's grown up understood the importance of the Bears and Packers," McCarthy said. "I've heard about the Chicago Bears and Green Bay Packers even as a kid. When I grew up in Pittsburgh, it was the Steelers and the Browns, and that was the big rivalry. And coaching for the Kansas City Chiefs, the Chiefs and the Oakland Raiders was such a big rivalry.

"But this is different. To say you're the longest rivalry in the history of the National Football League, and just the great players and the coaches and the teams that have been part of this rivalry. It's an honor and privilege to play in this game."

McCarthy and his red-hot football team couldn't wait.

16
Beating the Bears

Chicago Bears cornerback Tim Jennings isn't clairvoyant, but he admits, he saw this coming. Back on January 2, 2011, Green Bay had just rallied for a 10-3 win over the Bears in the regular-season finale. The Packers' victory gave them the sixth and final playoff spot in the NFC. As the Bears' bus rolled out of Lambeau Field that frigid night, Jennings had one overriding thought.

"I kept thinking we're going to see them again," Jennings said of the Packers. "I was thinking, 'Man, we should have knocked them out.' I wish we would have, too, because they're on fire. I kind of wish we'd be playing Atlanta."

Ah, what fun would that be? Instead, one of the most highly anticipated NFC Championships in recent memory was on the docket. Although Chicago was the No. 2 seed in the NFC and the Packers were seeded sixth, Green Bay was installed as a three-point favorite.

"It's going to be backyard football," said Bears defensive end Israel Idonije. "Man on man. They throw a punch, we throw a punch. We're going to slug back and forth, and the first one to flinch or drop is going to lose the game."

Chicago center Olin Kreutz, who had played in 24 Packers-Bears games, knew this contest would be unlike any other. "We don't like them and they don't like us," said Kreutz, a six-time Pro Bowler. "There's a tremendous amount of respect for each other. But it usually ends up the guy you respect the most, you hate the most. And that's how this is."

Green Bay and Chicago met twice during the regular season, with each team winning on its own home field. Overall, the

Packers and Bears had met 181 times in a rivalry that began in 1921. The Bears entered with a narrow 92-83-6 advantage in the series. Amazingly, though, these bitter adversaries played just once in the postseason. That came in 1941, when George Halas' Bears defeated Curly Lambeau's Packers, 33-14, in a Western Division playoff game played at Wrigley Field in Chicago.

"It's special," McCarthy said the day after he learned his team would face Chicago. "It's really a privilege and honor now to be part of this great history with the playoff game against the Bears. I know it's only the second time it's happened. Personally I'm honored to be a part of this and to be going down to Soldier Field to play for the Halas Trophy and for the opportunity to play for the Lombardi Trophy. It speaks volumes. It's great for both organizations, great for our fans. It's going to be a fun game to play in."

The game was a lot different now than 70 years ago, when these two organizations last met in a postseason contest. Back in the day, Chicago's George Halas and Green Bay's Curly Lambeau had no use for each other. It stayed that way for generations, as these two outfits continued an immense dislike for the other. Today, quarterbacks Aaron Rodgers and Jay Cutler were pals. Many players had the same agents and knew each other well.

While the rivalry had probably softened some in this new world of professional football, McCarthy insisted it still had plenty of fire. "We don't like their team and they don't like our team. I get all that," McCarthy said. "But I respect the way they play. They play the right way. We play the right way.

"But this is about winning championships. And we're going down there to play for the NFC Championship game. And you have to beat teams like the Chicago Bears to achieve that goal. That's really what it comes down to. But there will be plenty of energy on that field."

Rightfully so.

Both teams entered red hot, with Chicago (12-5) winning eight of its last 10 games. The Packers (12-6) had won nine of their last 12 outings, and both teams were excelling on each side of the ball.

Green Bay's offense was averaging 30.2 points over its last five games. Chicago's offense was averaging 29.0 points per game in its last four.

Green Bay's defense finished the year ranked second in points allowed (15.0 per game) and was fifth in total defense. Chicago was fourth in points allowed (17.9) and ninth in total defense.

The only time either offense was consistently stopped in the past month came when the Packers defeated the Bears, 10-3, in the regular-season finale. The Bears, with nothing to play for on that frigid night, showed no quarter and nearly knocked the host Packers out of the playoffs. Instead, Green Bay survived, and these two bitter adversaries were once again staring each other down.

"We could have buried them," Kreutz said of the season finale. "But here they are, and this is exciting. I can't imagine sitting here being more excited for any other team. So why not?"

When Bears coach Lovie Smith was hired in 2004, he listed his goals in this order:

1. Beat the Packers.

2. Win the NFC North.

3. Win the Super Bowl.

Green Bay had always been the measuring stick for Smith's Bears. Now, there was more at stake than ever before. "It just doesn't get any better as I see it than for the NFC Championship to come down to the Packers coming down on our turf this time," Smith said. "The Packers and Bears to finish it up. That's how it should be."

In Green Bay, McCarthy was more confident than ever. Sure, his team had averaged just 13.5 points per game against Chicago in 2010. But McCarthy knew if Rodgers had time, he could expose Jennings and the rest of Chicago's secondary.

On the flip side, Cutler and Bears running back Matt Forte gave the Packers cause for concern. But Chicago didn't have a true No. 1 wide receiver. And while the Bears offensive line was improving, it was well below average.

In the days leading up to the game, McCarthy came across more bold and self-assured than ever — even if he wouldn't admit as much. "I think it's just how I felt," McCarthy said. "I don't think I'm a very calculated individual. I don't think I could pull that off. Nobody's underdog. We're nobody's favorite, either. I think that's our motto today as a team.

"This group has a lot of confidence. We've never wavered from our goals. We've had challenges, everybody does. But we're here for a reason. We deserve to be here, and we're excited about getting to Chicago."

If McCarthy was excited about going to Chicago, think how he felt upon exiting.

Green Bay's performance in the conference title game wasn't always pretty, especially on offense. There were plenty of tense moments down the stretch. The Packers built a 14-0 lead, though, then held on down the stretch and posted a 21-14 win. McCarthy, who had talked about the Super Bowl since his arrival in Green Bay, had his team headed to Arlington, Texas, to play for the world championship.

The Packers, who had won more NFL Championships (12) than any team in football, now faced Pittsburgh—which had won more Super Bowls (six) than any other franchise—in Super Bowl XLV. And McCarthy was now coaching for a world championship against the team he'd grown up idolizing.

"I'm numb. It's a great feeling," McCarthy said. "I'm just so proud of our football team. You know, it's always tough coming into Chicago to win a football game. I have tremendous respect for the organization and Coach Love Smith. We felt we had them on the ropes there for a while. We just couldn't get the game to a three-score game.

"I think that says a lot about them as a football team. But it also says a lot about us as a team. Defense, special teams, people making plays down the stretch. It was the typical Green Bay-Chicago game with everything on the line. I'm very proud of our players and very proud of our coaches. As we stated, we have a goal of playing 16 quarters and we've completed 12. We're fired up and getting ready to go to Dallas, Texas."

The heroes on this night were rookie cornerback Sam Shields and second-year defensive tackle B.J. Raji, two players who came from different ends of the football universe.

The 337-pound Raji was the ninth overall pick in the 2009 NFL Draft and was given $18 million in guaranteed money on his rookie contract. The 182-pound Shields was given a paltry $7,500 in guaranteed money to sign with Green Bay as an undrafted free agent.

"It doesn't matter where you find guys," said Packers director of football operations Reggie McKenzie, who's now the general manager in Oakland. "Just so you find them."

The Packers did yeoman's work to find these two blossoming young players. And without their heroics in the NFC title game, the outcome may very well have been different.

Shields had a pair of interceptions, including one with 37 seconds left and Chicago driving for the potential game-tying score. Raji bailed out a struggling Green Bay offense with an 18-yard interception return for a touchdown midway through the fourth quarter.

"It's an unbelievable feeling," said Shields, who entered the game with one interception all year. "There's a lot of guys that wait a long, long time for this. Now, we're going to the Super Bowl."

The play of Raji, Shields and the rest of Green Bay's defense helped bail out a sluggish performance by the Packers offense.

Green Bay scored 14 points in the game's first 19 minutes. But the Packers offense didn't score again, leaving them thrilled with the win but frustrated by their own play.

"There are some things we are going to have to improve before we get down to Dallas," McCarthy said.

Packers quarterback Aaron Rodgers agreed. "We would have liked to put more than 14 points on the board obviously, but we're going to the Super Bowl," Rodgers said. "We've got a week to relax and get our bodies back and go enjoy Dallas and hopefully get a win down there."

The way the Packers started against the Bears, it looked like they'd breeze into the Super Bowl. On Green Bay's first drive, Rodgers led a seven play, 84-yard march that he capped with a one-yard TD run. Rodgers was 4-for-4 on the drive for 76 yards and hit Greg Jennings twice for 48 yards.

"Frankly, the first drive was the way we anticipated coming into this game," McCarthy said. "I thought we were able to get into a tremendous rhythm."

Green Bay stayed in rhythm and went ahead, 14-0, just four minutes into the second quarter. The Packers needed only five plays to cover 44 yards on that drive. Running back Brandon Jackson (16 yards) and wideout Jordy Nelson (15) both had big catches on the march, and running back James Starks finished the deal with a four-yard TD run.

"The way we started out, I thought we were going to put up 40 points," Packers right guard Josh Sitton said. "We came out and were running good, throwing good, just rolling like Atlanta."

Yes, for a little more than a quarter, this felt exactly like the NFC Divisional playoffs, when the Packers drilled the Falcons, 48-21. From that point forward, though, everything changed.

In Green Bay's first four possessions, it rolled up 181 total yards, had 12 first downs and averaged 7.9 yards per play. In the Packers' final 10 possessions, though, they had 175 total yards, 11 first downs and averaged just 3.9 yards per play.

"It was weird, man," Packers wideout James Jones said. "We don't feel like there's anybody out there that can stop us except us. And the rest of the game, I'd just say we stopped ourselves."

Chicago certainly had something to do with it, as well. Bears linebackers Lance Briggs and Brian Urlacher both intercepted Rodgers with the Packers in Chicago territory.

Briggs' came late in the first half after Green Bay had reached Chicago's 41-yard line and was looking to add to its 14-0 lead. But Rodgers threw low to wideout Donald Driver, the ball hit Driver's foot and bounced up and into the hands of Briggs.

Urlacher's pick came with the Packers at Chicago's 6-yard line and looking to add to a 14-0 lead midway through the third quarter. Urlacher read Rodgers' eyes, stepped in front of a pass intended for Driver, and totally changed momentum.

"It was a terrible throw," said Rodgers, who likely saved a touchdown by tackling Urlacher at the Chicago 45-yard line. "Once I threw it I started sprinting, and I was hopeful that I was able to at least catch up to him."

After scoring twice in their first four possessions, the Packers' final 10 possessions resulted in six punts, two interceptions and two kneel-downs to end halves. It was an unexpected turnaround for a Green Bay offense that had been smoking hot.

"I don't know what happened," Sitton said. "We were just really out of sync and lost all of our momentum. Thankfully our defense stepped up and made sure we're still playing."

No one stepped up more than Shields and Raji.

There were eight teams that wanted to sign Shields after he went undrafted, including Chicago. But he picked Green Bay because it offered the most money and the best chance to play.

Shields was officially listed as Green Bay's No. 3 cornerback, but he had performed like a No. 1 for weeks. The Bears tried picking on Shields at times during the conference title game, but the unflappable rookie didn't blink.

Late in the first half the Bears trailed, 14-0, but had just seized momentum after Briggs intercepted Rodgers. Two plays later, Chicago quarterback Jay Cutler took a shot down the left sideline for wideout Johnny Knox. Shields, who played wideout for three years at the University of Miami, ran stride for stride with Knox, then turned and almost became the receiver. Shields had inside leverage, got to the ball before Knox, and made a gorgeous pick.

"I just got my head around and went to the highest point," said Shields, who also had a sack.

Raji's play had been great all season, and it didn't change on this night.

With the Packers clinging to a 14-7 lead midway through the fourth quarter, Raji made a play that McCarthy called a "game winner."

The Bears had a third and 5 from their own 15. Raji lined up over center Olin Kreutz, showed blitz, then dropped into the middle of the field. Chicago third-string quarterback Caleb Hanie, who had replaced an injured Jay Cutler and an ineffective Todd Collins, was trying to get the ball to running back Matt Forte.

Hanie never saw Raji and threw the ball right into his enormous mitts. Raji caught the ball naturally, then waltzed to the right corner of the end zone to make it 21-7. Raji didn't have an interception in the NFL or college, so his timing was perfect for Packer Nation.

"It's just a great feeling," Raji said. "It was a great call. I was behind the back, and obviously he wasn't expecting that. I just caught it and ran it back."

Shields then capped Green Bay's huge defensive effort with a second interception, which was also the biggest play he had made as a Packer.

Hanie rallied the Bears back to within seven points. Chicago had driven to Green Bay's 29-yard line, had a fourth and five, and still 47 seconds to notch the equalizer.

Hanie worked out of the shotgun, the Bears sent out four receivers, and the Packers rushed five. Hanie took a shot down the middle for Knox, but Shields jumped the route, knowing safety Nick Collins was providing help from behind.

With his coaches screaming, 'Get down,' Shields returned the interception 32 yards. When Shields rose up, he was mobbed by teammates who knew their next stop was the Super Bowl.

"We need to work on that last play, getting on the ground a little sooner," McCarthy said afterward. "Sam, for a rookie—and I told a couple other rookies this—you have no idea what you've accomplished here in your first year in the league. He is going to be a great player for the Green Bay Packers for a long time."

Yes, Green Bay's defense was the No. 1 reason these Packers were going to their first Super Bowl in 13 years. McCarthy's decision to fire Sanders and bring in Capers two years earlier had worked like a charm.

Green Bay forced three Chicago turnovers, held the Bears' three quarterbacks to a combined passer rating of 45.2, and allowed just 132 total yards through three quarters.

Cutler had a miserable 31.8 passer rating before leaving the game with an MCL sprain. Collins was even worse, going 0 for 4, before the Bears tried door No. 3 and went with Hanie.

"We didn't even know who their third-string quarterback was," Packers defensive end Ryan Pickett said. "We were like, 'Who is that?' "

Amazingly, Hanie nearly rescued the Bears after three quarters of offensive ineptitude. Hanie threw for 153 yards and a touchdown in the fourth quarter alone.

"I ain't going to lie, when they put him in we were like, 'We don't know nothing about this guy,'" Packers defensive end Cullen Jenkins said. "But he did great."

In the end, though, Green Bay's defense made all the plays when it had to. "It seems the defense has put these last three games away," linebacker Clay Matthews said. "We had our backs against the wall a little bit, but we made the play to win the game."

For Thompson and McCarthy, this was utopia. For years now, there were websites calling for Thompson's firing. He'd been hammered for his approach to free agency, the Brett Favre fiasco, his reluctance to trade draft picks for proven commodities, and his refusal to ever divulge information.

Talk show hosts, columnists and virtually every "Joe Six Pack" had questioned Thompson's approach to building a team. So standing in the winning locker room shortly after the Halas Trophy had been presented to his Packers, Thompson had every opportunity to tell his critics "I told you so." But that had never been Thompson's style, and it wasn't on this day of celebration, either.

"It's nice to stand here now having won the NFC Championship and being able to take the Packers back to the Super Bowl," Thompson said. "But I don't get into this satisfaction of showing people up.

"I think most Packer fans are good people and they want the Packers to do good. And when we do good, they pat us on the back, and when we don't they don't. That's the way the NFL is."

Just more than a month ago, McCarthy's job security appeared tenuous, at best. Green Bay was 8-6 and on the outside looking in on the playoff race.

Now, McCarthy's bold approach and steady hand were instrumental in Green Bay's five-game winning streak. That surge now had the Packers 60 minutes from greatness.

"We've always felt that we are a very good football team," McCarthy said. "Now we have the opportunity to achieve greatness, and that is winning the Super Bowl down in Dallas. Bring the Lombardi Trophy back home. We never doubted that throughout the season.

"Really, the way that our season went—the trials and tribulations that we encountered, to me, that was how we were shaped. I think it's made us a better football team. It's challenged our character. I think we've really grown through it. Our players truly believe that we will be successful in Dallas, just like they truly believed that we were going to be successful here today. This was the path that was chosen for us, and I think it's really shaped a hell of a football team."

No one was arguing with the head coach of the NFC champs. McCarthy and his team were just 60 minutes from greatness.

Remarkably, it was Pittsburgh — the team McCarthy lived and died with as a child — that stood in the way.

17

Titletown Again!

The days leading up to a Super Bowl have terrified front offices for years. There is an endless string of temptations. Players have additional free time on their hands. And quite often, they make the wrong choices.

Cincinnati's Stanley Wilson went on a cocaine binge before Super Bowl XXIII. Oakland's Barret Robbins went on a drinking binge in Tijuana before Super Bowl XXXVII and wasn't allowed to play when he returned. And Atlanta's Eugene Robinson was arrested for soliciting prostitution the night before Super Bowl XXXIII.

Could one of the Packers do the same? "We're a young team but mature, and we have an opportunity to do something special," Packers wideout Jordy Nelson said. "Everyone knows that, everyone wants that. And I don't think anyone's going to jeopardize that."

Packers cornerback Charles Woodson was part of that Oakland team that lost Super Bowl XXXVII. And in case his teammates didn't know who Robbins was, Woodson informed them."It had a great effect on the team," Woodson said of losing Robbins. "He was our starting center. He was the captain of that line. It altered everything, especially for our offense. We didn't recover from it and ultimately lost the game.

"I talked to a few guys and reminded them of that story and to be careful. We know guys are going to have fun. That is just the nature of it, but whatever is in your power just stay out of that. Don't be that guy."

No one was. And a big reason for that was McCarthy and his even-handed ways. From the day McCarthy arrived in

Green Bay, he stressed consistency. There was always a steadiness to his approach, a regularity and dependability his team could count on. Week in and week out the Packers followed a similar routine. Now, just because the Packers were on football's biggest stage, that wasn't going to change.

"Everyone's an adult here, good group of guys," backup quarterback Matt Flynn said. "It's not like it's your first year in college and it's bowl week or something. Everyone's kind of done their thing. Sure, we're going to try and see what's going on around there, but I'm not worried about anything. This trip's all about football."

The biggest distraction Green Bay faced was with its official Super Bowl team photo. The Packers were originally scheduled to take their team picture on the Tuesday of Super Bowl week. Green Bay's 16 players on injured reserve weren't arriving until Thursday, though.

That meant the injured players would be left out of the shot. So players like linebacker Nick Barnett and tight end Jermichael Finley took to Twitter to voice their displeasure. "It's kinda sad," Barnett wrote.

"We got hurt playing for the team," Finley tweeted. "I never trip abt anything, but the way IR players are getting treated ... I guess its what have u done for me lately!"

Rodgers poured gas on the fire when he shot back at his injured teammates. "I was on IR back in 2006," Rodgers said. "I chose to stick around and finish out the season with my guys and be here every game. Some of those guys didn't. And so, we love them, we care about them, we don't wish injury on anybody, but this is a group of guys that's really come together and has been great to work with. Some of the guys who were injured, you know, they are still part of this team, but some of them didn't choose to stick around."

McCarthy called the entire situation "a total overreaction," which it was. He then settled it all by moving the team picture to Friday, when the entire team could be present. "If that's the biggest issue that we have in our preparation, we are going to have a hell of a week," McCarthy said. "So it's not that big of a deal."

The rest of the week went off without a hitch. McCarthy already started visualizing how he'd handle Super Bowl preparations back in 2007, when his team reached the NFC title game. Now, his No. 1 goal was to make this as close to a normal week as possible.

"My experience in coaching and life, people want discipline," McCarthy said. "People want structure. They want that in their life, especially in their professional life. It's very important.

"I do it every week that they get, OK, normal Wednesday, they know the schedule, but we go through it every week, and it's very important that everybody knows exactly where they need to be, what's going to be asked of them, and what the expectations are. So I think it's very important to group continuity, regularity. We talk about culture, we talk about environment, and scheduling is a big part of it."

The Packers were on board with that. They arrived in Dallas on Monday and checked into the Omni Mandalay in Las Colinas. Each player was given an individual room, instead of having a roommate, as they did during the regular season.

The Packers took part in the circus known as Media Day on Tuesday, before returning to their hotel for a walk-through that afternoon. "I'm just trying to get through this 60 minutes without saying anything stupid," Rodgers said of Media Day.

Much to McCarthy's delight, Rodgers and his teammates didn't make any waves. From Wednesday to Friday, Green Bay held a team meeting in the morning, met with the media, then had offensive, defensive and special teams meetings. Following a jog-through, the Packers ate lunch and went to practice.

Each night, the players had a few hours to themselves, and bed check was 11 p.m. In the end, there were no curfew violations or off-the-field incidents. Everything went off without incident — just like McCarthy had planned.

"This thing is a big deal, and we understand the reason it's a big deal is because of the trophy," nose tackle B.J. Raji said. "Everyone else can worry about who's performing the halftime show, who's doing this, who's doing that. We're worried about the game and ultimately winning that trophy. That's got to be our only focus."

On Saturday, the Packers had meetings and a walk-through in the morning, a team meeting in the evening, followed by a snack. On Sunday morning, the Packers held a final team meeting at 10:30, then boarded the bus at 2 p.m.

"That's how we've operated for five years," McCarthy said of the weekend schedule. "The players are in tune with that schedule. It's a schedule that definitely works for them, and we'll stay true to that."

For most of the week, much was being made of Pittsburgh's advantage in experience. The Steelers had 14 starters who had won a Super Bowl championship. Pittsburgh also had 10 players with two rings, and a total of 25 players who had competed in a Super Bowl.

Green Bay hadn't been in a Super Bowl since 1997. And the only Packers to ever play in a Super Bowl were cornerback Charles Woodson and defensive end Ryan Pickett — and both played on losing teams.

"It's meaningful," McCarthy admitted on the difference in experience. "But we're aware of it and understand that we haven't been there before, and that's something we'll talk about and make sure expectations and responsibilities (are) clear for everybody."

This was the Steelers' third Super Bowl appearance in six years. Pittsburgh defeated Seattle and Arizona, respectively, in Super Bowls XL and XLIII and many of its key cogs from those teams remained.

Hines Ward was the MVP of Super Bowl 40 after catching five passes for 123 yards and a touchdown. James Harrison had one of the most memorable plays in Super Bowl history with a 100-yard interception return for a touchdown in Super Bowl XLIII. And Ben Roethlisberger was the winning quarterback in each of those games.

Others like Pro Bowl safety Troy Polamalu, mammoth nose tackle Casey Hampton, steady tight end Heath Miller and splendid linebackers LaMarr Woodley, James Farrior and Larry Foote all played a role in Pittsburgh's recent dominance.

Even 38-year-old head coach Mike Tomlin, who was in his fourth year, had a Super Bowl win on his résumé. Pittsburgh's roster was packed with players who had enjoyed great success on Super Bowl Sunday.

The Packers weren't putting much stock into that, though. In 2009, a New Orleans team making its first-ever trip to the Super Bowl upset a veteran Indianapolis team. In 2007, a New York Giants team with little Super Bowl experience stunned New England, which had won three Super Bowls earlier in the decade.

"I believe if we stay calm and stay cool and understand what's going on, everything will work out," Packers running back Brandon Jackson said. "We've been on the big stage before, not as big as this, but as far as playoffs and everything like that, we've been on that type of stage. We're going to handle our business, stay calm and cool, and everything will work out."

McCarthy felt the same way. For weeks now, McCarthy had been more brazen than any other time in his coaching career. It started with the "Nobody's Underdog" statement. It continued through the final two regular-season games and only intensified during the playoffs.

Why would now be any different? "We've had an opportunity to play in five playoff-type football games," McCarthy said. "We feel that has really prepared us for this opportunity."

McCarthy had never been to a Super Bowl, and that was by design. Despite protests from his daughter, McCarthy didn't want to attend a Super Bowl until his team was in one. "My daughter Alex, it was something she always wanted to go to," he said. "And I said, 'Hey, we're going to go when we play in it.'"

It was here now, and McCarthy felt better than ever about his team. McCarthy felt so good, in fact, that he pulled a stunner less than 24 hours before the game.

On Saturday night, McCarthy made the bold move of fitting his players for the championship rings. Traditionally teams were fitted *after* winning a title. But the McCarthy Way was now much different than many of his peers.

"I felt the measurement of the rings, the timing of it would be special," McCarthy said. "It would have a significant effect on our players doing it the night before the game. I just told them, 'We're going to get measured for rings tonight.' Scheduling is so important during the course of the week. You want to do certain things at certain times. I thought that was a perfect time. I thought it would be special and give us a boost of confidence to do it the night before the game."

The Packers' confidence was sky high. And this only added to it. "That's pretty much how he coached us all year, and especially at the end," defensive end Ryan Pickett said. "He had a lot of confidence in us, and we had a lot of confidence in each other."

Cornerback Charles Woodson agreed. "No matter what anyone said about him, he never changed his focus on getting to this point," Woodson said of McCarthy. "When you have a coach who is unwavered by whatever is going on in the media or whatever is said about him, you know that you have a good guy at the helm. We followed him and his lead, and here we are with a chance to win the Super Bowl."

To many, this was a coin-flip game. On defense, the teams were remarkably similar. Pittsburgh finished No. 1 in the NFL in points allowed (14.5) and Green Bay ranked No. 2 (15.0). The Steelers were also No. 2 in total defense (276.8 yards per game) and the Packers finished fifth (309.1).

Green Bay was first in the NFL in opposing quarterbacks passer rating (67.2) and the Steelers were second (73.1). The Steelers also ranked No. 1 in sacks (48), while the Packers tied for second (47). Green Bay was second in interceptions (24) and the Steelers tied for fifth (21).

"They're just a team that knows how to finish," Packers running back Brandon Jackson said of the Steelers. "Those guys, they play four quarters hard every game, every day. You have to come strong against those guys or you won't beat them. We have to come out and play four quarters to have a chance."

The Packers finished fifth in passing offense (257.8), ninth in total offense (358.1) and 10th in points (24.3). Pittsburgh was 14th in total offense (345.3), 14th in passing offense (225.1) and 12th in points (23.4).

"They (the Steelers) are a great team, they've been doing it for years now, and we're just on the precipice of being good and potentially great," Packers linebacker Clay Matthews said before the game. "It's going to be a great game."

It was—for McCarthy and the Packers. McCarthy's game plan was centered around Rodgers and Green Bay's gifted band of pass catchers. McCarthy had talked often about being a great running team since arriving in Green Bay, but he knew the best way to win in today's NFL was through the air. Especially in this game.

McCarthy loved Green Bay's matchups against Pittsburgh cornerbacks Ike Taylor and Bryant McFadden. Safety Troy Polamalu was a star, but he also gambled often, while safety Ryan Clark was a big hitter with so-so speed.

The key to everything was blocking Pittsburgh's immensely talented front seven, where linebackers James Harrison and LaMarr Woodley ruined game plans week after week after week. That task would fall largely on tackles Chad Clifton and rookie Bryan Bulaga.

"They have a great defense," Rodgers said. "They're very well coached. Coach (Dick) LeBeau is one of the greatest coaches this league has ever seen, and he gets them prepared every week to play. It's going to be a tough challenge for us, and we'll be ready."

They were.

McCarthy and Rodgers went to work right away, throwing early and often. And on Green Bay's second possession, it hit paydirt. The Packers drove to the Steelers' 29-yard line, where on third-and-one, they lined up with two tight ends and Nelson the lone receiver split wide right. Pittsburgh anticipated a run, and that left Nelson one on one with William Gay, Pittsburgh's No. 3 cornerback.

Gay played press coverage at the line of scrimmage, but Nelson beat him after faking inside then releasing down the right sideline. The Packers offensive line did its job and Rodgers lofted a perfect fade to the right corner of the end zone.

Gay's coverage wasn't terrible, but Nelson had a step on him and won a hand fight between the two. Nelson then hauled in Rodgers' gorgeous toss to give the Packers a 7-0 lead with 3:44 left in the first quarter.

"It was just press (coverage)," Nelson said. "Aaron gave me a little signal if it was press to go deep. It was actually a screen play, but he checked to a go route. That's what we hit."

The hitting had just begun.

Pittsburgh began its next drive on its own 7-yard line following an illegal block penalty. And on the Steelers' first play, Roethlisberger made the game's biggest blunder.

Green Bay rushed four, but Roethlisberger was trying to hit a home run to Wallace, so he needed substantial time for the play to develop. That allowed beefy defensive end Howard Green, who was signed off the street in October when the Packers were ravaged by injury, to get home in 3.4 seconds.

Green whipped left guard Chris Kemoeatu, then drilled Roethlisberger as he let loose a bomb for Wallace. But Green's pressure caused Roethlisberger's pass to be severely underthrown, and Packers safety Nick Collins intercepted at the Steelers' 37-yard line.

The following season, Collins' Green Bay career ended when he suffered a neck injury in the second game of the year. On this play, though, Collins was magical.

Collins, who was named to three straight Pro Bowls, took off down the right sideline and made a nifty cut back inside. When Collins reached the 3-yard line, he jumped and reached the end zone. In a matter of 24 seconds, Green Bay had surged to a 14-0 lead.

"Oh man, that was the highlight of my day right there," Collins said. "I was able to read Big Ben (Roethlisberger) and got a nice jump on the ball. I made a couple cuts to get into the end zone."

Since the day McCarthy arrived in Green Bay, he had stressed turnover differential. To him, it was as important—if not more so—than any other statistic in the game.

The 2010 Packers had a turnover differential of plus-10. And in McCarthy's five years on the job, Green Bay had taken the ball away 45 more times than its opponents.

McCarthy stressed turnovers all week, and late in the first half, the Packers got another one from Roethlisberger.

Green Bay held a 14-3 lead, but Pittsburgh was on the move. Operating out of the shotgun, Roethlisberger threw short over the middle for Wallace, but cornerback Jarrett Bush read the crossing route, drove on the ball, and picked it off.

Bush had taken more than his share of grief from Packer Nation since arriving in 2006. But in 2010, Bush developed into a special teams stalwart. Now, this was undoubtedly the biggest play he made from scrimmage as a Packer.

"I didn't get to play much this season," Bush said. "If you keep working hard, keep working hard, keep working hard, when the time comes — and you thought it would never come — it comes, and you've got to be able to respond."

Rodgers did so on the ensuing drive.

Green Bay started on its own 47, and on its second play, Rodgers hit Nelson for 16 yards against nickel corner Bryant McFadden. Two plays later, Rodgers made one of his finest throws as a Packer.

On a first-and-10 from Pittsburgh's 21, Green Bay lined up four wide receivers, the Steelers rushed four and dropped seven. Greg Jennings lined up in the left slot and ran a deep seam route.

Jennings had gotten behind linebacker James Farrior and in front of safety Ryan Clark, but Rodgers' window was small and his pass had to be perfect. It was.

Rodgers delivered a dart that Clark missed by inches. Jennings took a wicked shot from Polamalu, but he was already in the end zone.

The Packers led, 21-3, with just more than two minutes remaining in the first half. Things were playing out just the way McCarthy envisioned.

"We know that they're capable of getting plays in chunks," Pittsburgh coach Mike Tomlin said. "We knew that they would throw the football quite a bit, and they did."

Shortly before halftime, though, the Steelers were given new life.

At the two-minute mark, Packers nickel cornerback Sam Shields left with a shoulder injury. Shields would return, but not until the fourth quarter.

One play later, cornerback Charles Woodson — Green Bay's best free agent since Reggie White—suffered a broken collarbone and wouldn't return. Earlier in that second quarter, wideout Donald Driver left with an ankle injury, and he wouldn't be back, either.

With the Packers shorthanded and scrambling defensively, Pittsburgh took full advantage. Roethlisberger threw for all 77 yards of the drive — highlighted by an 8-yard TD to Ward — and the Steelers pulled to 21-10 just 39 seconds before halftime.

During the 30-minute intermission, an emotionally distraught Woodson tried addressing his teammates. "I think I let out all of my emotions at halftime, knowing that I couldn't play the game the rest of the way," Woodson said. "I told the guys, before they went back out, they understand how much I wanted it."

His message was heard. "He could barely say much, he was very emotional and choked up," safety Charlie Peprah said of Woodson. "He got about three words out. He just said, 'You know how bad I want this,' and we knew what we had to do."

Added McCarthy, "I know Charles was very emotional at halftime. I know Donald was frustrated that he couldn't go. Our players just kept playing."

However, so did Pittsburgh's.

With Woodson and Shields sidelined, Green Bay was searching for defensive answers. But the Packers didn't have any early in the third quarter.

After the Packers went three-and-out to start the half — a series that included a drop from wideout James Jones that might have gone for a touchdown — the Steelers took over at midfield. Pittsburgh called five straight running plays and ripped off 50 yards, capped by an 8-yard Mendenhall TD run. Green Bay's lead, once as many as 18 points, had been whittled to 21-17.

"It was tough," Packers defensive coordinator Dom Capers said. "We were scrambling there for a while, because a big part of our game plan went out the window. We planned on playing a lot of man coverage, and when those guys went out, we had to become more of a zone team."

Green Bay's struggles continued. One series after Jones had a critical drop, Nelson had a drop of his own, one of his three in the game. Nelson had a marvelous night overall, with nine catches for 140 yards. But this drop led to a punt.

Green Bay's defense got a much-needed stop, but on its next offensive series, Packers No. 5 wideout Brett Swain had a brutal drop. McCarthy challenged the play — and lost — and the Packers punted from deep in their territory.

"I'd say the whole game was a little bit different, not a lot of flow to it," Rodgers said. "After the pick six, we were on the sidelines for a long time in the first half. Never really got our momentum back until the fourth quarter on those last few drives.

"In a game like this with the long TV timeouts, you lose your sweat. You lose your feel. You don't have those back-to-back plays, back-to-back possessions where you are still feeling like you are loose. You've got to kind of stay loose on the sidelines somehow."

Green Bay, loose and confident at the outset, was now in a battle for the ages. And with the fourth quarter set to start, Pittsburgh had reached the Packers' 33-yard line trailing by just four points.

Between quarters, Packers linebackers coach Kevin Greene went to his standout Clay Matthews and said, "Rally the troops. It is time. It is time."

It was time. And Matthews, who had quickly become one of football's elite defenders, came up huge.

On the first play of the fourth quarter, Packers defensive end Ryan Pickett and Matthews combined to blow up Mendenhall three yards deep. Matthews stood him up on the front side, knocked the ball free, and linebacker Desmond Bishop recovered.

"I was able to get around my guy and make a solid hit right on the football," Matthews said. "I wasn't sure that it had come out until I looked up and saw Desmond with the ball."

The Packers were back in business at Pittsburgh's 45-yard line, and Rodgers wasn't about to waste this golden opportunity. He proceeded to make three huge throws that gave Green Bay some comfort again.

The first came on a third-and-seven, when Rodgers rolled right and away from trouble. Jones ran a comeback route, and Rodgers drilled him for a 12-yard gain to keep the drive alive.

Then, after Nelson dropped a crossing route for a certain first down, the Packers faced a third-and-10 from Pittsburgh's 40. The Steelers rushed five but couldn't get close to Rodgers, in large part because running back Brandon Jackson stoned McFadden in the hole.

Nelson had single coverage and whipped Clark on an inside slant. The terrific blocking up front allowed Rodgers to step into the throw, and he delivered a strike to Nelson that went for 38 yards to Pittsburgh's 2-yard line.

"If you play this game long enough in this position, you are going to drop the ball," Nelson said. "You have to move on. We are level headed. We don't get too high and we don't get too low as a whole wide receiver core.

"We weren't panicking at all when Pittsburgh started coming back. We just said, ok, we have to go make plays. We knew it was going to be on us, and that is why we stepped up and made plays."

Rodgers and Jennings combined to make Green Bay's next big play.

After Rodgers took a sack, the Packers had second-and-goal from Pittsburgh's 8-yard line. Green Bay employed an empty backfield, and after the ball was snapped, Rodgers quickly looked left.

Rodgers had no intention of ever going left, mind you. He was simply trying to get Polamalu, the NFL's Defensive Player of the Year, to drift that way.

It was a continuation of a 60-minute battle that Rodgers waged—and won—with Polamalu.

"He's a guy that you have to be aware of him, where he's at all times," Rodgers said of Polamalu. "He's a great player, had a great season, but guys have to respect where my eyes are looking so it was important to me to use good eye control on the field and not stare anybody down because he can cover a lot of ground quickly.

"When he was down in the box, we made sure he was picked up in the protection schemes. A couple of times when he came on blitzes, we adjusted the protection to make sure we had him picked up, because he's a very talented blitzer and when he's high, a deep safety, you just have to make sure you are good with your eyes."

Rodgers was sublime on this play. Polamalu watched Rodgers' eyes and cheated back to the left, which allowed Jennings to come free in the right corner. Rodgers lofted another perfect ball, and Jennings' TD grab gave Green Bay a 28-17 lead.

"It was a corner route," Jennings said. "I had a corner route the entire time, and they dropped me and let me run free the play before. They dropped me on another corner route, and we came back to it and scored on that play."

Afterward, Polamalu took full responsibility. "That was completely my fault," Polamalu said. "Earlier in the game they ran Jennings down the middle and I was anticipating that same pass play and I guessed wrong."

Pittsburgh answered right back, though, as Roethlisberger engineered a 66-yard TD drive that took just seven plays and slightly more than four minutes. The Steelers' scoring strike came when Wallace got behind Shields, and Roethlisberger put the ball right on his fingertips for a 25-yard touchdown.

Antwaan Randle El scored on an option pitch for the two-point conversion, and the Steelers were within 28-25. There was still 7:34 left in what had become a Super Bowl thriller.

"I thought we were going to win," Wallace said. "We never think we are going to lose. We have no doubt in our mind that we are going to win the game."

Rodgers and the Packers took over on their 25, but after a sack and a false start penalty on Daryn Colledge, they quickly faced a third-and-10. Pittsburgh rushed just three, which meant Rodgers needed to be razor sharp to beat the eight-man coverage in back.

Jennings, working from the left slot, ran another seam route against Steelers' No. 1 cornerback Ike Taylor. The ball was out of Rodgers' hands in 2.8 seconds, and he had perhaps a 12-inch window to squeeze the ball into.

He did. It was the throw of Rodgers' life, one that went for 31 yards and kept the Steelers' offense grounded.

"It just got over the top of his outstretched hands," Jennings said. "It seemed like it brushed off the tip of Ike Taylor's glove, but it just got over the top enough where I could make a play on it."

A pair of runs by James Starks netted 15 yards. Then Rodgers threw a gorgeous back shoulder pass to Jones for 21 yards to Pittsburgh's 8-yard line.

On third-and-goal, though, Rodgers' fade for Nelson in the right corner of the end zone missed by inches. Green Bay was forced to settle for a Mason Crosby field goal, and its lead was a precarious 31-25 with 2:07 still remaining.

McCarthy and his offense were extremely disappointed after failing to put the game away. "On the last drive we had an opportunity to get the touchdown," McCarthy said. "It was an opportunity that was missed. You really just look at it as a missed opportunity."

In Super Bowl XLIII two years earlier, Roethlisberger led the Steelers 78 yards in the closing moments and hit Santonio Holmes with a 6-yard TD pass to win the game. Then in 2009, Roethlisberger and Wallace hooked up on a 19-yard TD on the final play of the game to defeat Green Bay, 37-36.

Now Roethlisberger would get a chance to repeat history.

"I think we knew that they had to go the length of the field, they had one timeout, and they needed to get a touchdown," Packers safety Charlie Peprah said. "I think we can do whatever it takes to keep them out. We just had to keep them out. Everybody felt that we were going to keep them out. We knew we had to stop them."

That was an immense challenge, though.

Pittsburgh began from its own 13, but two Roethlisberger completions quickly took the ball to the 33. The Steelers seemed to have communication issues, though, and Roethlisberger threw consecutive incompletions to Wallace and Ward on balls that weren't even close.

Suddenly it was fourth-and-five, and Super Bowl XLV came down to one play. For the Packers, it was simple: get a stop and win a title. "Everybody was just praying," Shields said.

Capers rushed five and ran a fire zone in the back. Roethlisberger threw to his left for Wallace, but cornerback Tramon Williams broke on the ball perfectly and knocked it to the ground. The Steelers wanted a pass interference call, but Williams' technique was perfect and no flags were warranted.

Green Bay had held. Only 49 seconds remained. "It was a great feeling because you knew that you had to go in and keep them from scoring a touchdown in the two-minute drill," Capers said. "A year ago when we played them up there, we had the same situation, and they scored on the last play of the game to beat us. So it was a great feeling to see the play get made. That's the best feeling in the world."

January 31, 2011: Fort Worth, TX. Green Bay Packers head coach Mike McCarthy at the Super Bowl XLV press conference at the Omni Mandalay Hotel. (Photo by Kirby Lee/Image of Sport-US PRESSWIRE)

There was one better: the kneel down. With Kuhn and Jackson huddled close, Rodgers took consecutive snaps and dropped to a knee. As the final seconds ticked off, Rodgers kept the ball in his hands, and that certainly seemed appropriate.

Of all the reasons Green Bay had won its fourth Super Bowl and 13th NFL Championship, Rodgers topped the list. Rodgers was as crisp as a quarterback could be, and his 304 passing yards might have been 450 if it wasn't for the drops. His passer rating of 111.5 was the fourth-highest in Super Bowl history. Most importantly, though, Rodgers was terrific at taking care of the ball. He threw three TD passes, didn't have an interception or fumble, and was an easy choice for MVP.

The player McCarthy helped mold and develop had led the Packers to their first Super Bowl championship in 14 seasons.

"He played great," McCarthy said of Rodgers. "We put everything on his shoulders. He did a lot at the line of scrimmage for us against a great defense. He did a hell of a job."

Truthfully, so did the entire 2010 Packers.

The Packers were left for dead when injuries struck. Most counted Green Bay out when it was 8-6 and on life support.

But the Packers never folded, as McCarthy's bold approach led to an improbable six-game winning streak and a Super Bowl title to finish the season.

"I did some things that were different, but frankly, just trust your instincts," McCarthy said. "I think the No. 1 responsibility as the head coach is to have your finger on the pulse of your football team and react and respond accordingly. That's what I felt myself and our coaching staff did. We stayed true to our operation. We didn't change the way we prepare for games, we didn't change the way we practice.

"I am not perfect, but the one thing I think the players truly know that they get from me, they get the truth and it comes from the heart. They know it is researched. They know our staff is very detail-oriented. We don't ever walk into a meeting unprepared.

"There is a belief in how we operate and I think that was the biggest key for us down the stretch. I just felt we were a consistent football team all year. I never felt we were as bad as our record may have been some time or as good when we had the blowout win. I felt we were just a very consistent football team, and I think that is why we ended up being the Super Bowl champions."

McCarthy had promised a Super Bowl title on the first day he arrived. To the amazement of many, he had backed it up. McCarthy and the Packers were on top of the football world.

18

From Hunter to Hunted

Mike McCarthy had been a Super Bowl champion for just 19 days. Green Bay's head coach had celebrated, rejoiced and reflected. He had also turned the page.

When McCarthy arrived at the NFL Combine in late February, he didn't focus on 2010 or the elation of being a world champion. Instead McCarthy chose to crank up the heat on his offense.

"I think the best offense in the league is the offense that scores the most points. That'll be our No. 1 focus," McCarthy said. "To break it down simply, run the ball better, pass protect better, have more production in the passing game. We plan on being a better offense." With good reason.

The return of tight end Jermichael Finley gave Green Bay its best stable of pass catchers in years. The running game also figured to improve with the return of Ryan Grant, the emergence of James Starks and the addition of third-round draft pick Alex Green.

The offensive line brought back four starters, and many believed it could be even better. Oh yeah, and quarterback Aaron Rodgers was coming off a magical 2010 postseason and figured to be in the hunt for league MVP honors. "We realize that it's going to be important for us to do things better than we did last year," Rodgers said.

Defensively, there was optimism Green Bay could also be just as good. The six-pack of Nick Barnett, Morgan Burnett, Mike Neal, Brad Jones, Brandon Chillar and Brady Poppinga were all defensive starters or key reserves at the start of 2010. By Week 8, all six were on the season-ending injured reserve list. Yet remarkably, Packers defensive coordinator Dom Capers got his unit to perform as well as almost any in football.

Barnett, Chillar and Poppinga never played in Green Bay again. But the other three were back.

The Packers' only significant loss from the Super Bowl lineup was defensive end Cullen Jenkins, who left for Philadelphia in free agency. Green Bay believed Neal was ready for that position, an opinion that wound up being completely inaccurate. But at the start of training camp, the Packers felt their defense wouldn't miss a beat.

"The young guys are going to have to step up and pick up that slack," Packers defensive coordinator Dom Capers said. "Any time you lose a good football player, then one of these young guys has to step their game up and fill it in."

The Packers, like every team in the league, lost four months of work due to the NFL lockout. That took away essential development time, time where McCarthy's young players have always made major strides.

When the Packers returned in late July, though, they were a consensus pick to repeat as Super Bowl champs. McCarthy knew he had to guard against complacency and smugness. So McCarthy took the approach that the Packers were still hunting — not being hunted.

"We're not defending anything," McCarthy insisted at the outset of training camp. "We've climbed Mountain XLV, it was a great climb, it was one that we'll have experience that we can probably pull forward to this year, but we don't get any wins, and there's nothing really to gain from being the champion last year. This is a whole new journey. This is a whole new football team.

"We're at the bottom of the mountain just like everyone else is right now. We're at the starting line, and we need to do the things that are necessary throughout training camp: build our team, select our football team and start the climb. There's a path out there for us to get to Indianapolis (home of Super Bowl XLVI). It's our responsibility and our focus, commitment to stay on that path. And that's the way we view it."

McCarthy always stressed handling success and stacking successes. With the rest of the league gunning for Green Bay, this would be the ultimate challenge. "You've got to ... understand that we're viewed differently now because we have won the championship," Packers quarterback Aaron Rodgers said. "We need to be the hunter in this situation because we're going to be hunted. Everybody plays their best game every week, they try to. I don't think it changes when you're playing a Super Bowl champion or you're playing a team that's in the bottom of the pack.

"We realize that it's going to be important for us to do things better than we did last year. We went 10-6, and we can start faster and hopefully get things jelling a little quicker than we did last year."

They did—and then some.

In the Packers' most thrilling season opener in recent memory, Green Bay notched a 42-34 win over New Orleans. The Packers built leads of 14-0 and 42-27 before the Saints came storming back.

New Orleans pulled to 42-34 and drove to the Packers' 9-yard line with three seconds left. Saints quarterback Drew Brees then threw for running back Darren Sproles in the end zone, and linebacker A.J. Hawk was called for pass interference.

Although the clock read 0:00, New Orleans was given one untimed play from Green Bay's 1-yard line. The Saints gave the ball to rookie running back Mark Ingram, but Green Bay's Clay Matthews and Morgan Burnett combined to deny Ingram and the Saints.

"This game was crazy, and I'm sure the networks aren't too upset it came down to that," Hawk said. "It was a fun game to be a part of. There were obviously a lot of ups and downs, so I'm just happy for our offense to score all those points for us."

Green Bay's offense was sensational. Rodgers, coming off a magical postseason in 2010, didn't seem the least bit affected by the lockout. Rodgers completed 27 of his 35 passes (77.1%)

for 312 yards and three touchdowns, and he posted a sensational passer rating of 132.1.

Rodgers threw a 7-yard back shoulder laser to Greg Jennings for a first-quarter touchdown. Less than four minutes later, Rodgers hit Jordy Nelson with a three-yard TD. And before the first quarter was over, Rodgers and rookie Randall Cobb hooked up on a memorable 32-yard TD.

Rodgers finished the first quarter with 188 passing yards, the most he's ever tallied in a single quarter. Rodgers completed his first seven passes and was 14 of 15 in the first quarter.

Talk about starting 2011 with a bang.

"The guy's outstanding," said safety Nick Collins, who was drafted in 2005, like Rodgers. "He put in the time, put in the hard work, and he brings it. He's a true champion and a true winner, and he knows how to lead the team behind him.

"We've got the best. It would be tough to have to defend him. I'm just glad he's on my team. You can put in the argument that he's the top dog right now."

Packers defensive end Ryan Pickett agreed.

"I might be a little biased, but there's just nothing he can't do," Pickett said of Rodgers. "He makes every throw. He makes you miss in the pocket. He can run and get first downs. His timing and release are quick. He can pick up blitzes. He's smart. He can handle everything the defense is throwing at him. To me, I don't see a better quarterback."

Cobb also made a grand first impression. He returned a kickoff 108 yards for a touchdown and had a receiving touchdown.

"You've got to be excited about Randall," McCarthy said. "He's shown that from the first day of training camp, his ability. When other players talk about a player having a chance to be special, he is one of those guys.

"He's very raw, he's picking up our system, but he knows what to do when he gets the football in his hands, and he knows how to get open. He's a gifted young man with a lot of good football in front of him."

Carolina rookie quarterback Cam Newton was another one of those gifted young players. And the Packers had to face Newton and the Panthers in Week 2. Newton, the No. 1 pick in April's draft, would go on to be named Rookie of the Year in 2011. And on this Sunday, Newton helped Carolina jump to a 13-0 lead early in the second quarter. In 2010, the Packers' greatest deficit was just seven points.

"That guy was the real deal," Packers linebacker Desmond Bishop said of Newton. But the Packers ran off 23 unanswered points, eventually stretched their advantage to 30-16, and notched a 30-23 win.

"It wasn't clean by any means," McCarthy said. "We can sit here and pick apart all the things that didn't go right, but most importantly, we finished it as a football team."

Newton threw for a franchise-record 432 yards in a sign of things to come for Green Bay's secondary. But the Packers did intercept three Newton passes, including two by Charles Woodson.

In two games, though, the Packers had allowed a remarkable 952 passing yards. Green Bay was saved — for the time being, anyhow — by terrific red zone defense. "Two weeks in a row our defense has stood up big in adversity situations," McCarthy said. "Red zone, fourth down. As long as we do that, we're going to be fine. The other things are correctable."

One thing wasn't correctable, and that was the status of Pro Bowl safety Nick Collins. During the fourth quarter, Newton threw to running back Jonathan Stewart on a third-and-nine. Green Bay's A.J. Hawk and Woodson had a chance to tackle Stewart but missed.

Stewart went airborne to elude Hawk, and when he did, his left buttocks hit squarely into Collins' helmet. Collins suffered a severe neck injury, was taken off the field on a stretcher, and was finished for the season.

"Losing Nick is rough," said Charlie Peprah, who took Collins' place. "But I think we've got the guys to do it. We feel we've got the best 53-man roster in the league, and we can overcome anything. You saw what happened last year, so hopefully we can make the plays we need to make it work."

The Packers didn't miss a beat the following week during their rematch of the 2010 NFC Championship game. Green Bay whipped host Chicago, 27-17, and improved to 3-0.

Second-year safety Morgan Burnett, who was thrust into the role of Green Bay's top safety, led the way with two interceptions. "We definitely can survive it ... and Morgan's a big reason for that," Packers cornerback Tramon Williams said of losing Collins. "The guy has been playing great all season long and we all knew what he can do."

Packers tight end Jermichael Finley was the offensive star, scoring three touchdowns. "He's a great player," Rodgers said of Finley. "I think his best ball is still in front of him, though. A couple of those plays he might not have been doing the right thing, but we made it work. He's a big-time player and incredible athleticism and the more he studies, the more he is going to get the ball."

Midway through the fourth quarter, though, a tweet with the following message came through on Finley's Twitter account: "Apparently the @NFLONFOX crew has not seen me live. Everyone needs a job, mine is proving people wrong."

Considering NFL players are prohibited from tweeting during games, Finley found himself answering more questions about his latest controversy than about his enormous performance. "It was just one of those tweets where I just tried to show my fans that I'm ready to play," Finley said.

The Packers were certainly ready to play, sitting at 3-0 with a trio of impressive wins. One week later, Green Bay played arguably its best game of the young season with a 49-23 thumping of Denver.

Against Denver, Rodgers became the first quarterback in NFL history to record 400 yards passing, throw for four touchdowns, and rush for two more in the same game. Rodgers also set a career high with 408 passing yards, which was the third-highest total in franchise history. "Aaron's really good,"

Packers right guard Josh Sitton said. "I wish I had him on fantasy."

Through four games, Green Bay had rolled up an NFL-best 148 points, breaking the old franchise mark of 140 set by the 1945 squad. The Packers had also scored 40-plus points in two of their first four games, the first time that had happened since Warren G. Harding was president.

McCarthy's offense, the one he challenged to become football's best, was doing exactly that. "This is the best offense I've been a part of in my career," veteran wideout Donald Driver said. "To have so many weapons on offense that the ball is spread all over the place and everybody can make plays.

"I played with a great quarterback in (Favre). He's a gunslinger, a true Hall of Famer and I love him to death ... and he had a lot of weapons. But he never had this many weapons. I can promise you that."

Green Bay was perfect at the season's quarter pole. And many were already buzzing about the prospect of an undefeated season. Truth is, though, that topic had been discussed by Green Bay's players before the lockout even ended.

"We started talking about going 16-0 before the season even began," Peprah said. "We feel we have the talent, the scheme, the coaching and the depth to do it. If we don't do it, it's really on us. Why not set your standards high? Shoot for the stars and land on the moon."

From the top on down, that's exactly the mindset these Packers now had. "Our goal is to win every game ... and I think we'll have a chance," said Packers director of football operations Reggie McKenzie, who's the general manager in Oakland today. "One thing I love about us is our depth. Then I think Coach Mike (McCarthy) does a great job of preventing those distractions. We've got a chance to be in every game, that's for sure."

One week later, talk of perfection seemed remarkably premature when the Packers fell behind in Atlanta, 14-0. Amazingly, though, Green Bay's defense didn't budge the rest of the night, the offense scored the game's final 25 points and the Packers emerged with a 25-14 win.

"We're building something here," McCarthy said. "That's what's special about this team: our ability to make the big plays when we need them."

Rodgers continued to make plenty of big plays, throwing for 396 yards. The highlights were a 70-yard TD pass to James Jones—a strike that gave Green Bay its first lead at 15-14—and later a 29-yard TD to Greg Jennings.

But the real stars on this night came on the defensive side of the ball. The Falcons scored touchdowns on their first two drives, and it appeared they'd make things look fantastically easy against the Packers' leaky defense. But Atlanta was blanked on its final eight possessions, and Green Bay improved to a perfect 5-0.

"I can see why people would be worried about the defense," Packers cornerback Tramon Williams said. "There's a lot of work to do. But traditionally, we've gotten better and better as the year goes on. We're all confident that can be the case again."

It was a huge statement for a Packers' defense that had been shredded by opposing offenses and its own fan base over the first month of the season. "There have been years where we've started slow, but then we just take off," Capers said. "Guys start to find their niche and they become more and more comfortable. I'm hoping that's what this team can be."

That seemed more probable one week later when the Packers dismantled the St. Louis Rams, 24-3. The Packers allowed 424 total yards, but many came with the game out of reach. For the second straight week, Green Bay's defense played top-notch football. "That's kind of been our thing all year—kind of bend, but not break," linebacker A.J. Hawk said. "We're definitely glad to hold them to three points, but we let them rush for too many yards on us. They made some big plays, but when it came down to it, when we needed stops, we got it."

Green Bay's offense produced its fewest points of the year, and the Packers also didn't score in the second half. By then, though, the game was out of reach. That's because Rodgers fired three touchdown passes within a 12-minute stretch of the second quarter as Green Bay built a 24-0 lead.

"(Green Bay) is, if not the best team in the league, one of the best," Rams coach Steve Spagnuolo said. "I've got a great deal of respect for the organization and the people here. They've got good football players, starting with the quarterback."

The Packers had one more test before their bye week, a trip to hapless Minnesota. The Vikings, who rolled the dice on a washed-up Donovan McNabb after Favre retired, were 1-5. McNabb had flopped and was being replaced by rookie first-round pick Christian Ponder.

On paper, this shaped up like a cakewalk for the Packers. But nothing is ever easy in this rivalry, and this trip to the Metrodome was no different. "They could be 0-14, 0-15. It doesn't matter," Packers wideout Greg Jennings said. "When they play in this building, you're going to get their best shot."

That's exactly what Green Bay got.

The Packers led, 33-17, heading to the fourth quarter. But Ponder rallied Minnesota back within 33-27, and Minnesota got the ball back with plenty of time to produce a game-winning score.

Green Bay's defense stiffened in the end, though, and the Packers moved to 7-0. "We're not going to swing from a rope around here as far as extremes, one way or another," McCarthy said. "We're very happy being 7-0, stating the obvious, but to a man we know we can play better. That's what's exciting."

The Vikings, fired up from the start, had built a 17-10 lead late in the first half. But Green Bay ran off 23 straight points — highlighted by a 20-0 third quarter — and took control at 33-17. Rodgers had another stellar game, throwing three touchdowns and completing 24-of-30 passes (80.0%). Through seven games, Rodgers was playing the quarterback position at an all-time level and was the odds-on favorite for MVP honors.

As the Packers entered their bye week, Rodgers was on pace for a record-breaking season in several categories, including:

- **Passer rating.** Through seven games, Rodgers had a quarterback rating of 125.7, well ahead of Peyton Manning's single-season mark of 121.1 set in 2004. Remarkably, Rodgers' *lowest* rating in a game was 111.4 at Chicago in Week 3.
- **Completion percentage.** Rodgers had connected on 71.50% of his passes, which would break Drew Brees' single-season mark of 70.62 set in 2009. It would also break Brett Favre's Packers record of 66.54% set in 2007.
- **Touchdowns.** Rodgers led the NFL with 20 touchdown passes and was on pace to throw 46 TDs. That mark would also break Favre's single-season Packers' record of 39 set in 1996 and rank fourth all time.
- **Yards.** Rodgers was on pace to throw for 5,422 yards, which would shatter Dan Marino's NFL record of 5,084 set in 1984 and Lynn Dickey's Green Bay record of 4,458 set in 1983. In addition, Rodgers was averaging an NFL-best 9.92 yards per passing attempt and had thrown just three interceptions.

As terrific as all those statistics were, Rodgers may have earned the ultimate compliment from McCarthy. Remember, McCarthy was Kansas City's offensive control assistant in 1993-94 when Joe Montana quarterbacked the Chiefs, and he also coached Favre in Green Bay in both 1999 and 2006-'07.

"(Rodgers) is clearly the best decision maker that I've been around, probably since my time in Kansas City with Joe Montana," McCarthy said. "(Rodgers) does not get bored throwing an easy completion, and that's a great tribute to have as a quarterback.

"He's clearly in tune taking what the defense gives you. He can throw the tight spots. He has the anticipation and arm strength and accuracy to attack the seams, but he does a great job of staying disciplined and staying within the offense." That didn't change in Green Bay's first week after the bye.

Rodgers made his first-ever start in his home state of California. And his four touchdown passes helped the Packers hold off hard-charging San Diego, 45-38.

Rodgers spends his offseasons in Del Mar, roughly 20 miles north of San Diego's Qualcomm Stadium. And he had plenty of ticket requests for this game. He didn't disappoint family, friends or Packer Nation.

"Consistency has been kind of a hot-button word for me over the past couple of years," Rodgers said. "I want to play consistently this season. I'm doing some good things. I'm throwing the ball the way I want to. I'm not turning the ball over."

No he wasn't. Instead, Rodgers hit four different receivers as Green Bay built a 45-24 lead early in the fourth quarter.

The Packers also had a pair of interceptions they returned for scores. Safety Charlie Peprah went 40 yards for a TD, and cornerback Tramon Williams had a 43-yard TD. In all, quarterback Philip Rivers was intercepted three times.

"When you give that quarterback and that offense 14 points," said Rivers, "it's tough to win."

Rivers did throw for 385 yards and four TDs, highlighted by a pair of fourth quarter scores to Vincent Jackson. But with San Diego trying to tie the game in the final minute, Peprah intercepted Rivers — his third pick of the game — and returned it 76 yards to end things.

Green Bay was now 8-0, although its defensive shortcomings were becoming a concern. Peprah was making his share of big plays, but didn't run well and was getting exposed. Williams had lost much of the strength in his shoulder and couldn't play the press coverage that made him so effective in recent years. Nickel back Sam Shields was struggling in coverage and with his tackling. Linebacker A.J. Hawk was a nonfactor, and the pass rush was invisable.

"Every year's a different year. Every game's a different game," Packers defensive coordinator Dom Capers said. "We felt going into that game it was going to be a challenging game because of the matchups you have. We had a number of different things where we were tying to match people up on receivers, now you add in all the formations adjustments, and it becomes more variables."

The Packers needed a complete performance, and facing lowly Minnesota was the perfect solution.

Rodgers threw four more touchdown passes, including two to Jordy Nelson, who continued his breakout season. Randall Cobb returned a punt 80 yards for a score and Green Bay held the Vikings to 266 total yards.

The result was a 45-7 destruction of a Vikings team that was in the NFC title game just two years earlier. "It's (our) best game, because of the margin of victory," Mike McCarthy said. "And at the end of the day, it's about points."

It was also another terrific game for Nelson, who had developed into one of football's premiere deep threats. Nelson was widely considered a possession receiver his first three seasons in the league. But in his last 10 contests, he'd caught five passes of at least 50 yards, and four of those went for touchdowns. Nelson, whose speed was always underestimated, had one theory for his emergence.

"To be honest, guys try me a lot because I'm white," Nelson said. "I'm definitely not trying to make it a racial thing, but it's the truth. And they can be fooled all they want, as long as it keeps going."

The Packers were going strong, now 9-0 and football's last remaining unbeaten team. Mediocre Tampa Bay (4-5) wasn't supposed to be a threat, but it was.

The Buccaneers pulled within two points of the Packers on two different occasions in the fourth quarter. But each time, Green Bay answered with touchdown drives on its way to a 35-26 win.

The Packers improved to 10-0 and stretched their winning streak to 16 games. Many of those games were tight, but remarkably, Green Bay never trailed in the fourth quarter of a single game.

Instead the Packers continued to make play after play to keep foes at bay.

"I think we have enough guys that have been around here long enough that lost the close games, and we don't ever seem to get down right now," Packers fullback John Kuhn said. "We understand that teams are giving us their best shots right now, and we're just trying to hang in there and battle 'til the end. And we feel if we play a consistent 60 minutes of football, then we should have a good chance of winning."

The last time Green Bay trailed in the fourth quarter was December 19, 2010. That was the infamous "Nobody's Underdog" game — one the Packers lost to New England, 31-27, in a game quarterbacked by Matt Flynn.

In addition, Green Bay was only tied once in a fourth quarter. That came in the 2010 season finale, when the Packers rallied past Chicago, 10-3.

"We expect to win, even though it's not always going to be pretty," said Packers cornerback Tramon Williams, who had two interceptions against Tampa Bay. "I think this team is experienced enough to know how to win, even when it's hard. Hopefully we'll continue to do that and get better at the same time."

Next up was Thanksgiving in Detroit. It marked the 20th time since 1951 the Packers and Lions met on Turkey Day, and this one was all Green Bay.

Rodgers threw for 307 yards and a pair of touchdowns as Green Bay cruised to a 27-15 win. The Packers also intercepted Detroit's Matthew Stafford three times.

Detroit had made tremendous gains since going winless in 2008. But the Packers showed the Lions how far away they were from joining the NFL's elite.

"We felt like we took a pretty big chunk of confidence out of this victory," McCarthy said. "It was a well-anticipated game, rightfully so. A lot of hype around the game. But at the end of the day, you've got to show up and play football.

"I thought our guys did a good job of just staying the course. We knew we were going to have bumps in the road. We talked about it exclusively the last couple of days and they just kept playing. It was a good victory for us."

This game also showed the difference between the two head coaches and the kind of teams they coached.

Since being hired in 2009, Detroit coach Jim Schwartz had changed the culture and instilled plenty of confidence in his team. But Schwartz had gone too far, and he now led one of football's dirtiest teams.

Arguably the Lions' filthiest player was second-year nose tackle Ndamukong Suh. Suh added to his horrible reputation during the game against the Packers when he slammed the helmet of Packers' guard Evan Dietrich-Smith into the turf three times and stomped on Dietrich-Smith's arm. Suh was thrown out of the game and later suspended for two more.

"We try to rise above anything that happens on the field," Rodgers said. "I'm proud of our guys, the way we played, the way we competed. It was a tough game. They're a good opponent, got a real good defense."

For the first time in team history, the Packers were now 11-0 overall and 6-0 on the road. Green Bay also tied the franchise record with its ninth straight road win.

The Packers' talent was undoubtedly a huge reason why they shined on the road. But many also pointed to McCarthy's consistency. When Green Bay goes on the road, very little changes. It doesn't matter what team they play or what day the game is played, McCarthy's schedule is always constant.

The Packers typically arrive in a visiting city between 3 p.m. and 5 p.m. the day before a game. Players get a few hours to themselves, and many use that time to have dinner with friends or family. There's a team chapel at 8:30 p.m. and a team meeting at 9 p.m. Curfew is 11 p.m., but most are tucked in well before that.

"Guys like the same routine … and you know what to expect when you go on the road," Packers kicker Mason Crosby said. "(McCarthy's) never going to change the schedule out of the blue. We always know what to expect and what's going on, and there's something to be said about that.

"It allows us to think about the game and not worry about what time a meeting is. We know all that. All that other stuff can create stress and panic ... and this way we can all just focus on the game."

The Packers needed all the focus they could muster the following week, when they headed to New York to face the Giants.

The Packers built leads of 28-17 and 35-27 only to see the Giants tie things at 35 with 58 seconds left. But Rodgers engineered a four-play, 65-yard drive, and Crosby drilled a 31-yard field goal as time expired.

Packers 38, Giants 35.

"I'm running out of things to say about him," McCarthy said of Rodgers. "He's a great quarterback. Playing against the pass rush they had tonight, he hung in there and made the plays."

Green Bay was 12-0, had set a new team record with 10 straight road wins, and appeared headed toward perfection.

The Packers' high-powered offense was sensational again, as Rodgers threw four more touchdown passes, including two to veteran Donald Driver. But the defense was showing cracks that hadn't been fixed four months after training camp began.

The Giants had 447 net yards, marking the eighth time in 12 games a Green Bay opponent had at least 400 yards. In 2010, the Packers allowed 400 or more yards just twice in 19 games.

The Packers led the NFL in interceptions, with 23. But when Green Bay wasn't taking the ball away, it was usually allowing teams to drive for points.

"Everybody needs to be accountable to one another," linebacker Clay Matthews said last week. "It's a very key word in football, especially on this team. Strictly speaking on the defensive side, everybody has to fit together and be responsible and accountable for your individual position.

"You notice when there's big plays or something goes wrong, it's someone or a few people who aren't staying accountable to their job, and that's usually what gets you hurt. We're not going to jump on each other because everyone makes mistakes."

Mistakes were few and far between during a 46-16 rout of visiting Oakland.

Running back Ryan Grant, a bit player most of the year, ripped off a pair of touchdown runs, including a nifty 47-yarder to start the scoring. Rodgers also threw two touchdowns, linebacker Erik Walden had a score, and the Packers built a 34-0 lead in this laugher.

Green Bay was 13-0, and McCarthy couldn't have been happier. "The script doesn't change for us," McCarthy said. "We go out there each week, and then by the time Friday rolls around we focus on ourselves and get ready to play. As long as we're taking care of things and keeping our focus on improving the quality of play, I don't think we can be beaten.

"And you could ask me that six years ago, I would have said the same damn thing. That's the way we think around here. So we expect to win every time we take the field and I would think any team in the NFL thinks that way."

Amazingly, tight end Ryan Taylor added a four-yard touchdown reception on his first-ever offensive play from the scrimmage. Taylor became the 19th Packers player to find the end zone in 2011, which broke the previous team mark of 18 set in 2008.

"That's something man," said Raji, who had a one-yard TD plunge against Tampa Bay in Week 11. "I guess it's just indicative of the season we're having. We preach team first, and that stat is really indicative of that."

Green Bay was now just three games from perfection, and talk of 16-0 was at a fevered pitch. "The most important thing will always be winning the Super Bowl," Grant said. "Whether that's at 19-0, 18-1 or whatever, that's the ultimate goal. But everyone in this room would love to get there without losing a game. That would be unbelievable."

Added Matthews, "We're embracing it. We're not shying away from it. The fact is, we've been able to do stay undefeated for a little while now."

The streak ended one week later, though, with a 19-14 loss in Kansas City. Former Bear Kyle Orton threw for 299 yards, and Green Bay's passing game struggled against the Chiefs' press-man coverage.

"It still sucks," Rodgers said of losing. "It's still not a fun feeling."

"The Streak" lasted a remarkable 364 days. It fell just a few hours short of reaching 52 weeks on the head.

It contained 19 consecutive wins, a franchise-best 13-0 start in 2011 and 10 straight road wins. It began the week after McCarthy's "Nobody's Underdog" statement and died in Kansas City.

It goes down as the second-longest winning streak in NFL history, behind only the 2003-04 New England Patriots (21). Most importantly, though, "The Streak" included a win over Pittsburgh in Super Bowl XLV.

"I've told so many people that this is something special," said Driver, who was playing his 13th season in Green Bay. "That streak is something I think the fans will cherish for a long time. And not just the fans, the players, too. We'll always cherish it."

McCarthy had downplayed the perfect season for weeks, largely to take pressure off his team. But after returning to Green Bay, McCarthy acknowledged his disappointment that "The Streak" was over.

"Very quiet plane ride home last night and understandably so," McCarthy said. "Everybody's disappointed with the loss and the opportunity to have an undefeated season. But the reality is upon us. We have the goal of getting home-field advantage right in front of us."

It took one week longer than McCarthy would have liked, but the Packers clinched the NFC's top seed on Christmas night.

Rodgers was in a league of his own, throwing five touchdown passes. Two went to Nelson and two more were to James Jones, and the Packers drilled visiting Chicago, 35-21.

Green Bay played its second straight game without No. 1 wideout Greg Jennings. But the offense didn't miss a beat.

The Packers won a 14th regular-season game for the first time in franchise history. Green Bay also wrapped up home-field advantage throughout the playoffs.

"Anytime I can ... talk about a record that stands in front of the great history and tradition of the Green Bay Packers, that's special," McCarthy said. "The goal was to get home-field advantage all the way through. We accomplished that."

The Packers were thrilled to bounce back from their first loss in nearly a year. And the 70,000-plus fans who packed Lambeau left with a nice holiday gift.

"We had three goals to start the season: win the division, clinch home-field advantage, and obviously win the Super Bowl," McCarthy said. "We wanted the path to go through Lambeau. We have a great home-field advantage here. There is nothing like our fans, our surface is in great shape, and we play well at home. I think everybody would like to play at home."

Green Bay still had one game left, but Rodgers' regular season was done. The Packers couldn't risk a potential injury to their franchise player. Also, Rodgers had put up numbers rarely seen in the NFL and had done enough to later earn MVP honors. He set franchise records for passing yards (4,643) and touchdown passes (45). His passer rating of 122.5 was a new NFL mark. He completed 68.3% of his throws and threw just six interceptions.

As for the regular-season finale, itself, it was the Matt Flynn Show. Flynn, Green Bay's backup quarterback, took the reigns and he had a day for the ages. Flynn set a new franchise record with six touchdown passes and powered the Packers to a thrilling 45-41 win over Detroit. Afterward, many fans and media members joked it might be hard for Rodgers to get his job back for the playoffs.

"It was clearly one of the best performances I've been a part of," McCarthy said of Flynn. "No doubt about it. I can't say enough about Matt Flynn. The whole world got to see what we see every day. He's a talented young man. He has full control of the offense. But just the way he plays, he's very even-keeled, he had some bumps in the road, and he just stayed the course."

In Green Bay, Rodgers, Favre, Lynn Dickey, Don Horn and Cecil Isbell had all thrown for five touchdowns in a game. Flynn became the first to ever throw for six.

Flynn also joined Y.A. Tittle (1962), Joe Namath (1972) and Joe Montana (1990) as the only quarterbacks to ever throw for 475 yards and six TDs in the same game. And Flynn's 480 passing yards broke Lynn Dickey's team mark of 418 set in 1980.

Flynn, who became an unrestricted free agent at the end of the year, put out one heck of an audition tape for the rest of the league to see.

"Wherever he's at, he'll be successful," Packers center Scott Wells said of Flynn, who later signed a free agent deal with Seattle. "He was successful in college, he was successful when he stepped in here. He's been waiting for an opportunity. He got that opportunity today ... and he did an outstanding job."

Flynn made every throw imaginable on a chilly day with wind gusts that exceeded 20 miles per hour. He threw a nifty jump ball that Nelson adjusted to, and hauled in for a 36-yard TD. He also threw a perfect ball down the seam to Nelson for a 58-yard score. Flynn hit Driver on a crossing route for a 35-yard TD and fired a gorgeous fade to Jones on the game-winning drive. Finally, Flynn capped off his big afternoon with a back shoulder bullet to Finley for the game-winning score.

Any team looking for a quarterback had to be talking about Flynn after his memorable performance.

"I'm not thinking about that right now," Flynn said when asked about his future. "But there's kind of a lot of guys jumping on my back, being goofy and saying things like that. But there's a lot ahead for this team right now."

That was certainly true.

Green Bay was the No. 1 seed in the playoffs for the first time since 1996, and there were many reasons to like their postseason chances.

The offense finished the year with 560 points, the second-most in NFL history. Green Bay was getting back tackles Chad Clifton and Bryan Bulaga, as well as Jennings, for the playoffs. And the Packers tied for the NFL lead with 38 takeaways.

On the flip side, though, the Packers finished 32nd — dead last — in yards allowed, at 411.6. Green Bay also ranked 32nd in pass defense, allowing an NFL record 299.8 passing yards per game.

"We have a lot of pride," defensive end Jarius Wynn said. "We know a lot of those (statistics) aren't acceptable. I still think we can turn it around in the playoffs."

The Packers also had just 29 sacks, which ranked 27th in football. The previous season, Green Bay had 47 sacks, which tied for second.

"I think the defense will be fine," defensive end Ryan Pickett said.

Was that a fair assessment or false hope?

The playoffs were here, and the Packers were about to find out what a 15-1 season was worth.

19
Adversity Strikes

Mike McCarthy dealt with a lot during his first six years as the Green Bay Packers head coach: the Brett Favre circus, job security issues and one of the NFL's most demanding fan bases. But nothing could prepare McCarthy and the Packers for what came their way before the NFC Divisional playoffs.

Michael T. Philbin, the 21-year-old son of Packers offensive coordinator Joe Philbin, drowned one week before Green Bay's game with the New York Giants. The Packers, a tight-knit group in the NFL's smallest city, were shaken to their core.

"Just a sad, sad time," said Packers left guard T.J. Lang, who lost his father the previous week. "Probably won't find a nicer guy on this staff than Joe. For that to happen to anybody is tragic, but to happen to a great guy like Joe makes it hurt that much more."

Joe Philbin, the father of six, was one of the most popular people in the Packers' organization for years. A devoted family man, Philbin spoke often of wife, Diane, and their children. He was also a grinder who paid terrific attention to detail and was known as one of the staff's finest teachers. But Philbin also maintained levity with his dry wit and pleasant demeanor.

Philbin didn't call the plays, but he had a huge role in game planning during the week. He was also heavily involved in coaching the offensive line, and on game days, he served as McCarthy's eyes and ears from the press box.

"He's an awesome coach," said Packers right guard Josh Sitton. "Smart as hell. He's fun to be around. Fun to have as a coach. He's an awesome guy, family man. Always talking about his wife and kids. Someone who truly cares about family."

When Philbin's name was brought up during one of McCarthy's press conferences that week, Green Bay's head coach stopped multiple times to fight back tears. On one occasion, McCarthy needed eight seconds between words. "A punch in the heart," McCarthy called it.

This was clearly a new challenge for McCarthy — and there was no road map.

"We talked about the importance of having the ability to separate personal challenges and your professional challenges," McCarthy said. "And it really goes in line with the family first philosophy. Everybody's feeling it. There's no question on what level. That's really for the individual to speak on. But professionally, I've been very pleased with what we've been able to accomplish."

Philbin coached for 19 years in the college ranks before former Packers coach Mike Sherman hired him to coach the offensive line in 2003. When Sherman was fired after the 2005 season, Philbin thought his days in Green Bay were done, too.

"I saw McCarthy's name come up on the ticker in my house," Philbin said during the 2011 season. "And I told my wife and kids at dinner that we'd be moving."

But Philbin impressed McCarthy during their interview. Philbin stayed on as the Packers offensive line coach, then was promoted to offensive coordinator in 2007.

Between 2007 and 2010, the Packers ranked fourth in the NFL in points scored and had the league's second-fewest turnovers. In 2011, Green Bay reached new heights when it scored the second-most points in league history (560).

When Philbin wasn't around the entire week of the Giants game, many Packers admitted it was virtually impossible to stay focused.

"I was constantly looking for him," said Packers defensive lineman Howard Green. "It's just a daily routine to see him. He gives me a hard time, I give him a hard time. That's my boy. I love him."

As Green tried to continue, his voice trailed off. He paused. His eyes welled up. Nearly a minute later, he continued. "I have my own kids," said Green, who has two daughters and a son. "It just kills me that this whole thing happened."

That reaction was commonplace at Packer headquarters throughout the week.

"It's important in this business to separate the personal from the professional, and when you're at work to try and focus on work," said Packers quarterback Aaron Rodgers, who had never been to a funeral. "But we're human as well.

"Everybody misses Joe and thinks about him and Diane and the kids, and we know it's a tough time for them right now. We're just trying to, when we're here, to focus on getting ready to play, and obviously we're thinking about him when we're not here."

McCarthy and his offensive staff split up Philbin's duties during the week. Many Packers attended Michael Philbin's funeral on Friday, then Joe Philbin rejoined the Packers for their divisional game with the Giants.

Months later, though, McCarthy said: "I don't know how you explain that week. It was like getting run over by a truck."

And run over by the Giants.

Four years earlier, the Giants stunned the Packers in the NFC Championship game and denied Green Bay a berth in Super Bowl XLII. It took McCarthy months before he could stomach watching that game again.

This one would be even more painful viewing.

Dropped passes. Fumbles. Shaky quarterbacking. And questionable coaching decisions.

The Packers had them all. The result was a 37-20 defeat to the upstart Giants.

Afterward, Green Bay's 15-1 regular season — the best in franchise history — was already forgotten.

"No one's going to remember 15-1," said Packers nose tackle B.J. Raji. "Now all they're going to talk about is the great letdown at home, in front of your home fans that love you and support you."

Green Bay had won 21 of 22 games, including a victory in Super Bowl XLV. The Packers won 15 of 16 games in 2011 thanks largely to an incredibly crisp offense.

But the Packers didn't resemble themselves against the Giants.

Green Bay, which lost just six fumbles in its first 16 games, lost three against the Giants. The Packers' receivers combined to drop eight passes. And Rodgers was off and threw just his seventh interception of the season.

The Packers, who were second in the league in turnover differential at plus-24, had four turnovers in a game for the first time since September 28, 2008.

"It doesn't feel good," McCarthy said. "It's not where I expected to be standing. It's very disappointing. It's a locker room that expected a lot more and rightfully so. I wish I would have done a better job tonight.

"It was an excellent regular season, but we clearly understand in Green Bay it's about winning championships. Just going to the playoffs is not enough. We're disappointed as a football team. We're disappointed for our fans. We had a heck of a run in the regular season. I thought we were playing very well down the stretch."

Back in 1997, the Packers were gunning for a second straight Super Bowl title. After that team lost to Denver, 31-24, in Super Bowl XXXII, Packers general manager Ron Wolf called Green Bay's two-year run "a fart in the wind."

The 2011 Packers would be remembered even less fondly.

The Packers won their first 13 games for the first time ever and set a franchise record for regular-season wins. But to a man, the Packers agreed the regular-season success would quickly be overshadowed by the postseason collapse.

"It's disappointing," Rodgers said. "We play to win championships. You win a championship and you're kind of at the top of the mountain, and you forget kind of how bad this feeling is. Had it after the 2009 season when we lost to Arizona, and it sucks.

"This team, this organization, this fan base expects championships. We had a championship-caliber regular season and didn't play well tonight."

Green Bay certainly wasn't the first team to have a historic regular season and then fall on its face in the postseason. Of the six teams to go 15-1 or better, only San Francisco (1984) and Chicago (1985) won the Super Bowl. Minnesota (1998) and Pittsburgh (2004) lost in the conference championship game, and New England (2007) lost in Super Bowl XLII.

The Packers, though, would now be remembered as the only 15-1 team that did not win at least one playoff game.

"No rhyme or reason to this," Raji said. "No one saw it coming. How could you? It definitely kind of ruins what we did in the regular season.

Linebacker A.J. Hawk agreed. "It's awesome, everything that happened during the regular season, all the records that different guys were setting and that," Hawk said. "But when it comes down to it, we didn't do it in the playoffs. It's almost like college basketball, you get in the tournament, it's how far you go in there. It's the same feeling. It almost erases what you did in the regular season."

What was most stunning in the loss was Green Bay's carelessness with the football.

Fullback John Kuhn, running back Ryan Grant and Rodgers all lost fumbles, while Rodgers threw an interception.

Green Bay finished minus-3 in the turnover department for just the third time in 104 games under McCarthy. Not surprisingly, the Packers were 0-3 in those games.

"We've been excessive, frankly, in handling the football in the winter weather preparing for the opportunity in playoff games, and we did not do a very good job handling the football," McCarthy said. "Turnover ratio is something that we don't lose very often."

That's for sure.

In McCarthy's first 96 regular season games, the Packers won the turnover battle 54 times (56.3%) and were even in another 16 games (16.7%). Green Bay lost the turnover battle in just 26 games (27.0%).

The Packers weren't quite as good in the postseason, where they had lost the turnover battle in four of McCarthy's first seven playoff games. Overall, though, Green Bay was plus-2 in turnover differential in those games.

Against the Giants, though, the Packers bottomed out in the game's most critical area.

Kuhn's fumble late in the first half set up a Lawrence Tynes field goal that gave the Giants a 13-10 lead.

On Green Bay's first drive of the second half, Rodgers pump-faked and had Greg Jennings wide open for a 30-yard touchdown. But a split second before Rodgers could release the ball, he was sacked by Giants defensive end Osi Umenyiora, fumbled, and safety Deon Grant recovered.

Then with the Packers trailing, 23-13, midway through the fourth quarter, Ryan Grant went 10 yards with a swing pass before fumbling. Chase Blackburn returned the ball 40 yards to the Packers' 4-yard line, and one play later New York had a 30-13 lead.

"We didn't get it done," Ryan Grant said. "We didn't make plays when we had opportunities, we turned the ball over. Across the board, we just weren't in sync. It's not a shock when you do that type of stuff, because that'll get you beat, regardless of whatever type of offense you have. They outplayed us."

Green Bay's pass catchers had a brutal day, as well. Tight end Jermichael Finley continued to struggle with dropped passes, which had plagued him all season. Jennings had a touchdown graze off his fingers. Jordy Nelson, James Starks, Tom Crabtree and Grant all dropped balls.

"It was just one of those days," Finley said. "I ain't God, so I couldn't tell you why we were out of sync today. We just didn't play our style for ball."

Per usual, Green Bay's defense was a mess.

The Packers were plagued by busted coverages, sloppy tackling and an inability to get off the field on third down. The

Giants even connected on a 37-yard Hail Mary touchdown pass to Hakeem Nicks on the final play of the first half.

McCarthy also had a curious game plan, first calling an on-side kick that failed early in the second quarter with the game tied at 10. Then with the Packers trailing 20-13 and with 13 minutes still left in the game, McCarthy went for it on fourth-and-five from the Giants 39, and Rodgers was sacked.

"No excuses," McCarthy said. "We practiced well. There's nothing in the preparation that led me to believe that this was going to occur today."

There wasn't a lot of data suggesting these Packers were about to implode. But that's exactly what happened in what became a Giant debacle.

"It sucks, that's all you can say," wide receiver Jordy Nelson said. "You're at a loss for words. We had one goal in mind and that was to win the Super Bowl. When you don't do that, you had an OK season. You didn't have a good season."

Fifteen and two now was an 'OK' season?

The bar couldn't be much higher for McCarthy and his team—which is just the way he wanted it.

January 29, 2012, Honolulu, HI. NFC head coach Mike McCarthy of the Green Bay Packers on the sideline against the AFC during the 2012 Pro Bowl at Aloha Stadium. The AFC defeated the NFC 59-41. (Photo by Kirby Lee/Image of Sport-US PRESSWIRE)

20

McCarthy's Way a Hit

Mike McCarthy's crazy schedule doesn't leave much time for the movies. Usually the only film he's watching is that of Lions and Bears and other NFL foes. But when McCarthy thinks about leadership and management style, he harkens back to Robert De Niro's *The Bronx Tale*.

"Great movie," McCarthy said. "One scene I really like is there's a gangster in there and he says, 'Is it more important to be liked or to be feared?' And his comment is to be feared. And if you asked me if I'd rather be liked or respected, I would much rather be respected."

Here's the rub: McCarthy doesn't have to pick. During his first six seasons in Green Bay, McCarthy became a box office smash on the field and in the locker room, as well. Innovative. Bold. Confident. Imaginative. This is Mike McCarthy between the hash marks. Organized. Consistent. Straightforward. Honest. This is Mike McCarthy during the week. That combination has made McCarthy one of the NFL's top coaches and a hit with players and staff alike.

"I really like how straightforward he is with the players," Packer right tackle Bryan Bulaga said. "He doesn't beat around the bush. He's straightforward and he tells it like it is."

Defensive coordinator Dom Capers, a head coach in both Carolina and Houston, agrees. "I think Mike's very consistent," Capers said. "I think he's had a plan since he's been here and a vision of what he wants this team to look like. This is a business that's a roller-coaster business, and we're all evaluated on what we do right now. What we did yesterday really has no relevance.

"So I think being able to be consistent with that message and be demanding and consistent in terms of the effort and the focus, in the meeting room and practice field and weight room and everything you do, you create a culture that's just standing operating procedure in the way we do business. And that benefits you in the long haul."

The McCarthy Way can be largely summed up in two words: consistency and communication. And McCarthy's players love his approach to both. McCarthy doesn't get too high or low. Whether the Packers are in the midst of a 13-0 start — like they were in 2011 — or struggling through a brutal season like they were in 2008, McCarthy is the exact same guy. No craziness. No unpredictability. No tirades.

"I'll just say this, when you lose your temper, I don't remember a whole lot of positive things happening," McCarthy said. Which is why McCarthy, who had a legendary temper two decades ago, has toned down that part of his act.

"I've seen him get mad ... but sometimes he's just really fired up, too," Packer defensive end Ryan Pickett said. "Coach has a lot of fire in him, and he gets the best out of us, but at the same time it's respect.

"That's why players love him. You won't find one player on this team that doesn't love playing for him. Everybody. He's just that kind of coach."

Packers tight end Jermichael Finley, who has received his share of tongue lashings from McCarthy, agreed. "My second year I saw him a lot," Finley said. "And seeing him helped me grow a lot. It was just like, 'Hey, he's telling me the truth.' I was talking my way through the papers.

"He's still got a temper, but to tell you the truth, his temper has come down a little. I just think he's a player's coach. That's all I can tell you."

The Packers' philosophy under McCarthy and general manager Ted Thompson has always been to draft and develop players. That has meant Green Bay almost always has more youth than most teams.

Therefore, McCarthy's steadiness is vital.

"He's consistent every week," former Packers center Scott Wells said of McCarthy. "He's clear, he's concise and there's no ifs ands or buts about it. You know exactly what's expected of you."

Thompson, the man who made the surprise move of hiring McCarthy, agreed. "He does a very good job of being organized," Thompson said. "He does a very good job of handling the chaos coming from the job, and he keeps a fairly even keel. I like all those things. I think those are good qualities."

From the start, McCarthy established a plan, stayed true to it, and his players bought into it.

One of the first things McCarthy did was try and improve communication throughout the entire building. Things had become fantastically corporate under former coach and general manager Mike Sherman, a man who many players said lacked a personal side or much personality at all, for that matter.

By the end of Sherman's regime, some players were terrified to make a mistake. There was tension everywhere. Morale was low. And coming to work each day had become a job, not a passion.

McCarthy did all he could, though, to change that. Today players rave about his communication abilities, and while they understand he's their boss first and foremost, they seem to have a bond that's greater than simply player-coach.

"Mike is a guy that has a great balance," former linebacker Brady Poppinga said. "He's intense when he has to be, but he's also relaxed. I was always nervous and on eggshells with Coach Sherman and thought like one mistake and I'm gone. Then (McCarthy) came in, and I thought he was just more relaxed."

Added quarterback Aaron Rodgers, "Coach (Sherman) was all business. I would have never just gone up to his office. I think (McCarthy's) a good communicator and there's an open door policy. He listens to people, and he's able to allow the other coaches on the staff to coach and to speak up, which I think is really important."

When it comes to schedules, players know what to expect weeks, sometimes months, ahead of time. And McCarthy almost never deviates from that plan. In the past, that wasn't always the case.

"I remember with (Mike) Sherman, we'd have off-days scheduled," Packer veteran wideout Donald Driver said of the former coach. "Then we'd play a bad game or something, and we'd be practicing on our off-day.

"That doesn't happen now. The schedule is the schedule. There aren't a lot of highs and lows, and (McCarthy) treats us like men."

To McCarthy, communication is a huge part of that. McCarthy tells every player on the roster — from Rodgers to those on the practice squad — that his door is always open. He means it, too.

"He's very approachable and really just a player's coach," Pickett said. "If you need anything, you can go talk to him. He's very understanding about things, kids, whatever. He's very good with that kind of thing, and I'm not sure other coaches are like that as much."

More often than not, McCarthy doesn't wait for players to come to him. He goes to them. Although McCarthy's office is on the third floor inside Lambeau Field, he'll spend much of his time on the first floor, where the weight room, locker room and training room are.

"It's the old bartender theory," McCarthy said. "You've got to be down there amongst them. The No. 1 responsibility I have as the head coach of the Green Bay Packers is I have to keep my finger on the pulse of the football team. That's how you make better decisions. And if you're not in tune to what's going on with the people that you're responsible for, your decision-making is going to be affected."

Not all of the communication is positive.

During training camp in 2011, McCarthy got tired of seeing Finley, an impending free agent, talking about a new contract. So McCarthy summoned Finley to his office, where the message was short and not-so-sweet.

The bottom line is problems are addressed.

"If he sees me in the media talking crazy, next thing I know I'm going to have someone sitting right here at my locker, waiting for me and saying, 'You know who wants you upstairs,'" Finley said. "And at the beginning of the season, he called me upstairs and just said, 'Watch your mouth.'

"That's why I say he's a great coach. He's going to tell you what's right and what's wrong and on the father level, too. And that's what I respect about him."

On the field, there's been a lot of respect earned, too.

McCarthy often used the term "stack successes," and his teams have done a terrific job of that.

Green Bay reached the postseason in 2009, then followed that with a Super Bowl championship in 2010. Then in 2011, the Packers went an NFL-best 15-1, before being upset in the playoffs.

"The mind-set at the start of the (2011 season) was 'We're not defending anything,'" former safety Charlie Peprah said. "We're hunting. And I think that mind-set really took hold in the locker room ... and we acted like we're just one of 32 teams just trying to win a Super Bowl.

"That's just another reason why I'd call him a great coach. He's one of the best coaches I've ever had, and it's because of how he adapts to situations. He's always growing as a coach, improving, and he listens to our needs. He's not one of these guys that says, 'I don't care what you say. We're doing it my way.' He listens to his guys and will change if it benefits the team."

Right now, the McCarthy Way is undoubtedly benefitting the Packers. His next challenge is to help Green Bay get back to the top of the football world.